MOUNTAINS OF THE GODS

High are the mountains.
Shiva lives in them.
This is my homeland;
It is more beautiful than heaven.
BHOTIAN SONG

MOUNTAINS OF THE GODS

BY IAN CAMERON

Facts On File Publications
New York, New York ● Oxford, England

Library of Congress Cataloging in Publication Data

Cameron, Ian, 1924–
    Mountains of the gods.
    Bibliography: p.
    Includes index.
    1. Himalaya Mountains. 2. Mountains—Asia, Central.
I. Title.
DS485.H6C28 1985   954   95-1656
ISBN 0-8160-1242-3

ORIGINATION BY IMAGO PUBLISHING LTD, THAME
PRINTED IN GREAT BRITAIN BY
PURNELL BOOK PRODUCTION LTD, PAULTON, BRISTOL,
MEMBER OF THE BPCC GROUP
10 9 8 7 6 5 4 3 2

ART DIRECTION AND DESIGN BY BOB HOOK
PICTURE RESEARCH BY JENNY DE GEX

FOREWORD

Looking across to Nanga Parbat bright in the sunshine it was hard to adjust to scale, to see it as the killer it is. We were flying at 18,000 feet in a world of glistening peaks and not a cloud in the sky. Apparently no wind either, no white banners streaming from the 26,660-foot peak, no crevasses showing dark veins in the glacier on its western slopes, the whole huge bulk of the mountain like an enormous feather bed that you could ski down in an afternoon. Only if you have been down there on the ground, only if you have experienced the staggering, exhausting difficulty of moving over the terrain on your own—only then can you begin to make the mental transition from the bird's eye view to the ground level reality.

I have had the same difficulty in other parts of the world. In Labrador, a delayed flight finding us dining in some luxury on a bright moonlit night in the depths of winter at over 20,000 feet and all the land below that I had travelled so laboriously laid out sparkling and clear, the ice-ridged esgairs, the dark of the jackpines, the frozen lakes, all unrolling beneath us with a magic facility. The same in the Andes, in the Rockies, in the Empty Quarter of Arabia; in all those places where the travel has been hard for those who have opened it up, air transport, and television too, has made us accept the impossible as the ordinary.

Here, in the half-dozen ranges known collectively as the Himalaya, we have the largest, the highest, the newest, the most spectacular mountain mass in the world. A mass that was formed, and is still being formed, by continental drift as India thrusts the colossal battering ram of its old hard rock into the underbelly of Asia. It took the Russians many years to drive their $2\frac{1}{2}$-mile-long tunnel through the Hindu Kush. It took over 20 years and 500 dead to construct the great highway through the Karakoram. The tunnel put Afghanistan at the mercy of the Soviets. The construction of the 488-mile-long Karakoram Highway brought the Chinese into a position of precarious check in what Kipling called the Great Game.

It is almost beyond belief that you can now leave London Airport for Rawalpindi and, if your bookings work out, and the weather is good, within 24 hours you can be sitting in the Rest House at Gilgit with the 25,551-foot peak of Rakaposhi towering above you, glimmering in splendour of snow and ice. It makes nonsense of all that has gone before, the tentative explorations, the military expeditions, the climbers, above all those early humans who acclimatized themselves and carved out an existence in the face of such natural odds. Toyotas standing ready for the tourist, brochures that speak in glowing terms of camera safaris in search of the snow leopard and the ibex, of fishing and pony-trekking, of sightseeing Buddhist rock engravings, the Karakoram Highway only six miles away, China a few hours.

The fact that for many the world is in the living room makes it imperative that the story of the opening up of areas that are now almost taken for granted is not forgotten, and of those areas the Himalaya is not only one of the most recent, but also the most condensed in time. It is a story in which the Royal Geographical Society has been deeply involved, almost as much as it was—and with as much publicity—as the opening up of Africa.

A full account, covering the whole sweep of history and back in time to the formation of these great ranges, has never been condensed into one volume before. In this work Ian Cameron has had the co-operation of the Society with access to the full accounts of climbing expeditions dating back to Graham's in 1883 and Conway's in 1892. Looking back now it seems hardly believable that before 1950 none of the great peaks over 26,000 feet had been climbed. And then in a single decade, following the French conquest of Annapurna, all the rest were achieved, including Everest.

The first of the four appendices gives the chronology of events, Mallory and Irvine 1924, Hertzog 1950, Hillary and Tenzing 1953. But further back there are the military expeditions, that dreadful slaughter of the Tibetans at Guru and the start of the great survey under George Everest in 1830 that culminated twenty-two years later in the triangulation that proved Everest the highest mountain in the world.

It is all here in *Mountains of the Gods*, illustrated with the best of the marvellous photographs in the Society's archives, and I for one am glad to set this book beside all the other climbing books on my shelves, something that I can turn to for a clear account of everything concerning the Himalaya. Also, like all Ian Cameron's work, it is produced in a very readable form.

HAMMOND INNES
December 1983

CONTENTS

———◆———

The Baltoro Glacier, Karakoram

INTRODUCTION

THE Himalaya are the most magnificent mountain range on earth. Yet they are no more than part of an even more magnificent complex, a vast ocean of peaks which covers an area more than half the size of Europe.

The different ranges that make up this mountain complex – the Himalaya, Hindu Kush, Karakoram, Pamirs, Tien Shan and Kun Lun – often merge imperceptibly one into the other, making it difficult to know where one begins and another ends. Pilgrims and traders, soldiers and spies, explorers, scientists and climbers have, from time immemorial, moved among these ranges without being conscious of crossing any definable boundary. Both geography and history would therefore seem to demand that this vast complex be treated as a single entity.

This I have tried to do.

Another reason for treating the area as a whole is that the whole of it is now under the same threat: the threat of change.

A hundred years ago the mountains of central Asia were virtually a blank on the map. Apart from Antarctica, they were the world's last and most formidable bastion of

The Potala, Lhasa, photographed on feast day, 1924

the unknown – Nepal was 'the land of mystery', Lhasa 'the forbidden city', the Pamirs 'the third pole'. It is very different today, with European package tours probing the approaches to Everest, Chinese troops dismantling the Tibetan monasteries, and Soviet engineers altering the course of the Pamir rivers. Those who live in the mountains have seen more change in the last couple of generations than their ancestors saw in the previous 1000 years. And this change has not always been for the better.

I have written *Mountains of the Gods* because it seems to me that the more we know about this threatened paradise and its fiercely independent people the better. No mountain or person today is an island. So the well that is drying up in the Karakum, the tree that is being felled in the Siwaliks, the bell that is tolling for the desecrated monasteries of Tibet, they are dying, falling, tolling not for some far-away people but for you and me.

CHAPTER ONE

THE FORMING
OF THE MOUNTAINS

Astronauts have said that 'the mountain complex of central Asia illuminates the heart of the continent like a circle of white fire', and one might have thought that so spectacular a feature in the earth's crust has been part of it for a very long time. This is not so. The Himalaya and their associated ranges are among the youngest mountains on earth. Three or four million years ago – at a time when the Urals, the Appalachians and the Rockies were already old – they didn't exist. In the place where they stand today, there was nothing but sea: the oldest and deepest sea in the world – the Sea of Tethys.

Hindu legend provides one explanation of how the greatest mountains on earth rose out of the deepest sea.

In the beginning, according to the *Mahabharata*, the god Vishnu, the Preserver-of-Life, lived on the northern shore of a great sea (which scholars have identified as the Sea of Tethys), his only companions being a pair of seagulls. Each year the female gull laid her eggs close to the shore, but each year the sea swept in and washed the eggs away. The gull tried building her nest farther inland, but it was no good: each year the sea advanced farther and farther over the land, seeking out and destroying the eggs. Eventually the gulls cried out in anguish to Vishnu to help them. And Vishnu opened his mouth and swallowed the sea, which vanished as though it had never been, and in its place lay the newly created Mother Earth. And to this legend the *Mahabharata* adds a postscript: that as Vishnu slept, exhausted after his bout of drinking, the demon Hiranyanksha leapt on the Mother Earth and raped her – raped her with such brutal violence that her limbs were broken and levered up, high into the clouds, thus forming the Himalaya.

It was at one time fashionable to dismiss this sort of legend as flight of fancy. Recent research, however, indicates that legend is often based on fact – witness the biblical story of the Flood. And indeed modern scientific textbooks give us what is basically an identical account of the birth of the Himalaya, albeit told in a different language.

Geologists are agreed that in the Jurassic era (about 80 million years ago, when the dinosaurs were beginning to disappear and the mammals to emerge) the earth consisted of two super-continents, Laurasia in the north and Gondwanaland in the south, with the great Sea of Tethys lying between them. Laurasia, we are told, gradually subdivided into two land masses, Europe-cum-Asia and North America-cum-Greenland; while Gondwanaland subdivided into five: Africa, India, Australia, South America and Antarctica. These land masses, with one exception, then drifted slowly into the positions they occupy today. The exception was India, whose movement was neither slow nor localized. For in the space of less than 50 million years India drifted clean across the Sea of Tethys, from the southern hemisphere to the northern, until it crashed into the underbelly of Asia.

The result was spectacular. For India was like a battering-ram. During its voyage north across the Sea of Tethys, it had passed over one of the hot spots in the earth's crust and a vast sheet of basaltic magma had been excreted on to it, so that by the time it collided with Asia it consisted almost entirely of rocks which were volcanic and hard – the granite, gneiss and basalt which today form the timeless and unyielding landscape of the Deccan. The underbelly of Asia, in constrast, consisted of rocks which were sedimentary and soft. For the sea bed of Tethys had been rolled up ahead of the advancing mass of India, rolled up against the plate of Asia into gigantic folds of sandstone, limestone, coral and clay. And it was these folds of sedimentary rock which, as the continents crashed together, were squeezed upward and ever upward – like toothpaste between the contracting walls of a vice – to form the mountains of central Asia. Indeed these same rocks are still being squeezed upward today at the rate of almost six inches (15 cm) a year; hence the old mountaineering joke that someone had better climb Everest quickly, before it got too high!

So within a span of not much more than 1.5 million years, the last remnants of the

'*The Snowy Range of the Himalaya from Landour,
India*', by Lieut. G.F. White, 1838

Sea of Tethys vanished (either swallowed by Vishnu or squeezed dry between the contracting land masses), and the most magnificent mountains on earth were prised up from sea level to 29,000 feet (8850 m) – either by rape or by unilateral pressure.

It is this traumatic birth which explains the basic structure of the Himalaya: their extreme height, and their alignment into a succession of roughly parallel ranges running east-to-west, conforming to the line of the old continental plate of Asia.

Two other factors have played a major role in making the mountains what they are today: rivers and the weather.

The Himalayan rivers are an anachronism, for they were there *before* the mountains. Indeed, they have almost certainly been flowing south from the Tibetan plateau ever since the Cretaceous era, draining originally into the Sea of Tethys and more recently into the Indian Ocean. This has led to a very unusual situation. In most ranges, the watershed lies along the line of its highest peaks: that is, if a range runs east-to-west, the rivers on its northern face flow down to the north, and the rivers on its southern face flow down to the south. This isn't the case with the Himalaya. Because the rivers were there first; and as the mountains welled up around them, they simply kept to

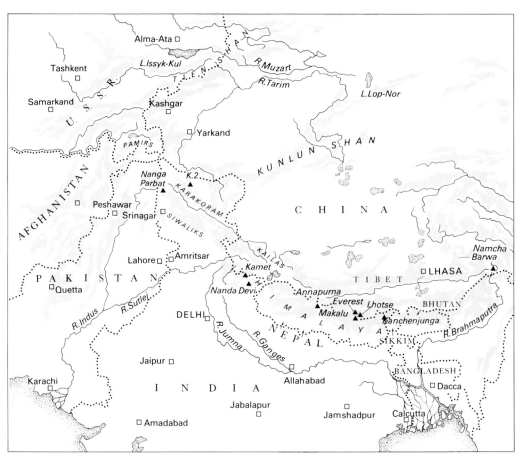

their original courses, cutting deep gorges through the soft upthrusting rock. Some of these, like the Kali Gandaki, a sheer 18,000 feet (5500 m) from riverbed to mountain peak, are the most spectacular on earth. This is why the watershed of the Himalaya is not where one would expect it to be – along the line of the great peaks Nanga Parbat, Nanda Devi, Annapurna, Everest and Kangchenjunga – but some 100 miles to the north and some 10,000 feet lower, in Tibet. This, in turn, explains why the great rivers of India – the Sutlej, the Indus and the Brahmaputra – all have their source not in India but far to the north of the subcontinent and far beyond the main chain of the mountains. The result of ranges running east-to-west and rivers running through them north-to-south has been to create a terrain of extraordinary complexity. For the rivers, as they cut deep through the mountains, have split them up into a jumble of individual massifs, each divided from its neighbours by a network of spectacular glacial valleys. The result is chaos! Nowhere else on earth can one so often climb what looks to be the highest peak in a range, only to find beyond it a sea not only of higher peaks but of higher ranges.

If the mountains' complexity is due mainly to rivers, their amazing contrasts are due mainly to weather. And here is a which-came-first-the-chicken-or-the-egg situation. For the weather both fashions and is fashioned by the mountains.

It would seem that a couple of million years ago the Tibetan plateau (then the coastline of Asia) must have been a veritable garden of Eden; for the southeast monsoon, as it swept in each year from the sea, deposited rainfall not only along the coast of Tibet but far into its interior – at least as far north as the Tarim and Takla Makan depressions.

However, as the subcontinents crashed together and the mountains started to rise, so the troubles of central Asia began; for the mountains pushed the monsoon rainclouds higher, and as they went higher, so they were forced to deposit their rain prematurely. As millennia passed, the rain, instead of reaching far into the heart of Asia, became increasingly confined to a narrow strip between the mountains and the sea; and with each passing year as the mountains rose higher, less moisture got through to the interior of the continent – until the garden of Eden became a desert.

This process is still going on today. To quote Himalayan authority, D. N. Wadia:

The once fertile and well-forested regions of the Tarim and the Takla Makan have been fighting against adverse climatic conditions since the end of the glacial period, and although they succeeded in preserving the remnants of their forests and cultivation until the early centuries of the Christian era, they have since steadily succumbed . . . Today their glaciers are wasting away, their river systems have decayed and withered, and a huge and waterless waste of sand has replaced the once fertile lowlands.

To those who live in their southern shadow, the Himalayas have brought life; to those who live in their northern shadow, death.

Such, in broad outline, are the mountains which were prised up as Asia and India collided. Their similarities are obvious: all came into being in the same cataclysmic multiple birth; all are young, complex, high and still thrusting higher; their southern slopes are alive with great forests and the most beautiful carpets of flowers; their northern slopes are lifeless, desiccated, and swept by winds of chill aridity.

It would, however, be misleading to stress the ranges' similarities without also pointing out their differences. For although the Hindu Kush, Pamirs, Tien Shan, Kun Lun, Karakoram and Himalaya do, in many cases, merge almost imperceptibly one into the other, yet each has an individual character of its own.

Kangchenjunga from near the Jongsong La Pass, photographed by Vittorio Sella, 1899

The most westerly of the ranges is the Hindu Kush. The name means 'Hindu-killer', because, we are told by the Arabian traveller Ibn Batuta writing in 1334, 'many of the slaves brought to us from India perish while crossing the high passes on account of the severe cold and the great quantities of snow.' Since it is the most westerly of the ranges, the rainfall of the Hindu Kush is modest for the monsoon, sweeping in from the Bay of Bengal, deposits less and less moisture as it moves northwestward: 123 inches (312 cm) a year at Darjeeling, 63 inches (160 cm) at Simla, 3 inches (7.6 cm) at Leh. The area is, however, nurtured by a succession of south-flowing rivers, chief of which are the Indus and its tributaries, and these rivers are for the inhabitants the warp and weft of life.

No one has described this part of the world better than W. K. Fraser-Tytler, a former British minister to Afghanistan. *It is*, he wrote,

> *a wild desolate country of great peaks and deep valleys, of precipitous gorges and rushing grey-green rivers; a barren, beautiful country of intense sunlight, clear sparkling air and wonderful colouring, as shadows lengthen and the rocks turn gold and pink and mauve in the light of the setting sun.*

And no one has painted it better than Atkinson, whose sketches have caught the very spirit of Afghanistan not only pictorially but historically. For the turbanned tribesmen who glare at us so fiercely from Atkinson's paintings are Muhammadans: men whose allegiance both geographically and culturally is to the Middle East; men who, from the dawn of history, have heard their mountain passes echo to the tramp of would-be conquerors on the march between the barren steppes of Asia and the fertile plains of India – Alexander, Genghis Khan, Tamerlane, nineteenth-century British mule trains, twentieth-century Soviet tanks. The Hindu Kush is a frontierland with a history of violence: a land of strong colours, strong passions and fierce independence.

North of the Hindu Kush, merging into it without recognizable transition and composed of the same Precambrian rock, are the Pamirs. The Pamirs are a paradox. They are still being born, still thrusting up at the rate of something like two-and-a-half inches a year; yet in the very moment of their birth, they are dying, for the ranges to the southeast are rising even faster and each year are blocking off more and more of their already inadequate rainfall, converting their already barren slopes to desert. This is one of the bleakest and least-known corners of the world: remote, mysterious and, at one time, dubbed 'the third pole'. Its mountains are rounded domes, divided by high, wide valleys which are very nearly as desolate as the peaks that surround them. A recent visitor, George St George, has left us this vivid description of a land in the grip of death:

> *There is less precipitation here than anywhere else in Soviet Central Asia – at Lake Karakul no more than an inch a year. This lake, one of the highest in the world, is surrounded not by ice and snow but by typical desert sand dunes . . . Not far away lie the bodies of horses and camels, the mummified relics of bygone caravans, perfectly preserved in the arid air.*

Among the animals of this unbelievably desolate land are the world's largest bears – *Ursus torquatus*, weighing anything up to 500 lb (225 kg); the world's largest cattle – *Bos grunniens* (the yak), weighing up to 2000 lb (900 kg); and the world's largest sheep (*Ovis poli*), the Marco Polo, whose horns are often more than five feet (1.5 m) from tip to tip. These creatures grow to so vast a size to counter the cold; for it is the largest animals, who have the smallest surface area in proportion to their mass, that lose body heat the least rapidly. The people of the Pamirs are nomadic Kirghiz: squat, gnarled men, and uncomplaining, flat-faced women who, because of the harshness of their environment,

Top: Hunters and Tibetan bear from Sven Hedin's expeditions to Central Asia and Tibet. Above: Tribesmen on the road to Lhasa by Capt. C.G. Rawling Right: Kirghiz, with Koumis bottle and bowl from T. W. Atkinson's 'Oriental and Western Siberia'

suffer the highest incidence of still-born babies in the world. Their allegiance, both geographically and culturally, is to the Soviet Union, though men seldom fight in the Pamirs – perhaps because they are too preoccupied with staying alive.

Eastward from the Pamirs run two of the least-known ranges in the world: the Tien Shan and the Kun Lun. The Tien Shan, the ancients' 'Mountains of the Spirits', may have been the last major range on earth to be discovered; not until the 1850s did a bona fide explorer set foot in them, let alone attempt to map them. This is another remote and inaccessible terrain, surrounded on all sides by barren deserts or by other equally barren ranges. Its distances are vast, its silences absolute. Until the present century, almost the only travellers to pass this way were merchants on the silk route from Peking to Samarkand; and they, we are told, hurried past the foot of the mountains as fast as they could, bewildered by mirages, and terrified by sounds not so much heard as imagined. 'Even by daylight,' wrote Marco Polo, 'men hear the voices of the Spirits, and often you fancy you are listening to the strains of many instruments, especially drums and the clash of arms. Travellers make a point of staying close together.'

Ice pinnacles on the Remu Glacier, East Karakoram, photographed by de Filippi

The Kun Lun, the 'Celestial Peaks' of Chinese mythology, lie to the south and east of the Tien Shan. They are a starkly beautiful range, sandwiched between the Tibetan plateau and the Takla Makan. 'These mountains,' wrote a Chinese traveller of the ninth century, 'are the coldest on earth,' a reputation confirmed by present-day climbers, who say that the Kun Lun are the only mountains in Central Asia where the icicles in their beards never melt even in full sun, where hot coffee freezes instantly as it is poured from Thermos to mug, and where the ink in their pens solidifies before they can write. In the past, the mountains used to be mined by nomadic Mongol herdsmen for silver, lapis lazuli and jade; today they are mined by Chinese engineers for iron and tin. The nationality of these engineers gives us a clue to the range's allegiance; for as the people of the Hindu Kush look to the Middle East, and the people of the Pamir and the Tien Shan look to the Soviet Union, so the people of the Kun Lun look to China. Indeed, the inhabitants of this little-known range have been nicely described as a sort of 'Sino-Celtic

*Top left: Shiwakta – one of the highest peaks in
the Chinese Pamirs – and, right, an un-named
peak in the Karakoram by Eric Shipton*

*Rhododendrons in the Zemu Valley,
Sikkim, photographed by Vittorio Sella in
1899*

Lhasa, the forbidden city, from Young-husband's album

Nuns outside a nunnery near Kampa Dzong – note the mantra on the stones behind them

The Dzongpen (headman or ruler of a village) of Kharta and his wife, photographed by Howard Bury, 1921

fringe': a border people who have for a long time acquiesced in the rule of Peking, who have often wanted and occasionally tried to reject it, but who have never been able to find a workable alternative.

◆

The hub from which these four great systems radiate is the Karakoram. This is the apex of the world: a spectacular wilderness of bare rock, black ice, sheer cliff and foaming river. No other range can boast such a concentration of mighty peaks – three out of the six highest mountains in the world, and 60 summits of over 22,000 feet (6700 m). Here is the earth's second-highest mountain, K2 (28,253 ft, 8611 m), the earth's largest non-polar glacier, the Hispar-Biafo (76 miles [122 km] from source to moraine), the earth's greatest concentration of ice outside the Arctic and Antarctic, and the earth's most spectacular scenery – witness Nigel Nicolson's description of the junction of the Hunza and Shimshal rivers:

> Lord, this is a dreadful place! On a summer's day, perhaps, the deep valley could acquire grandeur and even charm. But this was mid-January, and night was falling. The wind increased in force and bitterness, veering from point to point in violent gusts, as all around us the cliffs turned menacing and sullen-yellow. The two great glaciers ended in dirty snouts faintly visible in the gloom, and other ice-falls were clamped to chutes of fallen rock. Mist canopied the valley. There were no birds, no trees, no plants, no animals, no people.

Not surprisingly the Karakoram are seldom visited except by explorers, scientists or mountaineers. But what a challenge the range affords to those who *do* dare its heights! Here is the most impressive scenery on earth: a world too rock-girt for cultivation, too precipitous for grazing and too inhospitable to be inhabited. A world of almost lunar solitude – beautiful, but without life.

◆

East of the Karakoram lie the Himalaya. The Himalaya (the word is a compound of the ancient Sanskrit *hima* = snow, and *alaya* = abode) consist of three parallel ranges – the Siwaliks, the Lesser Himalayas (sometimes called the Pir Panjal) and the Greater or Trans-Himalayas. All three run roughly east-to-west.

The Siwaliks, the most southerly, are the youngest and least impressive: a line of gentle foothills, averaging no more than a couple of thousand feet in height, stretching from the Indus in the west to the Brahmaputra in the east. This is a lush, moist and fertile world, bordered by the *terai*, a heavily forested strip some 12 to 15 miles (19–24 km) wide, which provides sanctuary for a unique cross-section of Asian wildlife – chital deer, langurs, rhinos, leopards and more than half of the world's dwindling population of tigers. The *terai* contains a number of superb wildlife reserves and national parks, whose proliferation of life strikes the visitor as all the more impressive for flourishing virtually within the shadow of the highest mountains on earth.

North of the *terai*, rising steeply from the plains to some 20,000 feet (6100 m), are the Lesser Himalayas, arguably the most beautiful and exciting mountains in the world. One reason for their beauty is that they rise so quickly from a comparatively low-lying plain to so great a height. Another is that, because of the vast amount of rain which falls on them, every foot of their south-facing slopes is vibrant with colour and with life. What an amazing range of scenery one passes through as one climbs from *terai* to snowline! First comes the tropical rain forest, with its teeming and almost deafening insect life. Then the lower slopes of the foothills: a world of tall bamboo, stately sal and a superabundance of mammals – leopards, monkeys, bear, jackal, red panda, yak, goat, wild ass, deer, fox, hare, sambur, lynx and, of course, that most prolific and predatory of mammals, man. Then the middle slopes, clothed in quiet forests of pine and oak which, as one climbs, give gradual way first to juniper and rhododendron, then to birch. And finally, above the treeline, one emerges into a world of silence and of flowers: great banks of primulas, potentillas, anemones, aconites, eidelweiss, saxifrage and gentian, pushing through the melting snow, covering the upper reaches of the mountains, right up to 15,000 feet (4575 m), in great swathes of purple and blue, pink and white, scarlet and gold.

And to beauty is added excitement. For the Himalaya are being fashioned before one's very eyes: the peaks ever thusting upward (4 to 5 in. [10–12 cm] a year) only to be eroded by almost the same amount. And how spectacular the erosion can be; for this is a region of frequent earthquake, landslide and flood, a perpetual battleground where whole hillsides collapse overnight and fast-flowing rivers are forever carving out new gorges among the massifs. A world in transition. A world, too, where both creation and

Panoramic view of Everest, Lhotse and Nuptse, photographed by Eric Shipton

destruction are spectacular, for as the naturalist Joseph Hooker put it, 'upon what a gigantic scale does nature here operate!'

What is true of the Lesser Himalayas is true also of the Greater or Trans-Himalayas which lie immediately to the north. This is a fragmented chain of mighty peaks stretching for more than 1500 miles (2414 km) from Nanga Parbat (26,661 ft, 8126 m) on the Indus to Namcha Barwa (25,445 ft, 7761 m) on the Brahmaputra. This is a world of giants whose names are familiar not only to mountaineers, but to millions of vicarious adventurers throughout the world: Lhotse and Makalu, Nanga Parbat and Annapurna, Nanda Devi and Kamet, Kangchenjunga and Everest. Here we find the highest mountain in the world, the highest pass, the deepest gorge, the highest living animal, the highest flowering plant and the highest inhabited dwelling.

This last point highlights perhaps the greatest differences between the Himalaya and the other ranges of the complex. Whereas the population of the other mountains is sparse and nomadic, the Himalaya boast a population both sizeable and static. 'Life here in Ladakh,' writes John Keay, 'is peaceful. The people are Buddhists, many of them monks or nuns. In the still air the squeak of a prayer wheel is answered by the single resounding stroke of a gong which issues, pregnant with meaning, from an unseen monastery in the rockface. A charming world.'

A charming world and a charming people. It is often claimed that those who live amid the beauties of nature do not appreciate them. This certainly is not true of the people of the Himalaya. They adore and indeed worship their mountains. Everest they call the 'Goddess mother of the world'; Annapurna they call the 'Bringer of Life', they sing their praises in song:

> *High are the mountains,*
> *Shiva lives in them.*
> *This is my homeland;*
> *It is more beautiful than heaven*

This pantheism helps to explain why the Himalaya is not only one of the most beautiful places on earth, but one of the happiest.

◆

Apart from Antarctica, the mountains of central Asia were the last and the greatest of the blank spaces on the map, which for millennia had lain waiting to be unveiled. A vast natural fastness of some 750,000 square miles (almost the size of Europe, excluding the USSR and the Balkans): a fastness whose secrets would have been difficult enough to unravel if its only defences had been those of terrain and climate.

But another factor has given complexity to the unveiling of this forbidding region. For to the obduracy of nature has been added the intransigence of man.

Image of Kala Kharrah, Nepal,
photographed by Johnston and Hoffman,
1894

THE COMING OF MAN

I<small>T</small> is not known for certain who were the first men to set foot in the Himalaya, but it is possible to hazard a reasonable guess.

It is now believed that man (*Homo erectus*) developed from a primate (*Australopithecus*) something like 1.5 million years ago on the plains of east Africa. Our ancestors seem to have first survived and then prospered on the periphery of the great plains of the African rift valley, their success being due in the first instance to good eyesight, intelligence and the ability to communicate and act as a group. This background is relevant when we come to trace their subsequent migrations.

Civilization as we know it certainly sprang up along the great river valleys of the world – those of the Nile, Tigris, Euphrates, Indus and Yellow rivers – but this has been a comparatively recent development in man's evolution. Our earliest ancestors were creatures not of the river and valley, but of the waterhole and plain. They were at home not in the lowlands, but the uplands; and it is along the uplands that they almost certainly fanned out from their ancestral hearth-land of Africa.

The first people to set foot in the Himalaya were therefore probably a group of *Homo erectus* migrating some 500,000 years ago along the southern face of mountains which in those days were a good deal lower and less precipitous than they are today. And later – perhaps as much as 50,000 years later, because the route was colder and more difficult to find – other groups would have migrated along the northern face of the mountains; and if this, on present maps, looks a forbidding journey, it should be remembered that the northern face of the Himalaya was in those days both well-wooded and well-watered.

It would therefore seem that from the very dawn of history the mountains acted as a barrier, dividing those who migrated and settled to the south of them from those who migrated and settled to the north. This division helps to explain why today it is possible to move 100 miles (160 km) east-to-west *along* the mountains and not be aware of any great change, scenically, ethnically or culturally; whereas if one moves 100 miles north-to-south *across* them, one finds oneself in another world, inhabited by another and very different people.

It is unwise to make too many generalizations about early man and his migrations. It would, however, seem that the *Homo erectus* who settled south of the mountain complex evolved into Negroids – slim dark-skinned people, with broad flat noses and short black and often frizzy hair; while those who settled to the north evolved into Mongoloids – stockily built, light- to olive-skinned people, with little body hair, and with flat, wind-resistant faces and slit eyes, to protect their retinas from cold and snow glare. It would also seem that throughout the millennia the Mongoloids of the north remained by and large ethnically pure, having comparatively little contact with outside races; whereas the Negroids of the south were submerged by successive waves of other ethnic groups: not only Mongoloids and Caucasoids from the north, but also Australoids from the south. This is why the ethnic map to the north of the Himalaya is relatively simple, whereas to the south it is unbelievably complex – in Nepal alone (an area not much larger than England and Wales) there are no fewer than 19 major ethnic divisions.

This contrast between the simple north and the complex south has been accentuated by the nature of the terrain. In the north, the Mongoloid people have tended to lead nomadic lives in the wide-open plains, mingling freely and merging almost imperceptibly one with another. They are therefore basically similar: a Kirghiz from the Pamir would feel reasonably at home in the yurt of a Mongol from the Kun Lun. It is a different story in the south, where the Negroid people have tended to lead static lives in their valleys, cut off from the rest of the world by mountains often too high to be climbed. Here the valley has become the basic unit of life, supplying those who live in it with all they need: water, shelter, grazing, timber, food and, in some cases, even the name by which they are known. And in these secluded valleys the already divergent Negroids have tended to evolve, in isolation, their own individual life style, so that the people and customs of one valley are often quite different from those of the next: a

Tibetan beggars, photographed by Capt. C.G. Rawling during Younghusband's 'diplomatic mission', 1904

Pathan from the Hindu Kush would feel like a fish out of water in the longhouse of a Naga from the Arunachal Pradesh.

How fundamentally the various mountain peoples differ will be seen if each of the ethnic groups – Mongoloids, Primitives, Negroids and Caucasoids – is examined in turn.

◆

The heart-land of the Mongoloids is what is now the Takla Makan desert, but some 10,000 years ago was a fertile plain. Here, in the water holes and oases at the foot of the Tien Shan, there settled a short, olive-skinned, barrel-chested people. They were Shamanists, worshipping a god who revealed himself in natural phenomena: wind and fire, water and thunder, rock and ice. To start with, like most primitive people, they lived in caves, eking out a precarious existence by trapping the not-too-abundant wildlife of forest and plain. However, as millennia passed, they became increasingly dependent on animal husbandry, and it is this which set the pattern for their life style: a life style which is almost literally as old as the hills. Because the plains of central Asia

Tibetan yak drivers, photographed by Capt.
C.G. Rawling, 1903

were not fertile enough, even in those days, to support crops or large static herds of
domestic animals (and, with their decreasing rainfall, were becoming less fertile each
century), the Mongoloids took to driving their sheep, goats, oxen, camels and horses
from one seasonal grazing area to the next. They became nomads.

This need to be forever on the move has dictated their lives from that day to this. It
has meant that they built virtually no cities, but lived in collapsible tents which they took
with them wherever they went and that they became uniquely dependent on their horses.

Even today many Mongoloid people still live in *yurts* or *gers* (circular felt tents which
are built on a wickerwork frame and can be quickly dismantled and easily moved).
These are not primitive shelters, but large, comfortable and, indeed, sometimes
luxurious homes, with diameters of up to 30 feet (9 m), chimneys, double door-flaps and
rush floors. They can be taken down in no more than half an hour, and rolled into a
bundle of no more than 50 cubic feet. A thirteenth-century traveller tells us that seeing a
Mongoloid community on the move was 'like seeing a city on carts coming towards us';
while Stuart Legg in *The Heartland* paints an even more evocative picture:

> *Their* yurts *were mounted on a huge wagon with wheel-tracks of 20 feet and axles thick as a ship's
> mast. As many as 22 oxen or camels might be harnessed to a wagon in two lines abreast. Belongings
> were packed into chests and carried in carts, and a string of these might be hitched one behind the
> other, the whole train being driven by a single girl in the leading cart. So they would set out on
> another day's march beneath the blinding glare and furious winds of the steppe; the men and women
> riding herd on the animals, the children and* yurts *clustered on the wagons: a great self-contained
> land-fleet, sailing slowly across a grey-green ocean, the dust of its passage drifting away to the
> farthest horizon of the steppe.*

It is easy to see why the tough little horses of the steppe became indispensable to a
people who were forever driving large numbers of animals long distances from pasture to
pasture; easy, too, to see how, over the centuries, a bond must have developed between
rider and steed. What strengthened this bond into an almost mystical rapport was the
evolution of the horse into a weapon of war. It was Genghis Khan who brought this
evolution to its full flowering by creating the Golden Horde, the pillaging cavalry who
were arguably the most feared and most potent weapon of destruction the world has ever

Top: Building a yurt – the Mongols' portable home. Above: The Potala, viewed from inside the gate of the forbidden city, taken from Younghusband's album. Right: A Kargil woman, photographed by Capt. C.G. Rawling, 1903–1905

known. (Within a generation the Horde conquered half the known world, carving out for Genghis Khan an empire stretching from the Dneiper to the Sea of Japan and from Siberia to the Arabian Gulf.) Nothing cements a relationship more firmly than a military campaign, and from that day to this a Mongoloid's horse has been a great deal more to him than a cherished possession; even in the 1980s many a steppe-dweller would rather sell his wife than his horse. It is significant that a Mongol-Shamanist's soul-mate (his *alter ego* who appears to him in dreams predicting the future) is almost invariable a horse; and it is certainly no coincidence that the decline in the power of the Mongols has been paralleled exactly by the decline in the effectiveness of the horse as a weapon of war.

Mongoloids have one other trait which sets them apart from their mountain neighbours. They venerate water. It is difficult for us, accustomed as most of us are to a green landscape and water at the turn of a tap, to realize how much rivers and living plants mean to a desert people. George St George, in his book *Soviet Deserts and Mountains*,

Group of blackcap Lamas, photographed by
Chandra Das, 1879

describes how early one morning he saw an old man and a little girl staring at an acacia tree on the bank of a river. Suddenly the little girl ran up to the tree and kissed it. When St George asked why, he was told:

> *To a desert people every blade of grass is a dream, and every tree a miracle. Trees mean water and water means life. I've seen them bring their children for hundreds of miles to look at rivers. They stand on a riverbank as if hypnotized, looking at the flowing water. Afterwards they return to the desert. In desert settlements I've seen people share their last bucket of water with their plants . . . It may have something to do with Islam. Islam is a religion born in the desert. Muslims venerate water and every living green thing. Green is their favourite colour. When they fight for the Prophet they fight under a green banner. Green to a Muslim is the colour of Paradise – indeed the old Persian word* Pairidaeza *means simply 'garden'.*

How fundamental are the differences between these desert people who live to the north of the mountains, and the isolated pocket of rain-forest Primitives who live to the southeast.

Style of Tibetan hairdressing, photographed by Rev. Macleod, 1926

Long before the Mongoloids and their herds were fanning out from the Takla Makan, a very different and even older race were entrenched in the rain forests which in those days covered most of southeast Asia. They were a different people physically: taller, slimmer and more classically handsome, with pale skins, straight hair and regular features. They were different spiritually, for they practised ancestor worship (almost unheard-of in central Asia). And they were different culturally, for they led static lives, grouped together in enormous communal longhouses. Gradually, over the millennia, these Stone Age Primitives were driven more and more deeply into the secret places of the rain forest, until today they exist only in four isolated pockets – in the forests of Taiwan, the Philippines, Borneo and Assam. The rain forest of Assam, in north east India, is remote, isolated and difficult of access. Here is the lushest jungle on earth, nurtured by the heaviest rainfall, surrounded by the highest mountains. This is the home of the Naga.

The Tsin-tsar of Sinin, Tibet, photographed
by Capt. Kozloff, 1907

The Naga are divided territorially from the Mongols by no more than 100 miles, yet it would be impossible to imagine two peoples whose lives are more utterly dissimilar. The Mongols venerate water; to the Naga, water is a bugbear – they get over 300 inches (760 cm) of it a year, and it is forever washing away their crops and flooding their homes. The Mongols travel vast distances; a Naga seldom leaves the environs of the longhouse in which he was born. To the Mongol 'home' is a moveable family tent; to the Naga it is an exceedingly static 300-foot (90 m) wood-built longhouse occupied by up to 300 people. A Mongol's god shouts at him from mountain peak and thunderhead; a Naga's whispers from the skulls of his ancestors ever watching him from the wall of his longhouse. About the only thing the two races have in common is a love of freedom.

◆

Another very different people are the Negroids who live on the south-facing slopes of the mountains. At one time the whole Himalayan complex (the Siwaliks, the Pir Panjal and the Trans-Himalayas) was almost certainly populated by pure Negroids, descendants of the original *Homo erectus*: a race of slim, small-boned, graceful people with dark skin, dark curly hair and almond eyes. They became Hindus: a religion gentler than the Muhammadanism of the steppe, but prone to perpetuate division and caste. They lived in individual houses, grouped together in villages or towns, and their society was less male-dominated than that of their warlike neighbours to the north.

Over the last 2000 years these Negroids have been under pressure from both the Caucasoids in the west and the Mongoloids in the north. The latter, forced off the Tibetan plateau by its worsening climate, have been a particularly disruptive element. Migrating over the mountains, they dispossessed the original inhabitants of their valley settlements, so that today the predomenant strain in most Himalayan valleys is no longer Negroid but Mongoloid – a case in point being the Sherpas who, 600 years ago, were a Mongoloid community, living in northeastern Tibet.

This infiltration (which is still going on today) has brought about a situation of great ethnic complexity. In some valleys the newcomers took over completely, killing or driving out the original inhabitants and establishing a wholly Mongoloid community; in others, the newcomers mingled with and intermarried the people they conquered, establishing a Mongoloid-cum-Negroid community. While in a few places the Negroids resisted successfully, so that here and there one comes across a group that is still dark-skinned, almond-eyed and Hindu. The most obvious example are the Nuristani of Afghanistan, whose territory, surrounded on all sides by races of a different faith and different origin, was known for centuries as 'The Land of the Infidels'.

A further complicating factor has been that the people of the Himalaya have also been under pressure from the south. The Indo-Ganetic plain is one of the most densely populated areas on earth; in parts of it the climate is unhealthy, in most of it poverty is endemic. It has not therefore been only pilgrims who each year have flocked in their tens of thousands from the valleys to the hills.

The result of these ever-shifting, often-antipathetic racial groups living in a terrain where movement is difficult, has been to create a multitude of small, not-very-stable communities. In Nepal alone there are four basically Mongoloid peoples (the Bhotias, Sherpas, Gurungs and Thakals); nine Mongoloid-cum-Negroid peoples (the Brahmans, Kshatriyas, Newars, Thamangs, Mangars, Sunwars, Rais, Limbus and Rukhas) and six predominantly Negroid peoples (the Khas, Thakurs, Tharus, Indians, Garhwals and Kumaons). No wonder this part of the Himalaya has been dubbed 'the ethnic turn-table of Asia'. In the southwest segment of the mountains – the Hindu Kush – the ethnic scene is, if possible, even more confused, for to the mingling of Mongoloids and Negroids has been added another ingredient: the Caucasoids.

It is difficult to pin-point exactly from where the Caucasoid people originated; however, for millennia they have been entrenched in what is now loosely termed the Middle East, along the borders of southern Europe and Asia. Their skin is usually paler than the Negroids' but darker than the Mongoloids'; they have regular, somewhat aquiline features, and the majority of them are tall, strong and hirsute. They are Muslims, and religion is often the very essence of their lives; many of them still pray five times a day, and observe Ramadan – when food drink and sex are prohibited for much of the time. The henna-red beard is much in evidence, and *salaam alkeikum* is the never-failing greeting. Their society tends to be male-dominated and resistant to change.

For at least the last 1000 years, the Caucasoids have been expanding eastward. In

*Tibetan crowning ceremony, photographed by
Chandra Das, c. 1869*

the steppe they met the Mongoloids, who at the same time were expanding westward, and the two races intermingled, intermarried and became one – the Uzbeks and Tajiks of the USSR are examples of such composite races. In the Hindu Kush they met both the Negroids and the Mongoloids; and here, along the classic invasion route between the barren plains of central Asia and the fertile valleys of the Indus and Ganges, the three races did not so much integrate as split into little self-contained communities living uneasily cheek-by-jowl. This process of non-assimilation was due in part to the nature of the terrain, for a bleak unpopulated plateau intersected by the occasional fertile and densely populated valley is ideal territory for the creation of a series of small, isolated, self-contained, self-supporting, self-perpetuating communities. As long ago as the fourteenth century, a traveller in the Hindu Kush noted that 'here the inhabitants of one valley may be dark-eyed and have abundant hair, whilst the inhabitants of the next may be blue-eyed and have complexions fair as a Flemmings.' It is not to be wondered at that one of these remote and isolated valleys, the Hunza, was the inspiration for James Hilton's Shangri-la.

It is because the Hindu Kush is split up into so many frequently warring communities that its people have acquired a reputation for lawlessness and belligerence. 'They are proud' (to quote from *Peoples of the Earth*), 'and although they can be hospitable and friendly they are also aggressive and quick to avenge any injury. They enjoyed centuries of independence, and raised their sons to be warriors and hunters, first with spear and bow and later with rifles. Not so long ago a man's most prized possession was his Lee Enfield.' It is not perhaps surprising that more explorers have disappeared without trace in the Hindu Kush than in any other range in the complex.

◆

Such was the land and the people which lay for centuries on the periphery of the known world. A land of vast distances, breath-taking grandure and the most savage extremes of climate; a people of widely differing physique, faith and culture. A world not completely unknown but shrouded in mystery: enigmatic, challenging and dangerous.

30

CHAPTER THREE

THE PATHFINDERS

No single person can claim to have discovered the mountains of central Asia. It might be argued that their true discoverer was the *Homo erectus* who first set eyes on them some 500,000 years ago. It might equally be argued that not until the arrival of nineteenth-century scientists with their plane-tables and theodolites were the mountains truly delineated and therefore truly known. Whichever view one takes, discovery has been a matter not of sudden revelation but of gradual unveiling.

The first step in this unveiling took place well before the birth of Christ. The once-accepted view that our world was 'discovered' during a great burst of voyages and journeys in the sixteenth and seventeenth centuries is now recognized as fallacious. Christopher Columbus was preceded in North America by the Vikings, Vasco da Gama was preceded round the Cape of Good Hope by the Phoenicians, and the eighteenth-century explorers who claimed to have 'discovered' the Himalaya had, in fact, a host of precursors – pilgrims (both Hindu and Buddhist), the troops of a succession of campaigning armies (Alexander's, Genghis Khan's and Tamerlane's), a number of individual merchant-adventurers such as Marco Polo, and the ubiquitous Jesuit priests.

These might be described as pathfinders: men who passed through or skirted the mountain complex for reasons other than a wish to explore it. Their exploits are important not only for themselves, but also because they gave to subsequent exploration in the area an aura of *déjà vu*, the feeling of treading a path which had almost certainly been trod before . . . When Peary and Amundsen headed for the Poles, or Burke and Wills into the outback, they knew they were setting foot in virgin territory, that no fabled city or lost people lay waiting for them beyond the horizon. It has been just the opposite in the mountains of Asia, where the traveller always has the feeling that no matter how vast the distances and how bleak the terrain, beyond the next ridge he may always stumble across some city half as old as time: if not an 'Alexandria-the-farthest', at least a cluster of lamaseries glued to some improbable rockface.

◆

The first pathfinders to set foot in the Himalaya were pilgrims from the Indo-Ganetic plain. In many parts of the world, our ancestors regarded mountains as forbidden territory, the home of bitter winds and evil spirits. This was never the way the people of India thought of the Himalaya. As though realizing that their very existence depended on the water which flowed down from the mountains, they worshipped them; mountain tracks they lined with shrines, mountain slopes they adorned with prayer-flags, mountain peaks they thought of as gods. Year after year, they flocked to the high Himalaya as pilgrims, treading the snows with the same ecstasy as they plunged into the sacred waters of the Ganges. And one peak they believed was particularly sacred, a holiest of holies: Mount Kailas. At first sight a surprising choice.

This is what Hindu legend (*The Mahabharata*) tells us of Kailas:

It is the monarch of all mountains, an eternal refuge of asceticism and a never-tiring worker for the common good . . . It is covered with the most beautiful forests; its rivers are sweet as ambrosia, and adorned with golden lotus. On its upper slopes is the assembly hall of Brahma, a hall rich with fountains out of which is forever flowing the elixir of life.

All of this is certainly a surprise to those who visit Kailas today, and find it a starkly beautiful but relatively small mountain, with not a tree or a river in sight, much less a golden lotus or a fountain! One wonders why this remote and not very impressive peak should have been singled out for such devotion. There is, I think, only one possible answer: that the early pilgrims recognized Kailas as being the fountainhead from which stemmed the river system of virtually the whole Indo-Ganetic plain. For it is here, within a few miles of this holiest of mountains, that the four great rivers of India (the Indus, Sutlej, Ganges and Brahmaputra) all have their source.

So what *The Mahabharata* tells us is, symbolically, true. As with the story of the seagulls, legend turns out to be based on fact. And the only conclusion that can be made

Group of Lamas, photographed in Sikkim, 1894, by Johnston and Hoffman

is that long before the birth of Christ, Hindu pilgrims must have crossed the main ranges of the Himalaya, penetrated deep into present-day Tibet, and traced the great rivers of India to their source. How else could they have known that Kailas was the fountainhead from which all four rivers flowed? So as Webb and Draper stood triumphant at the source of the Ganges, and Kinthup at the source of the Brahmaputra, they were simply opening up a trail so old that it had become forgotten.

It is these links with the semi-legendary past which give those who explore the Himalaya the feeling that, as they climb a supposedly inviolate peak, they may always find at the top not only the most magnificent vista but a prayer-flag!

◆

The next pathfinders were a very different people from the pilgrims, and they came from a very different part of the world. The first Europeans to set foot in the mountains of central Asia were the troops of Alexander the Great. The ghost of Alexander broods like a Colossus over the mountains of Asia, his influence still a force to be reckoned with after

more than 2000 years. He did a fair amount of pure exploration, leading his armies
through several thousand square miles of unknown territory, two of his greatest feats
being his crossing of the Hindu Kush and his scaling of the Kor-i-nor.

The object of his winter traverse of the Kush was to catch his adversary Bessus
unawares by mounting a spring offensive at a time when the Persians believed him to be
the other (i.e., the Indian) side of the mountains. In November, 330 B.C., he led his army
of some 35,000 men into the foothills north of Kandahar: here his troubles started. The
hills were bleak, the weather bitter, food scarce. To quote his biographer, Robin Lane
Fox:

> The winter skies hung morosely over the thick-lying snow, and the more the soldiers climbed the more
> they were distressed by the thinness of the atmosphere. Stragglers were soon lost in the murky light
> and left to frostbite and certain death; others blundered into snowdrifts which were indistinguishable
> from the level whiteness of the ridges. Shelter was sought wherever possible, but it needed sharp eyes
> to pick out the native huts of mudbrick whose roofs, as nowadays, were rounded into a dome above the
> deepening snows.

It was the sort of crisis Alexander revelled in, and he boosted the morale of his men by
sharing their hardships, helping the lame, carrying the fallen, giving his own food to the
starving.

Early in 329 B.C., his army paused briefly in the high valleys beneath the summit
ridge. Here they founded a garrison town, which the troops misnamed Alexandria-in-
the-Caucasus,* its theatres and wrestling rings defiantly raising the banner of Greek
culture in the most unlikely of Afghan valleys. Then in March came the climax: the
crossing of the northern buttress of the mountains, almost certainly via the Khaiwak
Pass, which rises to 11,500 feet (3500 m) before dropping into the plains of central Asia.
It was a nightmare journey. The snow was still deep, the cold was intense, food was
scarce and fuel non-existent. The men, struggling through drifts up to their armpits,
suffered terribly from exhaustion, snowblindness and frostbite. Literally in their
thousands they were frozen solid to the rocks as they leaned against them. The horses and
pack-asses suffered an even higher ratio of casualties, but at least their bodies, eaten raw
because there was no fuel to cook them, provided the troops with food. Alexander lost
more men and more animals crossing the Hindu Kush than in all his subsequent
campaigns in central Asia.

But if one asks 'was it worth it?', the answer in military terms has to be 'yes'. For it
had never occurred to Bessus that a scouting party, let alone an entire army, would
attempt to cross the Kush in winter. As the Greeks came pouring into the plains of
Bactria, the Persians fled north in confusion over the Oxus, burning timber and boats in
an effort to delay pursuit. Alexander, however, was in no mood to be thwarted. His men
stitched together their leather tents, stuffed them with straw and floated them across the
Oxus as rafts. Bessus was captured, stripped naked except for a wooden collar (the mark
of a slave) and publicly flogged. Later his nose and ears were cut off, and later still his
head – cruelty being an ingredient never missing for long from the history of the north-
facing slopes of the mountains.

Soon after he had defeated the Persians, Alexander turned his attention to the
Sogdians, at the approaches to the Pamirs. Here he founded 'Alexandria-the-farthest'
(present-day Leninabad), and a little to the east of this, the most farflung outpost of his

---

* The misnomer arose because the Hindu Kush and the Caucasus both boast a legendary eagle. Many of Alexander's troops knew the legend of Prometheus who,
because of his theft of fire, was believed to have been chained by Zeus to a rock in the Caucasus, with a great eagle gnawing eternally at his liver. When Alexander's
native guides pointed out a cave in the Hindu Kush where *their* eagle was said to live, and showed the troops a great slab-sided rock scoured by the marks of its
claws, many assumed it must be the Caucasus they were crossing.

empire, he carried out his famous assault on the Kor-i-nor rock: an assault which gives us our first description of climbing in the mountains of central Asia.

Sogdian troops had taken refuge in a natural fortress which they thought impregnable, a vast bastion of rock, 15 miles (24 km) in circumference and three miles (4.8 km) in height; and when Alexander called on them to surrender, they laughed at him and told him to go and find troops with wings. Robin Lane Fox's description of what happened next cannot be bettered:

Alexander hated to be mocked, let alone told what he could not do. Heralds invited mountaineers to stand forward from the ranks. Their rewards were [to be] in keeping with the danger. The first to scale the rock would receive twelve talents, twelve times the bonus paid for four years' Asian service: the rest would be paid according to their position in the race to the summit. The three hundred experienced climbers who volunteered were told to equip themselves with flaxen ropes and iron tent- pegs; and that same winter's night, by the pale light of the stars, they moved round to a rockface far too forbidding to be guarded. They climbed with the patience of hardened alpinists. Every few feet they hammered tent-pegs into the crevices and frozen snow drifts, lassoed them, and hauled themselves up on the end of their ropes. On their way to the top, 30 of them slipped to their death and buried themselves beyond recovery in the snow beneath; but as the first streaks of dawn showed through the sky, the remainder attained the summit.

When the Sogdians saw them, they thought they must be more than mortal, and surrendered. They were neither the first people nor the last to learn that to Alexander nothing was impossible: that no peak was so steep it couldn't be climbed, no river so broad it couldn't be crossed, no people so warlike they couldn't be tamed.

But soon after his capture of the Sogdian citadel he was dead.

By extending the map of the known world by 2000 miles (3200 km), Alexander made Europeans aware for the first time of what the more romantic of our ancestors called 'the mysterious East': the golden temples of the Indians, and the fabulous pavilions of the Mongols. He also managed to bring about a genuine marriage between East and West, for 18 cities named Alexandria which he founded east of the Euphrates not only survived for many centuries, but survived as centres which actively disseminated the Hellenic way of life. And although in the years which followed his death, the links that he forged were loosened, they were never altogether severed; so that when, more than a millennium later, explorers from the West began once again to push into the mountains, they had the feeling that they were not so much breaking new ground as rediscovering old: a lurking suspicion that beyond the next ridge they might stumble across some ruined Alexandria, its gymnasiums and Corinthian columns an abiding epitaph to the man who for a brief moment made Europe and Asia one.

◆

Little is known about the role played by China in the early exploration of central Asia, but the travels of Hsuan Tsang underline China's long-standing links with the area.

Hsuan Tsang was born in A.D. 602. We are told that, as a boy, he was 'rosy as the evening mists, round as the rising moon and sweet as the odour of cinnamon', and that he grew into a 'tall, handsome man with beautiful eyes, a gentle expression, and a manner sedate and serious'. He seems to have been one of those exceptionally gifted but faintly irritating people who excel in whatever they undertake; and soon after his ordination into the priesthood of the Pure Land Buddhists, he set out on a journey of unbelievable difficulty and danger.

Wishing, he tells us, to study the fountainhead of Buddhism at first hand, he decided to travel from China to India by land. It says much for his courage that he planned to make at least the first part of the journey alone, and much for his good sense that before he set out he learned at least three of the languages he was likely to encounter *en route*. His friends did their best to dissuade him. 'The roads to the west', they told him, 'are bad. Oceans of sand stretch far and wide. There are evil spirits and burning winds. Even large caravans lose their way and perish. How can you hope to accomplish such a journey alone?' But Hsuan was not to be put off, and in 629 he set out on the journey which was to earn him the title 'Prince of Pilgrims'.

His start was hardly auspicious. He hired a guide to see him across the frontier, and the guide, on their first night alone in the desert, tried to murder him! *Avoiding this danger*, his biographer Hui-Li tells us,

> *Hsuan made his way across the sandy plain with nothing but bones and horse-droppings to guide him. Suddenly he thought he saw a troop of several hundred horsemen. They were wearing furs, and one moment seemed to advance and the next to halt. After them came camels, and the glitter of standards and lances. He took them for robbers. But even as he stared at them, their shape changed – now growing larger, now smaller – until they suddenly dissolved into thin air.*

He had seen one of the mirages for which the Takla Makan is notorious.

At the frontier he was mistaken for a spy, and shot in the leg by an arrow; but this setback likewise failed to deter him. And soon he was heading northwest, across the 300 miles (480 km) of waterless plain, his first objective the distant foothills of the Tien Shan. It was a terrible journey. 'There are no birds in the sky,' he wrote in his diary, 'no beasts on the ground, no vegetation and no water. By night demons and goblins burn torches as numerous as the stars. By day winds whip up the most terrible sandstorms.' He lost his water-bottle, and for four days and five nights had nothing to drink. Eventually, more dead than alive, he staggered into the oasis at Hami.

Here, when he had recovered from his ordeal, he was faced with an unexpected problem. The local ruler was so impressed with his erudition that he refused to let him go; Hsuan must, he said, remain in the oasis and give instruction to his monks. When the pilgrim demurred, he was told that he would be held, if necessary, by force. Hsuan however, had a twentieth-century answer to a seventh-century problem. He went on hunger strike, fasting to such good effect that the ruler eventually relented and let him continue his journey.

After various adventures in the oases which lie scattered along the northern periphery of the Takla Makan, including a hair's-breadth escape from massacre by bandits, Hsuan came to what was perhaps the most difficult part of his journey: the crossing of the Tien Shan. *These mountains*, he wrote in what is the earliest eye-witness description we have of them,

> *are steep and treacherous. They reach to the skies, and ever since the beginning of the world snow has been accumulating on them: snow which has been converted into ice which never melts, either in spring or summer, and whose glare is blinding. Even heavy fur-lined clothes cannot prevent the wind and the driving snow from freezing the body. There is nowhere dry where one can eat or sleep: for a bed one can only lay a mat on top of the ice.*

He added that it took the party he had joined seven days to cross the range – probably via the Bedel Pass – and that 14 men were frozen to death in the crossing.

North of the Tien Shan he found himself in a world both barbarous and magnificent. A world of bleak mountains, deep, unexpectedly fertile valleys, and great lakes like the Issyk-kul – 'almost 300 miles [480 km] in length, blue-black in colour, bitter in taste, and in its depths great fishes, dragons and scaly monsters'. The people of this little-known part of the world were, he noted in his diary, ever dressed in magnificent furs, ever mounted on camels or horses, and ever inviting him into huge pavilions, 'so decorated with gold that they dazzle the eye'. This was his first introduction to the nomadic Mongols of the steppe: a people shifting as dust, and as resilient; a race whose way of life has been dubbed barbaric, but who have survived and prospered while ephemeral, city-based civilizations have withered and died.

Hsuan spent several months among the Mongols. Then once again he was heading for India, following the traditional trade route from Samarkand to the Oxus, from the Oxus to Balkh 'the Mother of Cities', and finally from Balkh over the high passes of the Hindu Kush and south into the plains.

His description of Balkh is particularly interesting. The city was then one of the most famous centres of Buddhism; almost every other building, it seemed to Hsuan, was

Hsuan Tsang returning from India on his elephant,
from an early eighth-century fresco at Tun-huang

a temple, lamasery or shrine, almost every other artefact a sacred relic. 'I rested awhile,' he wrote, 'in this truly privileged and prosperous part of the world, marvelling at its many monasteries, fertile plains and well-wooded and watered valleys.' Yet those who visit the Mother of Cities today find its surroundings more desiccated than well-watered – evidence that in the last thousand years the north-facing slopes of the mountains have suffered a considerable deterioration of climate.

Finally arriving in India, Hsuan spent 13 years in the subcontinent, travelling extensively and being involved in enough adventures, escapes and religious confrontations to fill a volume. Indeed his travels *do* form the basis of the famous Chinese legend told in the famous legend *Monkey*, that unique combination of beauty and absurdity watched by millions on television.

Eventually he returned via the Hindu Kush and the Pamirs to his native China, 'laden with many gold and silver statues, 150 relics of the true Buddha, and 657 learned books'. He is the first traveller on record to have set foot in all the ranges of the complex – except possibly the Karakoram – and lesser mortals from the West can only agree with his biographer that he does indeed deserve the title 'Prince of Pilgrims'.

*Top: Tullajoo Temple,
Khatmandu*

*Above: Bhadgaon Temple,
Nepal*

Of the people Hsuan met in his travels it was the Mongol herdsmen who impressed him most. And it was these herdsmen who made the next incursion into the mountain complex: an incursion as violent, scouring and catastrophic as the flood that follows the bursting of a dam.

Genghis (the name means 'ocean-to-ocean') Khan was born near the Onon River in China in 1162. When he was nine, his father, a local chieftain, was killed in a blood feud; and in the years that followed the boy had to call on all his cunning, ruthlessness and powers of endurance to survive. It was during this blood-soaked adolescence that he developed those qualities which were to make him the most successful military commander the world has ever known; for in less than 20 years Genghis Khan was to carve out for himself an empire almost double the size of Alexander's.

Above: A thirteenth-century portrait of Genghis Khan and, left, a Khan's tent surrounded by a wooden stockade

The Mongol 'invasions' of Europe and southern Asia were brought about by several factors: a progressive deterioration in the climate of the steppe which made it increasingly difficult for the herdsmen to support themselves by traditional grazing; the metamorphosis of the horse from a pack-animal into a weapon of war; and by the fact that early in the thirteenth century Genghis Khan persuaded the various Mongol factions to stop fighting one another and fight their neighbours instead. This he did by unifying them under a single law, the *Yassa*, which laid down a strict code of conduct for 'believers' and proclaimed a holy war against everyone else.

In 1208 the Mongols invaded China. One after another the great cities of the Chinese empire fell to the Horde; they were looted and razed to the ground, and their inhabitants were massacred. Eventually Peking, the capital of the Ch'in empire, one of the richest and most beautiful cities of the ancient world, was starved into surrender. When the Chinese laid down their arms, every man, woman and child within the capital was put to the sword; 'it was,' wrote a Mongol eye witness, 'the most prolonged and glorious slaughter'. The city was then burned to the ground; the fires smouldered for more than a month, and when at last they subsided the Mongols raked the ash level so that not even the outline of a building could be traced. Over the next five years every army that took the field against the Mongols was decimated; prisoners – sometimes as many as 50,000 at a time – were massacred; and eventually the Chinese emperor was forced to accept the Khan's suzerainty.

Having 'purified' the Buddhists of the East, the Horde turned their attention to the Muslims of the West.

The Muslims put up a more spirited resistance than the Chinese, but their fate was the same. They were massacred with incredible brutality, not only to the last man, woman and child, but sometimes to the last man, woman, child and animal.

The reign of terror started in 1219 when Genghis Khan, with a force of almost 200,000 cavalry, advanced westwards over the steppe. Muslim writers have left a vivid description of the Horde and the terror they inspired:

> *They are all compleat Men: vigorous and looking like Wrestlers; they breathe nothing but War and Blood, and show so great an Impatience to fight that their Generals can scarcely moderate it; yet tho' they appear thus fiery, they keep themselves within the bounds of a strict Obedience to Command, and are entirely devoted to their Prince. They are content with any sort of food, and are not curious in their choice of beasts to eat. As to their members, they are like the Grasshoppers, impossible to be number'd. The neighing of their steeds is enough to make Heaven shut its ears, and their arrows convert the sky to a sea of reeds.*

The first skirmish of the campaign set a pattern to be repeated many times in the years to come. In a narrow pass in the Tien Shan a detachment of Mongol horsemen found themselves confronted by a well-entrenched army of the Shah. Everything was in the defenders' favour: numbers, terrain and a formidable network of redoubts. Yet the Mongols attacked with such ferocity that, in a few hours, the Shah's troops were cut to pieces. To quote from Wilfrid Blunt's excellent book *The Golden Road to Samarkand*:

> *As a result of this engagement the Shah, who narrowly escaped with his life, acquired a healthy respect for the bravery and tactical skill of the barbarians. He no longer felt inclined to challenge them in the open, preferring to surrender the initiative and to use his troops to garrison his principal cities. To besiege a well-fortified city was apt to be a long and costly business; and [he hoped that] the Mongols would be content to ravage the countryside and then return home with their plunder.*

This suited Genghis Khan very nicely. He picked the plums at his leisure, one at a time.

The great centres of the Muslim world – Ottrar, Bukhara, Merv, Balkh, Kandahar, Samarkand, Tabriz and Baghdad – fell one after another to the Horde. Some cities held out for months, other surrendered in days, but their fate was always the same: they were looted, fired and razed to the ground and their inhabitants were massacred. '*Amadand, u kandand, u suktand, u kustand, u burdand, u raftand*' (they came, they uprooted, they burned, they slew, they despoiled, they departed), lamented a contemporary historian in an epithet reminiscent of Caesar's '*Veni, vidi, vici*', 'Our splendours are effaced from the earth as writing from paper, our palaces have become the abode of the owl and the raven.'

For almost a decade the north-facing slopes of the mountains reverberated to the thunder of hooves, the clash of arms and the death agony of millions. Then the holocaust subsided almost as suddenly as it had erupted.

The man who described himself as 'The Scourge of God' died in 1227. His funeral epitomized his life. He was buried with much pomp on a hill overlooking the Onon River not far from the village where he was born; and then, in order to keep the location of his grave a secret, every man, woman and child in the great multitude who had joined his funeral cortège was put to death.

It is difficult to judge the long-term effect of the Mongols' brief but bloody reign of terror. One view is that, since they plundered rather than occupied, their influence was transitory. There is, however, another and, I think, more discerning view: that their ravages accelerated a decline in prosperity which was already under way because of the area's worsening climate. Certainly contemporary writers did not underestimate the effect of their visitation. 'With one stroke,' wrote Juvaini, 'a world which billowed with fertility was laid desolate, and the regions thereof became a desert, and the greater part of the living, dead.' Many great cities like Balkh never recovered; they were never rebuilt, and for centuries their ruined palaces and desecrated shrines bore silent witness to the fact that on the north-facing slopes of the mountain complex the reality of the present had overtaken the splendour of the past.

Tibetan masks: 'the Goblins of Hell'

Of the travellers who passed through the mountains in the wake of the Mongols, the best known is Marco Polo. It is easy to see why. The story of a brave, handsome and intelligent young man (Marco was only 17 when he set out from Venice) journeying through strange lands and among strange people makes exciting reading. Also Marco was lucky enough to have as a friend a professional writer who recorded his adventures. As soon as he returned to Europe from his travels he was taken prisoner by the Genoese, and, while in not very rigorous captivity, dictated his memoirs to a literate fellow-prisoner named Rusticiano or Rustichello. His ghost writer, in fact, did almost too good a job for Marco's *Description of the World* was considered too entertaining to be true, and the Venetian was accused of exaggerating and dubbed '*el Milione*'. It is only recently that his 'tall stories' – his Garden of Dreams, his fire that gave no heat, and his sheep with five-foot (1.5 m) horns – have been recognized as fact.

We can follow his route with some accuracy. The three Polos (Marco, his father and his uncle) started their journey in 1271 and took nearly a year to reach Ormuz, on the Persian Gulf. From here they had planned to continue their journey to China by sea but,

'Distant view of Mount Kinchenjunga from Darjeeling', from a painting by Marianne North, c. 1877

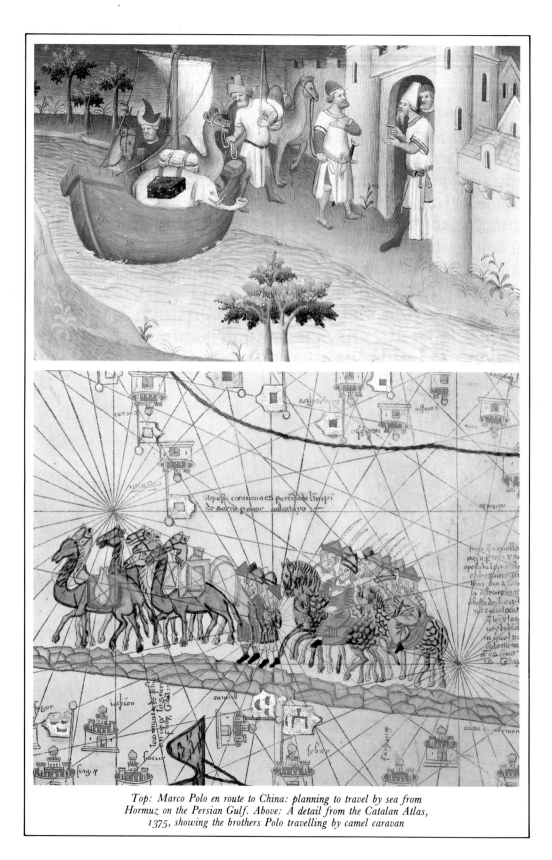

Top: Marco Polo en route to China: planning to travel by sea from Hormuz on the Persian Gulf. Above: A detail from the Catalan Atlas, 1375, showing the brothers Polo travelling by camel caravan

Top: Genghis Khan (with sceptre) outside his tent. Above: Mongol warrior plaiting his horse's tail

Dr H.A. Oldfield's watercolour of the Mayabouddha Temple in Khatmandu

finding, to their horror, that the local ships were held together by nothing more substantial than wooden pegs and string, they had second thoughts and decided to travel by land, through the mountains of central Asia. In fact, their original plan was the safer, for the Arab *dhows* which criss-cross the Indian Ocean are among the most seaworthy vessels in the history of sail.

To start with, their route lay over the deserts of eastern Persia. Here the wells were few and far between; 'and what water there is in them,' wrote Marco, 'is brackish and green as meadow grass. Drink one drop of it and you void your bowels ten times over.' North-east of the deserts, they came to a country of bleak hills, intersected by the occasional steep-sided and fertile valley. One of these valleys, Marco said, was the home of the Old Man of the Mountains, head of the notorious Assassins.

> *Here the Old Man ordered there to be built the most beautiful garden the world has ever seen, planted with the finest fruits, and containing the most splendid palaces and mansions, lacquered in gold. He also ordered there to be built four conduits, one flowing with wine, one with milk, one with honey and one with water. Also in the garden were fair ladies and damsels, the loveliest in the world, unrivalled at playing every sort of instrument, at singing and dancing, and ready to minister to every desire.*

Into this earthly paradise, Marco would have us believe, the Old Man enticed groups of carefully selected teenage boys, and these he instructed in the art of murder. When their training was finished, the boys were given an assignment – usually the assassination of some potentate who refused to pay the Old Man protection money. If the boys succeeded, they were told they could return to their earthly paradise; if they failed, they would go to their Heavenly paradise: they couldn't lose. 'And so,' Marco adds, 'they went joyfully about their business.' It does indeed sound a tall story, until Marco explains the boys were tempted into the garden in the first place by gifts of cannabis, and that once inside they were given increasingly heavy doses until they became so addicted they were willing to commit murder to get their hands on more. Another name for cannabis is *hash-hish*, and it is from this that the world 'assassin' is derived.

Crossing into present-day Afghanistan, the Polos passed through Balkh. 'Here,' wrote Marco, 'there used to be many fine palaces and mansions of marble, but these now lie shattered and in ruins. Grass grows in the streets, and wild goats browse in the deserted fields' – more proof, if it were needed, of the effect of the Mongols' spoliation. Continuing east, they noted that in the upper reaches of the Oxus the men appeared to have a predilection for women with big buttocks – 'she is considered the most glorious who is stoutest below the girdle. The girls therefore pad out their breeches with up to 300 feet [90 m] of cotton or silk, thickly pleated and scented with musk.' And so to the Pamirs: 'On the tops of these ranges are broad plains, a great abundance of grass, few trees, and springs of the purest water. This is said to be the highest place in the world. So high you see no bird flying, fire burns with a pale flame and gives off so little heat that you may put your hand in it, and there are an abundance of great sheep with horns of up to six palms in length.' These supposedly tall stories didn't enhance Marco's reputation with his contemporaries. It is only in recent years that ornithologists have confirmed the almost total absence of bird life in the upper reaches of the Pamirs; that mountaineers have confirmed, much to their discomfort, that the lack of oxygen in the air renders flames largely inaffective; and that zoologists have classified the giant sheep, *Ovis poli*, and found their horns measure every bit as much as 'six palms in length'.

In the autumn of 1273 the Polos descended from the Pamirs into the plains of Sinkiang, a desert region laced with the occasional skein of oases. They were now on the last stage of their journey, the Silk Road which skirts the periphery of the Takla Makan.

They had a happy knack of noticing and recording interesting facts about the places through which they passed. In Yarkand, for example, they noted that 'many of the inhabitants have a strange swelling on the side of their neck'; it is now know that impurities in the local water make the people of Yarkand particularly susceptible to goitre. In Tun-Luang they noted that 'in this place are many abbeys and monasteries and secret places all full of idols of diverse forms'; this was the site of the Cave of the Thousand Buddhas which 600 years later yielded so rich a harvest to the archaeologist Sir Aurel Stein. A few months later, not far from the Great Wall of China, they noted that 'in these parts if a stranger comes to a man's house, that man will straightway leave his home and his family and will not return until the stranger has gone. This custom is believed to ensure much wealth, good crops and healthy children.' '*Et les femmes sunt beles et gaudont et de soules*' (and the women are beautiful, compliant and derive much pleasure from the custom) adds the French translation of *Description of the World* – although this seems to have been not a contemporary observation, but the interpolation of a latter-day male chauvinist!

Temple of Devi Bhowanee, Bhadgaon,
photographed by Dr H.A. Oldfield, 1860

Four years after setting out from Venice, the Polos came at last to the end of their travels, being escorted with much pomp and circumstance into the Kublai Khan's summer palace on the outskirts of Kaiping. For Marco's father and uncle it was the end of a great adventure. For the young man it was the start of an even greater one, for he was to spend the next 17 years in the service of the Khan.

The Polo family's travels and the enormous public interest aroused by Marco's *Description of the World* did much to strengthen the trading links between Europe and Asia, but there was more to their journey than that. According to H. A. L. Fisher in his *A History of Europe*: 'Marco's story made an intellectual revolution in Europe quite as important as that great expansion of human knowledge which two centuries later proceeded from the discoveries of Columbus.' Westerners now learned to their astonishment that there was, in the farthest reaches of Asia, a civilization every bit as advanced as their own, and this provided a very considerable stimulus to the expansion of Europe. As Alexander had made Europeans aware for the first time of the splendours of India and the Steppe, so Marco made them aware for the first time of the opulence of China, an opulence to which distance added an aura of enigma and mystique.

In a thousand-and-one ways, this awareness of China enriched European life. To give one unexpected example, in 1274 Marco wrote:

> The palace of the Kublai Khan is built of stone and marble, with halls and rooms painted with hunting scenes and landscapes. The great surrounding wall encompasses an area of sixteen square miles, which can be entered only through the palace gates. Therein are sacred rivers, great fountains, fair stretches of lawn and groves of beautiful scented trees. Here are kept beasts for the chase, and here the Great Khan goes hunting with his falcons and tame leopards. In the middle of the park is a pavilion built of bamboo, its columns and tiles gilded with gold, all braced against the wind by more than 200 ropes of twisted silk and so constructed that it can be dismantled and moved hither and thither at the will of the monarch.

In 1616 this passage was repeated more or less verbatim in the famous travel book *Purchas, his Pilgrimage*. And in 1798 a visitor walking into Samuel Taylor Coleridge's cottage near Porlock in Somerset would have found the scent of opium, Purchas's book open at the above passage, and the first draft of the famous lines:

> In Xanadu did Kubla Khan
> A stately pleasure-dome decree:
> Where Alph, the sacred river, ran
> Through caverns measureless to man
> Down to a sunless sea.
> So twice five miles of fertile ground
> With walls and towers were girdled round;
> And there were gardens bright with sinuous rills,
> Where blossomed many an incense-bearing tree.

If Marco Polo's influence was beneficial and unifying, that of our next pathfinder was very much the opposite. Tamerlane, 'that monster who hath drunk a sea of blood, and yet gapes still for more', has the doubtful distinction of almost certainly having caused mankind more misery and suffering than anyone in history; a conservative estimate of the deaths for which he was responsible is 17 million.

He was born near Samarkand in 1336. In his youth he suffered arrow wounds in his right arm and leg – his detractors say while stealing sheep – and these left him lame for life; hence his name Timur-i-leng (*timur* = iron, *i-leng* = the limper). His career was a succession of ruthless, highly successful campaigns. Russians, Mamelukes and Turks all fell before his armies and were massacred with clinical efficiency, and in the last decade of the fourteenth century he turned his attention to India. He is quite explicit about his motives: 'I came to Hindustan,' he wrote, 'to lead a campaign to the death against the infidels, to convert them to the true faith, to purify their land from the abomination of idolatory and misbelief, to overthrow their temples and idols, and to seize their riches, since plunder taken in war is as lawful to our people as mother's milk.' In all this he succeeded.

He entered India by the classic invasion route, the Hindu Kush, following Alexander's tracks in reverse and suffering, as Alexander had suffered, the most appalling casualties. Throughout the spring of 1398 his troops crawled on hands and knees through glacier and snowdrift, dragging their pack-animals behind them on wooden sledges, and swinging their horses across the open ravines by means of rope bridges lassoed round projecting rocks. Something like 20,000 are believed to have perished; but by June the survivors stood triumphant on the banks of the Indus, before them the riches of the Indo-Ganetic plain, ripe for plunder.

What followed was not so much a campaign as a holocaust. Tamerlane advanced on Delhi, leaving in his wake a trail of looted temples and massacred garrisons – in the fortress town of Bhatnir, his troops are said to have killed 11,000 Hindus in less than an hour. On the plains of Jumna, in front of their capital, the Indian army made a last desperate stand. They fought with a bravery that won the respect even of Tamerlane; but in spite of their courage and their 125 elephants, coated in mail, loaded with

Tamerlane: reconstructed from a scientific study of his skull by Professor Gerasimov

firecrackers, and with poisoned blades lashed to their trunks, they were defeated. Delhi surrendered. In the hope of saving the lives of the inhabitants, a huge ransom was handed over; but the Mongol army got out of hand and, having collected the ransom, proceeded to massacre the entire population. 'Clearly,' wrote Tamerlane, 'it was the will of God that this calamity should befall so evil a city.'

Throughout the next year the rich towns of the plains were systematically looted and razed to the ground. Centres of the Hindu faith such as Hardwar (then believed to be the source of the Ganges) were singled out for special treatment – 'on the banks of this abominable river, every man, woman, child and living creature was despatched to the fires of hell.' By the summer of 1399 the Mongols had accumulated such a vast treasure in gold, silver, pearls, precious stones and silk that some 10,000 extra pack-mules were needed to transport it. It was time, Tamerlane decided, to transfer this plunder to the centre of his empire, his beloved Samarkand. So, laying waste the rich farmland of the

Siwaliks, the Horde retraced their steps into the Hindu Kush. One moment they were plundering and pillaging, the next they had disappeared into the Afghan valleys as suddenly as they had emerged.

In their wake, they left a world in ruins: crops burned, irrigation systems shattered, towns reduced to rubble and ash, something like five million dead, and a legacy of disorder, famine, poverty and disease from which the people of the plains needed a hundred years to recover.

Soon after he returned to his capital, Tamerlane began to prepare for what was probably the greatest festival the world has ever known. Huge pavilions, lacquered in gold and glittering with rubies, pearls and emeralds, were built on the banks of the Zarafshan. The different Mongol guilds vied with one another to produce the most exotic – and often erotic – set-pieces: the cotton-makers wove a minaret of pure cotton over 100 feet (30 m) high, the butchers dressed up human beings as animals; the saddlers attached a litter to a camel 'in which were seated two of the loveliest girls in Samarkand, posturing delightfully for the entertainment of the crowd'. In comparison, Henry VIII's Field of the Cloth of Gold would have looked like a tawdry bazaar.

It was the Mongols' swan song, one last glorious and defiant display of transitory splendour. For centuries they had grown rich on plunder, and their tents were now magnificent with the gold and rubies of India, the silk and jade of China, the furs of Siberia and the perfumes of Arabia. But their heartland, the arid wilderness of the steppe, was dying through lack of rain. And ephemeral plunder is, in the long term, no substitute for a sound economy.

The festival was also Tamerlane's swan song. For that autumn he decided to invade China. 'So when the leaves had fallen,' his biographer tells us, 'and the nights grew cold upon the meadow, Tamerlane rolled up the carpet of pleasure and turned his thoughts to the destruction of China. Wine and unlawful pleasures were once more prohibited; the great pavilions were dismantled; the smaller tents were folded up; and the Horde prepared to ride once again with those sisters of victory, fire, pillage, murder and rape.' It must have seemed to Tamerlane that success could be taken for granted, for in the previous 30 years the greater part of the known world had succumbed to his armies. But he was now to meet an adversary even more deadly than himself. Winter.

His generals tried to persuade him to remain in Samarkand until the following spring. However, he brushed their advice aside, and, at the head of a force of something like 250,000 men, headed northeast for the Jaxartes (the Syr-Daria), his plan being to winter in the upper reaches of the river, then invade China the following spring. The winter of 1404/5, however, turned out to be the coldest in living memory, and Tamerlane found the Jaxartes covered by three feet (1 m) of ice. The warning could hardly have been more explicit. But none the less he pushed on.

Then winter unleashed his raging tempests, raising over the roof of the world the tents of his swirling clouds. The serpents fled for refuge to the depths of their Gehenna, lions hid in their dens, and gazelles sought the shelter of their lairs. Fires subsided and were snuffed out, lakes froze, leaves were torn from the trees, avalanches rolled into the valleys, and the earth grew pale with fear . . . But Tamerlane ordered extra coverings to be made for his tents, and extra-thick shirts and breastplates for his men. 'Fear not,' he said, 'for Winter cannot harm you' . . . But Winter was not to be mocked. 'If you are one Infernal Spirit,' he cried to Tamerlane, 'I am another and Greater. We have both grown grey in the destruction of men. But the breath of my frost is more deadly than the heat of your fire; I have slain more men than you; and not all the heat from your piled coals shall save you.' Then he struck [the Horde] with great cataracts of snow and with a cold so great that it split breastplates and dissolved joints of iron. The wind blew upon the camels and they died. When a man breathed, his breath congealed on his beard so that he became covered in ice. When a man spat, though the spittle was warm as it left his mouth by the time it hit the ground it had frozen to a solid ball. Seared by the cold, men's noses and ears fell off. They froze to death as they rode.

Thus Winter destroyed both the noble and the base.

Yet Tamerlane cared not for their dying, nor grieved for those who had fallen.

Winter, however, had the last laugh. It killed him, too. According to Wilfrid Blunt:

Tamerlane's health had suffered from the severity of the journey, and before long he became seriously ill. Each day he grew worse; not all the furs of Asia could bring warmth to his chilled body, nor arrack laced with drugs and spices allay his shivering fits. When orthodox treatment had failed, his doctors attempted to drive out cold with cold, laying ice-packs on his chest and belly till he coughed and foamed like a strangled camel. Soon he began to spit blood, and the doctors were obliged to confess that all their remedies were unavailing. 'We know of no cure,' they said, 'for death.'

He died, reciting the Koran, in the middle of a violent thunderstorm.

Such was the terror that Tamerlane inspired in his life, it is hardly surprising that after his death there grew up a legend about him: that if ever his body was disturbed, a catastrophe greater even than any he had wrought in his lifetime would befall the world. During World War II, a distinguished Soviet scientist, Professor Gerasimov, obtained permission to exhume Tamerlane's body. (It is from the measurements Gerasimov made of his skull that the portait was reconstructed.) Gerasimov exhumed the body on 22 June 1941: the day that Germany invaded Russia.

Tamerlane's career underlines two basic facts about the mountains of central Asia. First, that although they present a formidable barrier between north and south, this barrier *can* be breeched. This is why when the people of Pakistan and India look north, they have the uneasy feeling that what happened once could happen all too easily again. Second, it emphasizes the fact that weather is king: that all man's courage, tenacity and expertise are unavailing in the face of the elements, a fact brought home to us nowadays by the annual death roll of those who challenge the great peaks.

◆

Our pathfinders so far, with the exception of Alexander, have passed through the mountains without showing the slightest inclination to tarry, much less to settle. We come now to a group of people who *were* anxious to put down roots – the Jesuits.

The Jesuit priests were men of high courage and formidable intelligence; and in just about every corner of the world – in the headwaters of the Mississippi, the peaks of the Andes, the oases of the Sahara, the beaches of Japan and the high valleys of the Himalaya – they blazed trails considerably in advance of those who are often regarded as discoverers.

In the Himalaya they carried out three journeys of particular interest. Between 1603–7 Bento de Goes travelled from Lahore to Chiaucuon in the Great Wall of China; between 1624–28 Antonio de Andrade attempted to set up a mission at Tsaparang (then one of the great cities of Tibet) a little to the west of Mount Kailas; and between 1661–62, Fathers Grueber and D'Orville made an epic trek from Peking to Agra, crossing directly over the Nepal Himalaya and almost certainly being the first Europeans to sight Mount Everest.

Jesuits were initially drawn to the Himalaya by reports that pockets of Nestorian

*Top: Tongsa Penlop of Bhutan with
his Council and, above, Tibetan
nuns*

Christians were still eking out a precarious existence among the mountains; and in 1602 a merchant gave the Fathers of the mission at Goa information too specific to be disregarded. 'Beyond the mountains,' he told them, 'there lives in Xambalu in Cathay a great Khan who rules over an empire in which many of the people are Mohammedans and many Isavitae [followers of Jesus].' He added that he had seen with his own eyes 'church services which involve the wearing of white robes, ritual singing, the use of incense, the taking of communion and the worship of one god.' What the merchant had in fact seen were not Christian rituals but Buddhist; he had been deceived by the many superficial resemblances between the two faiths. The Jesuits, however, had visions of restoring lost flocks to the fold of the Catholic faith, and they decided to send one of their number to 'Xambalu in Cathay' to make contact with these far-distant Christians.

The man they chose was Bento de Goes: a great if little-known explorer.

Bento de Goes' caravan attacked by bandits in the Hindu Kush, from an engraving by Pieter vander Aa, 1707

In February 1603 Goes joined the annual caravan from Lahore to the plains of central Asia. His biographer's description of his departure sums up the difficulties of would-be explorers in the Himalaya: 'Realizing that as a European he would meet opposition, Goes let his hair and his beard grow long, and donned the garb of a Persian trader . . . from the moment they left Lahore the caravan had to protect themselves not only against the severities of terrain and climate, but against bands of marauders attracted by their merchandise.'

Throughout the spring the caravan literally fought its way up the Chitral valley and into the foothills of the Hindu Kush. 'In these mountainous ravines,' Bento de Goes' biographer C. J. Wessels wrote, 'the beasts of burden were driven along the lower tracks, while the escort made their way along the upper, to prevent brigands from crushing them to death by rolling rocks on to them . . . Eventually they were compelled to hire an escort of 400 soldiers as a defence against the attacks of the natives. Many were wounded, and some lost their lives trying to save their valuables.' It was mid-summer before they struggled through to Kabul. At this stage, several of Goes' companions, unnerved by danger and hardship, returned home, but Bento and his servant Isaac pressed on. They crossed the Hindu Kush, probably by the Parwan Pass, and headed east into the Pamirs, where they came across the phenomenon which has intrigued so many travellers: 'In several villages that we passed through,' wrote Goes, 'the people had brown hair, blue eyes and fair complexion. They are called Calciàs, which means "ravens who have been driven high into the mountains".'

Because the greater part of Goes' diary was subsequently lost, it is not known by which route he crossed the Pamirs. All that can be gleaned is that he had a difficult journey, that five of his horses died of cold, that he was unable to make a fire to warm himself, and that 'the uncongenial state of the atmosphere made it almost impossible for men and animals to breathe, hence both felt oppressed beyond endurance and gasped continuously for breath' (as good a description of altitude sickness as one could wish for). It must have been a relief, in late November, to descend to Yarkand at the approaches to the Takla Makan.

Goes was one of the first Europeans to set foot in this remote and tantalizing emporium. John Keay's description cannot be bettered.

With the merchants of Central Asia Yarkand was highly popular. Bukhara might be the noblest city, Merv the oldest and Samarkand the finest, but Yarkand was the naughtiest; it was their Paris. Western Turkistan was oppressively Mohammedan; but Yarkand was ruled by the Chinese. The Chinese vetted their visitors carefully. But their rule was fair – and so too were the ladies of Yarkand. Mohammedans they might be, but they wore no veils and hid from no man. On the contrary, from their high-heeled boots to their elaborate medieval head-dresses, they invited the very glances for which in Bukhara a man could be arrested. Some were prostitutes. There were streets of brothels, and they were well patronised. But for the visiting merchant, who might spend months in Yarkand assembling his caravan, there were pleasanter arrangements. He got married. Four wives was the accepted maximum; but a most convenient institution known as a 'nicka marriage' limited conjugal rights to a fixed period: it might be a year, it might be just a week. By the time she was thirty, an attractive Yarkandi girl might have had a hundred husbands.

Goes' earnest biographer tells us that the priest 'was obliged, much against his wishes, to spend nearly a year in this sinful and uncongenial city, his patience being sorely tried.' However, it should in fairness be pointed out that it was not the ladies of Yarkand who detained Goes, but the Chinese officials, who refused to let him join an eastbound caravan until he had paid a succession of hefty bribes.

By the winter of 1604/5 he was again on the move, skirting the Takla Makan via the skein of oases which lie within the rain shadow of the Tien Shan. It was a bleakly beautiful world through which the caravan moved in a silence so absolute it could almost be felt: a vast ocean of sand, ringed to the north, south and west by mountains which 'rose on three sides of us like the unscalable walls of a prison'. Often the mountains would be hidden by 'loess', fine dust particles which hang in the air, defying gravity, until dispersed by wind or rain. It is this loess which gives Asia its imagery of yellow: the dusty yellow air, settling on the yellow soil, impregnating the yellow rocks, seeping into the yellow rivers (the Huang Ho, of course, is known as the Yellow River), emptying into the Yellow Sea which lies between Korea and China, home of the yellow people. The loess is also responsible for the name 'Celestial Mountains', given by early travellers to the Tien Shan; for when the upper layers of the dust disperse, the peaks of the whole 1200-mile (1930 km) range often appear to be floating on a layer of heavenly cloud.

To the difficulty of the terrain was soon added Goes' travelling difficulties. His Mohammedan companions allowed him a place in their caravan only on sufferance. At every oasis there were scruples to be overcome, delays to be endured, an endless succession of officials to be bribed. He began to run short of money, and his health deteriorated.

He seems to have spent the better part of two years struggling across the Takla Makan, before coming at last to the Great Wall of China. Here there were more delays; and it was while he was waiting for permission to press on to Xambalu that he became seriously ill – some believe that he was poisoned. On 10 April 1607, in spite of the ministrations of his devoted Isaac, he went into a coma; and the next day, to quote a contemporary Jesuit, 'in search of Cathay he found heaven'.

His fellow travellers promptly seized the last of his money and possessions. They also tore up and burned his diary, only a few fragments being saved.

Bento de Goes was the first European of modern times to make the journey from India to China and the first to prove that the legendary Cathay was synonymous with China. These achievements have never won the recognition they deserve.

During his travels Goes failed to come across the hoped-for Christian communities. Yet rumours that such communities existed continued to filter through to India, and in the spring of 1624 Father Antonio de Andrade set out in search of an enclave which had been reported in the western Himalayas.

Andrade, like Goes, was a member of the Jesuit mission at Goa, and he was accompanied on his travels by two servants and the lay brother Manuel Marques. The four men disguised themselves as Hindu pilgrims, and joined a party bound for the sacred springs which rise near the headwaters of the Ganges. Their disguise was soon seen through, and they were arrested and thrown into prison as spies. They managed, however, to talk and bribe their way out of trouble – a pattern to be repeated many times by many travellers in the years to come – and after only a few days were allowed to continue their journey. Soon they were passing through the vale of Kashmir, 'that jewel set in a ring of pearls', on which Andrade's biographer waxes eloquent:

> *Before them rose the Lesser Himalayas. As yet no European had set foot among these huge fastnesses. Their ascent proved extremely difficult, ridge rose beyond ridge, and the paths were so narrow they could advance only by inches, clinging to the walls of rock, while far below the sacred Ganges seethed and foamed through its gorge-like bed. At every favourable point along the track stood tiny temples, jewels of architecture, many of them occupied by the fanatical Hindu self-torturers. The scenery was beyond belief: the slopes covered with primeval forests – gigantic pines two or three times the height of the church tower at Goa, many cinnamon bushes, cypress, lemon and chestnut trees, and flowers without number.*

Beyond Kashmir they came to the Greater Himalayas, a chain of mighty peaks rising higher and ever higher until their snows disappeared into the clouds. It must have seemed to Andrade and his companions that the Christian communities of Tibet lay beyond human reach. However, they struggled on. *Now*, wrote Andrade,

> *the road became terrible indeed. The snow was so deep that we sank into it up to our waists, sometimes even up to our shoulders. We had hardly camped for the night when we were overtaken by a snowstorm so violent and thick that we could not see one another, even though we were lying side by side. The intense cold made our hands, faces and feet numb and brittle; so that knocking my finger against something hard, I found I had knocked the tip of it altogether off. Having no sense of pain, I should not have believed it, had not a copious flow of blood shown it to be a fact. Our feet became so frozen and swollen that we felt nothing when they were touched with a piece of red hot iron.*

Next day they managed to drag themselves over the Mana Pass, and saw before them the vast plains of Tibet, 'all one dazzling whiteness to our eyes, which had become so weakened with snow-blindness that we could not make out the road we should follow.' They would almost certainly have died of exposure if the local ruler had not heard of their predicament, and sent a guide and pack-animals to rescue them. Eventually, in the last stages of hypothermia, they were carried into Tsaparang.

They found no Christian community in Tsaparang and no Christian church – once again the reports which had filtered through to India had mistaken Buddhist services for Christian. Andrade, however, was a man to be reckoned with. He founded his own church: a Jesuit mission, the first Christian community to put down roots in the Himalaya. It was a gesture as brave, if nothing like as enduring, as the founding of the Alexandrias. For several years the mission flourished; then the ruler who had befriended the Jesuits was defeated in a local war, the priests were driven out, the mission was closed, and subsequent efforts to re-open it met with such opposition they had to be abandoned.

'Such was the sad ending,' writes Andrade's biographer, 'to a day that had begun so brightly'; although to an unbiased observer the failure of this first attempt to impose an alien creed on the Tibetans might not seem altogether a disaster.

Letter from Lamas ordering all Tibetans to turn the foreigners back, from an earlier expedition by St G.R. Littledale, 1895

Throughout the seventeenth century the Jesuits continued to probe the Himalaya, pioneering routes which explorers were to follow in the eighteenth century and climbers in the nineteenth. Perhaps the most impressive of their journeys was that made by Fathers Grueber and D'Orville, who in 1661 travelled from Peking to Agra not by the usual caravan trails, but by cutting directly across the Nepal Himalaya, a route of extreme difficulty through virgin territory.

The Austrian Johann Grueber is one of the most enigmatic figures in the history of exploration. In his chosen subjects, theology and mathematics, he was a man of formidable erudition – his analysis of Buddhist and Christian doctrine was a treatise of rare scholarship, while his survey work was so accurate that many of the latitudes and longitudes which he fixed in 1661 have proved more reliable than those made 200 years later. But he was, alas, to quote the then President of the Royal Geographical Society, Sir Clements Markham, 'not very communicative'. In the whole of his diary there is not a single description of landscape, not a word of admiration for the majestic ranges of the

Himalaya; there is also very little about the people through whose cities he was often the first white man to pass. He seems to have been more interested in statistics than beauty, more at home with dogma than with people.

With the Belgian Father Albert D'Orville, he left Peking early in 1661, determined to travel to Rome 'by a route no man hath yet attempted'. From the moment they left Sining-fu on the Great Wall of China, the fathers were heading into the unknown.

To start with, their route lay over the arid 'Tartar desert' at the approaches to the Kun Lun. About the only distinctive feature on this part of their journey was the Koko-Nor (the name means 'blue sea', although the lake – the largest in Tibet – is usually a brackish-grey); they skirted its shores in mid-summer and headed southwest into a lunar world where range after range of featureless mountains lay strewn across their path like the waves of a petrified sea. Grueber, in what for him is a purple passage, describes it as 'an impossibly barren land, whose bleak hillsides are broken only by the occasional cluster of black felt tents, home of the predatory Mongols'. Three months after leaving

Drawing by Kircher of the Potala at Lhasa

Sining-fu, they came to the highest of the ranges, the Kun Lun, which they crossed by a 15,000-foot (4575 m) pass before descending into the plains of central Tibet. Here the distances were vast, and progress slow and uneventful. Day after day, week after week, the fathers plodded along a little-used caravan route, through a world of desiccated rock and unremitting wind: a harsh environment where even the deepest valleys were 10,000 feet (3000 m) above sea-level. By autumn they were approaching Lhasa, the 'forbidden city', the Mecca of travellers in which no European had set foot for more than 300 years.

They entered the Tibetan capital in early October; and how one longs to find in Grueber's diary some description of the architecture, the customs, the everyday life of the people in a city which for centuries had been the epitome of mystery and inaccessibility. He did, it is true, make a number of sketches of the city – his drawing of the Potala was once derided as a forgery because in the foreground is a wheeled carriage, a form of transport which did not exist in seventeenth-century Tibet; it is now, however, generally agreed that the carriage represents nothing more than the obligatory foreground material which most artists of the day incorporated into their landscape, and that the Potala itself is a faithful reproduction of the actual building.

He also made one or two interesting observations on Tibetan life. For example, he gives the first description of the prayer wheel, and of the much-repeated phrase *Om mani padme hum* (Hail, oh jewel in the lotus!) which is the Tibetan equivalent of 'hello' and 'good-bye'. He was the first to report 'that bloody and most detestable custom whereby on certain feast-days a youth in gay habit, decked with banners and armed with a sword, quiver and arrows, wanders about the streets killing people at his pleasure, none making the slightest resistance.' And he was the first to note with horror that the much sought-after 'curative pills', sold at an exorbitant price by members of the royal household to those who were seriously ill, were made not from special herbs but from the excrement of the Dalai Lama! Most of his diary, however, consists of a long dissertation on Tibetan politics, and a highly technical comparison between Buddhist and Catholic dogma. The latter he summed up with the words:

> *It is amazing how their religion agrees with the Romish. They too celebrate the sacrifice of the Mass with bread and wine, they too give extreme unction, bless those who are married, say prayers for the sick, make processions, sing in choirs, honour the relics of idols, have monasteries and nunneries, observe fasts, undergo severe penances, consecrate holy men and send out missionaries who live in extreme poverty and travel barefoot.*

No wonder casual observers often mistook Buddhist services for Christian.

Grueber and D'Orville left Lhasa in November on the last and most hazardous part of their journey, the crossing of the Himalaya. Here again how one longs for even a brief description of the terrain through which they passed. The fathers must have clung to some of the most perilous paths and gazed at some of the most spectacular scenery on earth, almost certainly passing within sight of Everest; yet in Grueber's diary there is not a single description of landscape, not a word of admiration for the majestic peaks that lined their route. It must be said in his defence that an appreciation of the natural world is a characteristic of the nineteenth not the seventeenth-century, but one cannot help regretting an opportunity lost.

The priests reached Agra almost exactly a year after setting out from Peking, and within a few weeks the patient and self-effacing D'Orville was dead; 'the hardships and privations he had endured had,' we are told, 'altogether drained away his strength, and midway between China and Europe he departed for his heavenly home.' Grueber continued his journey alone, his arrival at the Vatican in 1663 ending an impressive if little-known feat of exploration.

The Jesuits were a link between ancient and modern, a bridge between the medieval pathfinders and the explorers of the eighteenth and nineteenth centuries. It was the Jesuits who were the first to try, albeit without much success, to put down roots. It was the Jesuits, too, who were first to covet something the mountain people had: not material possessions, but their souls. In this they set an unhappy precedent. For millennia the mountains of central Asia had been like a great rock which the waves had lapped and sometimes beat against but had never even remotely threatened to engulf. It was Jesuit priests who made the first small penetration into this rock. After them came the deluge.

From the middle of the eighteenth century, the outside world became increasingly interested in the mountain complex, and soon explorers, traders and government agents were making systematic inroads into terrain which for centuries had been shrouded in mystery.

CHAPTER FOUR

THE EXPLORERS

BY the end of the eighteenth century, three great and predatory empires were advancing on the mountains: the Russians from the northwest, the Chinese from the northeast, and the British in India from the south.

Of the protagonists in the drama about to unfold, the Russians were initially the least active – not until the middle of the nineteenth century were their explorers pushing into the Tien Shan and the Pamirs. The Chinese were the most powerful and the most firmly entrenched – their influence had been a major factor in the life of the mountain people for 1000 years before, in 1811, the first Englishman struggled through to Lhasa. The British were the most active.

It was the East India Company, and in particular its president Warren Hastings, who triggered off British interest in the Himalaya. Hastings was the archetypal imperialist: energetic, shrewd, far-sighted and utterly dedicated to the task of spreading British influence into the far-flung corners of the earth. Taking advantage of a quarrel between local rulers, he decided 'to send an English gentleman into Tibet for the purpose of exploring this unknown region, of opening mutual communications of trade, and of making a treaty of friendship'. The man he chose for this formidable task was not in fact an Englishman at all, but a 28-year-old Scot, George Bogle.

Bogle, a revenue collector for the East India Company, left Calcutta in May 1774. His route lay initially up the lush valley of the Brahmaputra, then through the *terai* where he was 'much hampered by thickets of reeds, brushwood and long interwoven grasses, and plagued by an abundance of frogs and watery insects'. It took him a fortnight to reach the foothills of Bhutan where, he relates with disarming candour, he 'for some days sojourned with a female pedlar, with good features and shape, fine teeth and Rubens' wife's eyes . . . her only garment one blanket wrapped around her.' Soon he was approaching territory in which few Europeans had set foot, and as the mountains became steeper and the trail more precipitous he was obliged to recruit porters. *The only way of transporting goods in this hilly country,* he wrote,

> *is by coolies; the roads are too narrow steep and rugged for any other conveyance, and the rivers too strong and rapid for boats. The carriers are pressed into service from among the local inhabitants, and receive an allowance at the pleasure of the person by whom they are employed. This is a custom so well established that the people submit to it without murmur. Neither sex, youth nor age exempt them from it. One day a girl of eighteen travelled with us, carrying a burden of 75 pounds – more than I could with comfort lift.*

Bogle's immediate goal was Tassisudon, the capital of Bhutan; but while he was still several days' journey from the city, he received a letter from its ruler advising him to abandon his mission and return to Calcutta, 'since no Moghuls, Hindustani, Patan or Feringies [Europeans] may be admitted into our realm'. Bogle, however, was a determined character; he pushed on, and little more than a month after leaving Calcutta entered the Bhutanese capital.

Tassisudon in those days consisted of a cluster of farms and a single monastery-cum-palace: an enormous two-storey building which was the home of 3000 men (including 1000 monks) but not a single woman. Bogle was given comfortable accommodation 'in one of the better houses near the residence of the Rajah', and here he waited patiently for an audience. On 6 July the hoped-for summons reached him.

It was an historic moment, the first official meeting between a Himalayan ruler and an accredited envoy from Europe, and Bogle's letter to his sister captures the bizarre pageantry of the occasion.

After passing through three courts and climbing two iron ladders, I was carried into an antechamber hung with bows, arrows, swords, matchlocks and other implements of war, and filled with a large number of priests. Having waited there for about half an hour, I was conducted to the Rajah. He was seated upon a throne or pulpit, raised about two feet above the ground. On entering, I made him three low bows, instead of prostrating myself according to the etiquette of the court; I then gave him a white satin handkerchief, while my servants laid out my presents of spices, cloth and cutlery, after which I was conducted to a cushion prepared for me at the opposite end of the room. All this passed in a profound silence. Several copper trays with rice, butter, tea, walnuts, apricots and cucumbers were then set before me, together with a little stool and a china cup . . . The Rajah, a pleasant-looking old man, was dressed in scarlet cotton, with a gilded mitre on his head; an umbrella with fringes was constantly twirled above him. The panels of the room and the ceiling were covered with Chinese landscapes and different coloured satins. Behind where I sat, several large Chinese images were placed in an alcove, with lamps of butter burning before them, all ornamented with elephant's teeth, little silver ornaments, china-ware, silks and ribbons . . . Soon there came a man carrying a large silver kettle, with tea made with butter and spices, and having poured a little into his hand and drunk it, he filled the Rajah a cup, then went round to all the ministers and priests, who are always provided with a little wooden cup, black-glazed on the inside, which they carry wrapped in cloth and lodged within their tunic next to their skin, which keeps it warm and comfortable; and last of all the cup-bearer filled my dish. The Rajah then said grace, in which he was joined by all the company. When we had finished our tea, and every man had well-licked his cup and deposited it in his bosom, a gown like what Aunt Katy used to wear, was brought and put on me, and a red satin handkerchief was tied round me as a girdle. I was then conducted to the throne, where the Rajah bound my temples with another handkerchief and muttered some prayers over me, after which I was led back to my cushion. We had next a cup of whisky, fresh and hot out of the still, which was served round in the same manner as the tea, of which we had yet more helpings and as many graces, and last of all betel nut.

There followed a great deal of complimentary but largely meaningless talk, before Bogle, resplendent in his Aunt Katy gown, was escorted back to his quarters. Here he was to spend the next three months trying to obtain permission to enter Tibet.

A less patient man would have become frustrated; a less observant one, bored. Bogle, however, passed the time contentedly enough studying and recording a way of life which up to now had been unknown to Europeans.

It says much for his common sense and pleasant personality that he quickly established a happy relationship with his hosts. Initially he seems to have made a conscious effort to create a good impression. 'In order to fulfil my commission,' he wrote in his diary, 'I had to gain these peoples' confidence and goodwill. With this in mind I assumed the dress of the country, endeavoured to acquire a little of their language and manners, drank a deluge of tea-salt-and-butter, ate betel nut, took snuff, and would never allow myself to be put out of humour.' There soon developed, however, another reason for Bogle's content. He genuinely liked the mountain people. Subsequent explorers were often critical of the filth and squalour of the Bhutanese and Tibetans and the procrastination of court officials, but Bogle was more tolerant. He noted but did not condemn the widespread lack of cleanliness, adding that it must be difficult in so cold a climate to wash oneself frequently; as to the leisurely pace of negotiations, he remarked that it made a pleasant change from the bustle and rush of Calcutta. 'The more I see of these people,' he wrote to Hastings, 'the better I am pleased with them.' He was especially pleased, in mid-October, to be given permission to enter Tibet.

There are two schools of thought about Bogle's journey into Tibet. One that it was uneventful, unproductive and therefore unimportant. The other that, since it provided the world with its first glimpse of an unknown land and people, it was very important indeed. There is truth in both viewpoints, although perhaps more in the latter, since Bogle's observations are both meticulous and perspicacious, and on the strength of them the British initiated a policy towards the Himalayan kingdoms which was followed for the better part of a century.

Cane bridge over the Teesta River,
photographed in the late nineteenth century

He left the Bhutanese capital on 13 October 1774 with a sizeable retinue of porters, heading for the gap in the Trans-Himalayas a little to the east of Kangchenjunga. It was a cold and difficult journey. Soon they were toiling up a path so high that they had to pause every few yards panting for breath, and so rough that even the sure-footed mules stumbled and fell. The surrounding peaks were covered with snow – a phenomenon unfamiliar to Bogle's Bengali servants who asked the local porters for an explanation and were told that God in his mercy had dropped white cloths on the mountains to keep them warm!

On crossing into Tibet Bogle was impressed by the Arcadian simplicity of life. According to his biographer, George Woodcock:

The character of the people at once touched his heart, and in this part of his journal one is aware of his mounting delight at having discovered a race he found utterly congenial . . . This feeling appears very strongly when he rode one afternoon into a village where the people were working in the fields, stacking their straw and singing as they worked. He stayed the night in a polyandrous household of two brothers married to 'a very handsome wife and sharing three of the prettiest children I ever saw'. Bogle was astonished at the sheer natural happiness of this family, organized on principles so very different from those that governed domestic life in Scotland. He entertained his hosts to tea and sugar-candy, and after dark the whole family reciprocated by dancing for two hours, chanting the folk songs of the region.

By mid-November, when Bogle and his retinue struggled through to the palace of the Panchen Lama at Desheripgay, it was clear that the hard-headed Scot had fallen under the spell of Tibet and the Tibetans. And in Desheripgay something happened which made this spell more binding. He formed a deep and lasting friendship with the Panchen Lama.

Cynics have pointed out that the two men doubtless found it politic to be on good terms, but there is plenty of evidence that their relationship was based on a genuine personal rapport. Bogle wrote to Hastings: 'I endeavoured to find in his character those

Baggage horses in Sinkiang, China,
1899

defects which are usually inseparable from humanity, but I had no success; not a man could find it in his heart to speak ill of him.' In turn, the Lama offered his guest far more in the way of help and companionship than was called for by mere diplomatic courtesy; he made every effort to get him a permit to visit Lhasa, and took him with him when he moved to his winter palace at Tashilhunpo.

Tashilhunpo was another of those great monastic institutions, more like a town than a building, its temples climbing tier after tier up the steep-sided valley of the Tsangpo. Here for the next three months Bogle was torn between delight and frustration: delight in his surroundings and the knowledge he was acquiring, frustration at being continually refused permission to continue his journey. The difficulty was that Hastings had believed the Panchen Lama to be the ruler of Tibet, and had provided Bogle with presents and letters of introduction for him alone; Bogle now discovered that the real ruler of Tibet was not the Panchen Lama in Tashilhunpo but the Dalai Lama in Lhasa; the latter was very much under the influence of the Chinese, and he used Bogle's lack of credentials as an excuse to refuse him permission to come to Lhasa. The fact was that 'Feringies' were *persona non grata* in the capital, for the Tibetans were perfectly happy with the trade links they already had with China, Siberia and Kashmir, and the East India Company had nothing to offer them. Bogle found that neither pleading, persuasion, persistence nor all the good offices of his friend the Panchen Lama could gain him the hoped-for permission and in April 1775 he returned to Calcutta.

It might be said that he had failed, for he brought back no treaty of friendship, and never even saw the ruler he had travelled more than 1000 miles (1600 km) to meet. He did, on the other hand, bring back a vast amount of information about Bhutan and Tibet, and although this information was not widely disseminated, it was studied with great care by the East India Company. As a result of what Bogle told them, the company initiated a policy towards the Himalayan kingdoms which has been followed by successive British governments from that day to this: a policy which set its face against

The Dalai Lama, 1910

military occupation, attempted to foster trade, and respected the way of life of the people. Many explorers who are better known accomplished less.

Sadly, Bogle never returned to the country he loved. With Hastings' backing he was preparing for another attempt to reach Lhasa in 1779 when, within a few days of one another, both he and his friend the Panchen Lama died, the one of cholera in Calcutta, the other of smallpox in Peking.

For Hastings the deaths of Bogle and the Lama were major setbacks. However, he continued to seek ways of promoting British interests in the Himalaya, and in 1783 an opportunity presented itself. Hearing that the incarnation of the Panchen Lama was believed to have been found in a small child, he decided to send another envoy to Tibet to congratulate the Lama on his return to a new body. The man he chose was his cousin, Samuel Turner, a lieutenant in the military division of the Company.

Turner was to prove a tactful and intelligent emissary, although he lacked Bogle's warm-hearted rapport with his Tibetan hosts. The highlight of his mission was his audience with the child Lama: an occasion which he describes with real feeling.

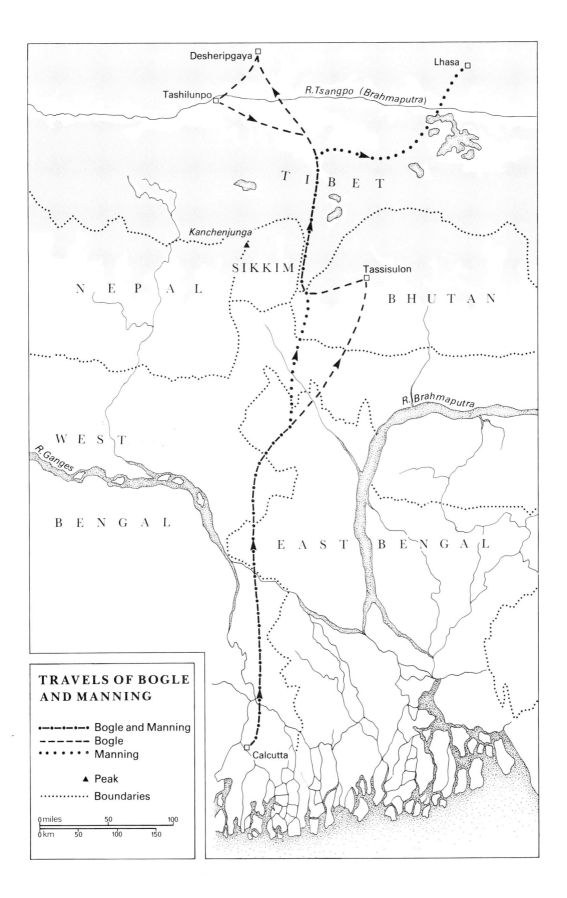

Desheripgaya

Lhasa

Tashilunpo

R. Tsangpo (Brahmaputra)

T I B E T

Kanchenjunga

SIKKIM

Tassisulon

N E P A L

BHUTAN

R. Brahmaputra

W E S T

R. Ganges

B E N G A L

E A S T   B E N G A L

**TRAVELS OF BOGLE
AND MANNING**

•—•—•—•— Bogle and Manning

– – – – Bogle

•••••••• Manning

▲ Peak

•••••••• Boundaries

Calcutta

0 miles   50   100

0 km   50   100   150

The Lama was only 18 months old when he received his visitor in a monastery near Tashilhunpo. Turner had been told that although the child was not yet able to speak, he could understand all that was said to him; he therefore addressed him as an adult, explaining how 'the Governor-General [Hastings], on receiving the news of his decease in China, had been overwhelmed with grief and sorrow, and had long continued to lament his absence from the world; but that now he had reappeared, his joy was even greater than his sorrow had been. The Governor-General,' Turner went on, 'anxiously wished that he the Lama might long continue to illumine the world by his presence, and was hopeful that the friendship which had formerly existed between them might become still greater.' It was a scene that had all the elements of farce: the young British officer in full-dress uniform earnestly delivering a succession of platitudes to the incongruously robed child. Turner, however, didn't find it absurd, for he was deeply impressed by the Lama's precocity. *While I spoke,* he wrote to Hastings,

the little creature looked steadfastly towards me with the appearance of much attention, nodding repeatedly as though he understood every word . . . When my cup was empty he appeared uneasy, and, stretching out his arm, made a motion to his attendants to give me more . . . Though unable to speak, he made the most expressive signs and conducted himself with astonishing dignity.

In fact, Turner was so impressed that he wondered if there might not be some truth in the Tibetans' belief that the child was indeed a reincarnation of the Lama. As for the Tibetans they seem to have been almost equally impressed with Turner. 'Although our visitors were not knowers of the niceties of religion,' wrote a Tibetan monk, 'by merely gazing at the young Panchen an irresistible faith was born in them, and they said to one another "in such a little frame are activities of body, speech and mind that are greatly marvellous." They therefore addressed him with great reverence.

Unfortunately for Turner his hosts were not sufficiently impressed to let him continue his journey to Lhasa; and eventually, like Bogle, he was obliged to return to India having accomplished little. He did, however, achieve one distinction which eluded his more illustrious predecessor; he managed to find a publisher for his diary, and his *Account of an Embassy to the Court of the Teshoo Lama* was for 100 years almost the only account of Tibetan life to appear in Europe.

Soon after Turner completed his mission, Tibet was invaded, first by the Gurung and then by the Chinese. The British, preoccupied with the Napoleonic wars, were unwilling to become involved, and in the early years of the nineteenth century interest in the mountains was at a low ebb.

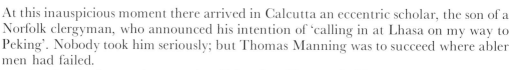

At this inauspicious moment there arrived in Calcutta an eccentric scholar, the son of a Norfolk clergyman, who announced his intention of 'calling in at Lhasa on my way to Peking'. Nobody took him seriously; but Thomas Manning was to succeed where abler men had failed.

It is hard to know what to make of Manning. He was a brilliant scholar, yet he never took a degree; he had a warm if mercurial personality, yet he made few friends. 'He was the most wonderful man I ever knew,' wrote Charles Lamb, 'more extraordinary than either Wordsworth or Coleridge,' yet he died an unrecognized recluse in the shadow of paranoia. He was a man who promised much but achieved nothing: nothing, that is, except the distinction of being the first Englishman to set foot in the Forbidden City – and even this was something of a failure, since his real objective was Peking.

He left Cambridge in 1800 with the reputation of being the finest scholar of his generation but, typically, without a degree, since he found the formality of repeating the religious oaths required of graduates repugnant. Abandoning a promising career in mathematics, he became obsessed with Chinese culture: an obsession which was to last for the rest of his life although, again typically, he never published anything to consummate his years of research. In 1806 he arrived in Canton, determined to travel to Peking and obtain an audience with the Emperor. 'I have been petitioning the Mandarins,' he wrote to Lamb, 'for leave to go to Peking as ASTRONOMER and PHYSICIAN. They refuse as yet to send my petition to the Emperor; but I have not given up, and they shall hear from me again.' He was soon to discover, however, that Peking was as much a forbidden city as Lhasa, and failing to get the permission he hoped for, he hit on the scatterbrained idea of being landed secretly on the coast of Conchin disguised as an Annamese trader. This scheme also foundered because the Royal Navy frigate in which he embarked decided to chart the Paracel Islands instead of the south China coast, which Manning found 'a terrible waste of time and a grievous bore'. Thwarted in his efforts to penetrate China via the Pacific, he decided to try via India and Tibet, hence his arrival in 1810 in Calcutta.

This background pinpoints the *raison d'être* of Manning's journey. It was *not* an official mission, and it was *not* a journey of discovery; it was simply a very long and very arduous walk, carried out by an eccentric individual who wanted to get from A to B and found that Lhasa happened to lie on his route. It is not, therefore, very fair to Manning to complain that his diary tells us more about his character than about nineteenth-century Tibet.

He emerges as a tenacious but inexpert traveller, ever at odds with his servants and guides, and ill-equipped both physically and mentally for his momentous journey. His diary is full of trivia.

Wet, wet, wet; why is it always raining? I find going up-hill does not agree with me – perhaps because I am going down-hill! . . . My Chinese servant has changed our silver spoons into pewter ones. I told him I would not go on till I got my spoons back. Now it seems my porter is a party to this iniquity. At last he went and returned with one silver and one pewter [spoon]. But I swore I would not move till I had the other. I am in bad bad hands. Now my Chinaman is as cross as the devil and will not speak. A spaniel would be better company!

How on earth, one wonders, did he ever get to Lhasa?

Probably the main reason for his success was that he had considerable skill as a physician; and although his remedies often strike one as more than a little bizarre – 'I gave her a few papers of bark, opium, and a good dose of arsenic' – he never seems to have been short of patients. It also helped that he was a Sinophile. His diary (at least to start with) is full of sycophantic references to the Chinese: 'they are really civilized and do not live like cattle . . . what a comfort it is, after having lodged in smoke and dirt with the native animals of Tibet, to take shelter in a Chinaman's house, where you can be sure of urbanity and cleanliness.' The Chinese controlled the approaches to Lhasa, and they were as susceptible as the next race to flattery. Another thing in Manning's favour was, to give him his due, that he never minded making a fool of himself. Bogle, when introduced to dignitaries, had been reluctant to bow; Manning, in contrast, grovelled – 'in order to dispel any thoughts that I might be an Englishman, I performed the most humble kow-tow, falling to my knees and touching the floor three times with my brow. I was always asking when I could kertse or kneel, and if there was an option between one kertse or three, I invariably chose to give three.'

The Chinese soon recognized him for what he was: a harmless, highly-strung eccentric. It seemed hardly worth their while stopping him from reaching Lhasa; so early in December 1811 – the exact date is not clear from his diary – Manning became the first Englishman to enter the Forbidden City. Here he was to remain for four months, trying unsuccessfully to obtain permission to push on to Peking.

One cannot help wishing that the mysteries of Lhasa could have been unveiled by a less neurotic traveller. What a Burton with his scholarship or a Vigne with his easel would have made of such an opportunity! As it is, much of Manning's diary consists of either trivia or introspective passages describing his terror at the prospect of being poisoned and tortured. To start with he didn't have a good word for either the Tibetans or their capital. 'The habitations,' he wrote, 'are begrimed with smut and dirt. The avenues are full of dogs, some growling and gnawing bits of hide which lie about in profusion and emit a charnel-house smell, others starving and dying and pecked at by ravens. In short everything mean and gloomy. Even the laughter of the inhabitants I thought unreal and ghostly.' However, as the months passed his attitude changed; he became increasingly disillusioned with the Chinese and increasingly grateful for the crumbs of comfort offered him by the Tibetans. For the Chinese refused to let him continue his journey; he became convinced they were trying to poison him, and was obsessed with the thought that he was about to be arrested and tortured. He turned, in terror, to the people he had formerly despised: the Tibetans. He never understood them – from the first day of his stay in Lhasa to the last he referred to their prayer wheels as 'whirligigs' – but he did begin to realize that there was more to their way of life than met the eye. Before he left he was able to see the kindness that lay behind their not-very-prepossessing façade. Eventually he too, in his idiosyncratic way, came to love them.

In April 1812 he was forced to admit that his dream of reaching Peking was a chimera. Disillusioned, he left the Tibetan capital and retraced his steps to India.

Back in Calcutta his journey caused less of a stir than might have been expected, partly because, in 1812, fighting the French was considered more important than exploring the Himalaya, and partly because his eccentric behaviour alienated the hierarchy of the East India Company. Eventually he returned to England, complaining, with some justification, that his exploits never won him the recognition he deserved.

A few years later, Bhutan and Tibet sealed off their borders to foreigners.

Bogle, Turner and Manning were not truly great explorers. They did, however, give Europeans the first glimpse they had had for many centuries of the Himalaya and its people. And all three of them fell under the spell of the Tibetans. 'Farewell, ye honest and simple people,' Bogle wrote on leaving Tashilhunpo. 'May ye long enjoy that happiness which is denied to more polished nations, and while they are engaged in the endless pursuit of avarice and ambition, defended by your barren mountains, may ye long continue to live in peace and contentment and know no wants but those of nature.' It is easy to dismiss this as naïve. Yet it is worth remembering that Bogle and his fellow explorers did establish a rapport with the mountain people, a rapport which, with one unfortunate exception, has characterized Anglo-Tibetan relations from that day to this. Other nations have sometimes had less rapport – and less sympathy.

With the Himalaya in the east now forbidden territory to travellers, the British turned their attention to the Hindu Kush in the west.

◆

Exploration in the Hindu Kush has a different flavour to exploration in the Himalaya, one more spiced with danger. For a fair proportion of those who traversed the bleakly beautiful ranges of the Kush met violent deaths, including its first and arguably its greatest explorer, Moorcroft.

William Moorcroft has been variously described as 'a horse dealer', 'an adventurer' and 'a spy'. There is truth in each epithet, but it would, I think, be fairer to call him a trader, a trader who was brought up in and imbued with the ideas of the eighteenth century, but whose travels spilled over into the nineteenth. He was born in Lancashire in 1765, and as a young man took the then unprecedented step of abandoning medicine in order to study veterinary surgery in France. In 1788 he became the first qualified veterinarian to set up a practice in England, and quickly acquired an excellent reputation and a sizeable fortune. What happened next gives a clue to both his character and his career. He invented and patented a machine-made horseshoe, sank most of his money in marketing his invention, and lost the lot. Moorcroft was a man of vision, ability and great enthusiasm, but he did not always have the knack of seeing his projects through to fruition.

Moorcroft and Hearsay riding yaks on their
way to Lake Manasarowar

In 1808 he became manager of the East India Company's stud farm in Bihar, an important and lucrative job in the days of cavalry. Much was expected from the appointment of so distinguished a man of science, and Moorcroft did not let his employers down. He was a hard worker and a great innovator, introducing oats and equine innoculation to India, and within a couple of years he could claim that, whereas when he had taken over the stud there had been an average of 100 animals sick at any one time, there were now less than ten. Determined to improve the quality of his horses still further, he asked the company for new breeding stocks, either a herd of stallions from England or a herd from Central Asia – an area whose horses had long been renowned for their speed, agility and endurance. Since the former was not forthcoming, in 1819 he decided to go in search of the latter.

There was, however, a great deal more to Moorcroft's expedition than a quest for horses. It was also a quest for trade, and a conscious effort to extend British influence into *terra incognita*.

'Trade with central Asia,' says John Keay, 'was the inspiration behind all

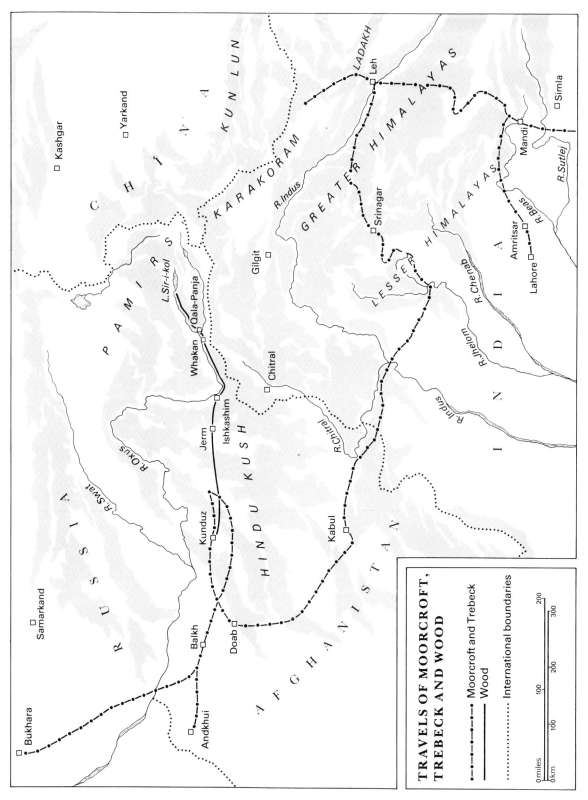

RUSSIA

Bukhara

Samarkand

Andkhui

Balkh

Doab

R.Swat

R.Oxus

PAMIRS

L.Sir-i-kol

Qala-Panja

Whakan

Jerm

Ishkashim

Kunduz

HINDU KUSH

Kabul

AFGHANISTAN

CHINA

Kashgar

Yarkand

KUN LUN

KARAKORAM

R.Indus

Gilgit

Chitral

R.Chitral

R.Indus

GREATER HIMALAYAS

LADAKH

Leh

Srinagar

LESSER HIMALAYAS

R.Jhelom

R.Chenab

Mandi

R.Sutlej

R.Beas

Amritsar

Lahore

INDIA

Simla

TRAVELS OF MOORCROFT, TREBECK AND WOOD

•—•—• Moorcroft and Trebeck
——— Wood
········· International boundaries

0 miles   100   200
0 km   100   200   300

Moorcroft's schemes. He saw the area between China and the Caspian as a vast political vacuum. British influence, in the form of a network of trading interests, could (in his opinion) bring prosperity and order while making of the region an outer rampart in the landward defences of India.' Also Moorcroft had a real liking and respect for the people of India, and he believed (to quote his own words) 'that the lot of the common folk could be much alleviated by the improvements and benefits which would spring from healthful trade'.

While Moorcroft's motives for making the journey were simple, the same could not be said of the motives of his sponsors, the British government and the East India Company. And we come now to one of the imponderables in the exploration of the Hindu Kush: to what degree were the travellers who pushed into the area officially supported? The British government had good political reasons for trying to extend their influence into the mountains, for the Chinese were already entrenched in the northeast of the complex and the Russians were advancing on the northwest. The East India Company, however, had doubts as to whether expansion could be achieved without rousing the animosity of the hill tribes in general and the Sikhs in particular, and therefore everything had to be done 'unofficially'. When Moorcroft set off in search of his horses, he was provided with company stores and company muskets, but he was denied official status; he was not even given letters of introduction to the various potentates through whose territory he intended to pass. This ambivalence casts a spell of uncertainty over the exploration of the Hindu Kush and the Karakoram. Soon even bona fide French botanists and fanatical Jewish preachers were suspected of being British spies. As for British explorers, as often as not they were murdered on the spot, the assumption being that even though they did not behave like spies, they probably were!

Moorcroft's expedition left Bareilly (some 150 miles [240 km] east of Delhi) in October 1819. And what an expedition it was! One can only wonder that so experienced a traveller as Moorcroft – who a few years earlier had successfully scoured the headwaters of the Ganges in search of the goats from whose wool the famous Kashmir shawls were woven – should have allowed himself to be burdened with so cumbersome an entourage. He took with him more than £3000 worth of merchandise, most of it heavy bales of cloth; this necessitated the use of scores of porters and muleteers, and was to prove a sore temptation to the hill tribes of the more unsettled areas, while the hordes required to carry it caused consternation. Wild rumours began to circulate that a 'Feringhi' army had crossed the Sutlej and were claiming that the hill states had come under British protection.

So one can picture Moorcroft, early in 1820, floating his unwieldy entourage over the Sutlej on inflated buffalo skins, and striking into the unknown ranges of the western Himalaya. His immediate goal was Leh, where he hoped to contact Chinese officials and, with their co-operation, plan the next stage of his push into central Asia. He was 55 years old, an unlikely age at which to be setting out on one of the longest and most hazardous journeys in the history of Asian exploration.

The start was not auspicious. At Mandi, less than 100 miles (160 km) beyond the Sutlej, he was halted first by the local rajah's army – 'a tatterdemalion rabble armed with swords matchlocks bows and arrows' – then by revenue-collecting Sikhs. The rajah was prepared – at a price – to let Moorcroft through, but the Sikhs were not; he was told he would have to go to Lahore to seek permission to proceed. Halfway to the Sikh capital he was arrested and thrown into the local jail, strategically sited next to the town's cesspit. Here he sweated it out for the better part of a month before a guard arrived to take him to Lahore. The journey must have been a considerable ordeal for the ageing vet, who was weakened by dysentery and reduced to eating three vegetarian meals a week; most of the way he had to be carried in a makeshift hammock. Nor were his troubles over when he got to Lahore, for he met not so much opposition as non-co-operation; permission to proceed was first given, then withdrawn, and eventually Moorcroft thought it prudent to slip away to the neighbouring kingdom of Kangra.

There his reception was altogether different, partly because within a few days of his arrival he managed to cure the rajah's brother of apoplexy, and partly because he and his host were united by a mutual dislike of the Sikhs. The rajah offered Moorcroft anything he wanted: any tract of land from his farms, any horse from his stables, any girl from his dancing troupe. The first two offers were refused; but Moorcroft was not too old to be interested in the *nautch* girls, the famous courtesans of northern India; he dallied six weeks in Kangra, and before he left he gave 'a fine gold-embroidered muslin to Jumalo, my favourite'.

His expedition, meanwhile, had been bogged down in Mandi during the hottest three months of the year. Mandi is only 2000 feet (610 m) above sea-level, is surrounded by arid grey mountains falling steeply to the Beas River, and is not, in the hot season, a good place to camp in – 'the air is so still that smoke and smells just hang there, the flies so lethargic they have to be pushed away.' It says much for Moorcroft's second-in-command, George Trebeck, that he managed to keep up the morale of the porters and muleteers. There were no desertions; and indeed throughout Moorcroft's long and arduous travels one is impressed by the loyalty of his followers. His enthusiasm may at times have disconcerted his superiors, but his kindness never failed to earn him the affection of his subordinates. He was a good man.

By mid-July his expedition was again on the move, heading into the western reaches of the Trans-Himalayas.

This was territory no European (except perhaps some of the ubiquitous Jesuit priests) had yet set foot in; and how one wishes Moorcroft had described the beauties of the scene which unfolded daily before him. But he was, alas, a wretched travel-writer, ever glossing over his difficulties and never indulging in those personal anecdotes that bring a travelogue to life. This is due partly to the fact that he was reticent by nature, and partly to the fact that, as a trader, he was anxious to minimize the hazards of the route he was pioneering. Moorcroft and Trebeck's *Travels in the Himalayan Provinces* reads, therefore, more like a gazetteer than the narrative of a great adventure. Page after page is taken up with a painstaking analysis of the crops, domestic animals and agricultural techniques of the villages through which they passed. Four pages are devoted to the properties of Ladakh's barley, three pages to the cultivation of its rhubarb; their crossing of the Bara Lacha Pass, 16,500 feet (5030 m) above sea-level, in a blinding snowstorm, is dismissed in half-a-dozen lines. Seldom can so spectacular a journey have been so prosaically recorded.

We have therefore to picture for ourselves Moorcroft's unwieldy caravan as it wound its way first up the Rohtang Pass and over the Lesser Himalayas, then up the Bara Lacha Pass and over the Greater. We are told that the column, moving in single file because of the narrowness of the trail, stretched out for more than a mile. First would come the 60-odd mules, the gentle tinkling of the bells round their necks not so much disturbing as intensifying the silence of the hills. Next would come the 100-odd porters, each with a load of some 70 lb (32 kg), bent double as with many a pause for breath they plodded ever-upward into the clouds. Near the middle of the column would be the two Indian pundits, recording every step they took in an effort to measure the distance covered each day. (In his use of these pundit-explorers, as in many other respects,

Moorcroft was an innovator far ahead of his times.) Sometimes the column would be guarded by the troops of the local rajah; other times it relied on the fire-power of its Company flintlocks, which had one great advantage over the matchlocks used by the brigands forever harassing them: they could be used in wet weather. Moorcroft and Trebeck, on horseback, spent most of their time keeping the column together and surveying – the latter no easy task with primitive instruments in zero temperatures.

Week after week they forced their way north through the mountains, until in September 1820 they reached their first objective, Leh, the capital of Ladakh, which Moorcroft describes as 'an intricate labyrinth of streets and houses, situated in a narrow valley, bounded on the northern and southern sides by a double chain of mountains' – the Trans-Himalayas to the south and the Karakoram to the north.

So far the expedition had been a success. Moorcroft had crossed the Himalaya, and had pioneered a difficult but perfectly feasible trade route to Leh; he had also done valuable survey-work. But from now on things began to go wrong.

Rope bridge in the Himalaya

Moorcroft was to spend three years in Ladakh trying to extract permission from the Chinese to proceed to Yarkand, which he correctly identified as the key to the trade routes between China and Kashmir. But he had no luck. It was a story to be repeated many times in the years to come. The Chinese were there first; their merchants had a trading monopoly, and they were not prepared to give this monopoly up. The 'Feringhies' were met first with procrastination, then with polite refusal, and finally – if they still had not got the message – with physical violence. Towards the end of their stay in Ladakh, there were attempts on both Moorcroft's and Trebeck's lives.

It was not in Moorcroft's nature to sit about and do nothing, and while waiting on the Chinese he explored Ladakh thoroughly and dabbled in its politics injudiciously. His exploration took him not only among the great peaks of the Trans-Himalayas, but also through the barren valleys of the Spati and Dras, and the desert wilderness of the Changthang. And in the course of his travels he came to love Ladakh: a harsh skeletal land, where the lowest point of the warmest valley is 9000 feet (2745 m) above sea-level. And even more than the country, he came to love its inhabitants; for everywhere he went he was met with kindness. *The people*, wrote John Keay,

> *were the antithesis of their surroundings, warm, gentle and welcoming. His medical work brought him a flood of patients who turned his house into a market-place with their offerings of vegetables and livestock. In gratitude for a minor operation, a patient's old mother would come a week's march to present him with a sheep. He was as well received in the lama's monastery as in the shepherd's shelter.*

An artist's impression of an expedition crossing the Alai mountains, from Gabriel Bonvalut's 'Through the Heart of Asia', 1889

In fact the people so loved and respected him that they offered to make him their king.

Moorcroft may have been a visionary, but he was not without common sense, and he very prudently turned down the offer. He did, however, do what he believed to be best for the people of Ladakh: he advised them not to pay their customary tribute to the Sikhs, but to place themselves under the protection of the British government in Delhi. With this in mind, he negotiated and signed a commercial treaty with them in the name of the East India Company, and encouraged the drawing up of a political treaty in the name of the British government.

He did this from the best possible motives, and indeed in the long-term his dreams of Ladakh as a British protectorate is exactly what was most desirable and exactly what came about. His superiors, however, were only interested in short-term considerations. Ladakh to them was in another and impossibly distant world; *their* concern was to keep on the right side of their immediate neighbours, the Sikhs. Moorcroft's proposals were disadvantageous to the Sikhs, and his meddling was therefore condemned, his treaties were repudiated and he was recalled.

However, by the time the order to return got through to Ladakh, the intrepid old man was heading west into the lonely reaches of Afghanistan. Rumours of official wrath did finally catch up with him in Kashmir. 'It is a strange tale that Mr M. has been recalled by the Directors,' wrote the loyal Trebeck. 'If it were a fact, they knew him not who suppose he would obey the summons.' Moorcroft indeed had no intention of admitting defeat. Blocked by the Chinese in the northeast, he headed northwest, hoping to find in the plains of Turkestan the horses in search of which he had already travelled 1000 miles and was to travel 1000 more.

But by now his already hazardous mission was fraught with additional dangers, for the Chinese were convinced he was a spy, the Sikhs were convinced he was their enemy, and the British had washed their hands of him. The writing was on the wall.

Moorcroft left Ladakh in September 1823, and his diary for the next year again reads like a gazetteer of all the remote and mysterious places which Europeans had for centuries longed to visit: Peshawar and Jalalabad, Kabul and the Khyber Pass, Balkh and Bukhara, the Oxus river and the Hazara desert. Everywhere he went he recorded in meticulous detail the mechanics of the peoples' life: the shape of the bowls they drank from, the size of the barley grain they planted, the weight of the paper they wrapped their tea in. And in between great tracts on husbandry, there is the occasional passage which gives the first description of the Trans-Himalayas – not scenic descriptions, for Moorcroft was unmoved by the beauties of nature, but technical accounts of how the great peaks were being sculpted before his very eyes.

About two-thirds up a hillside half-a-mile distant, a little dust was from time to time seen to arise; this presently increased, until an immense cloud spread over and concealed the summit, whilst from underneath it huge blocks of stone were seen rolling and tumbling down the slope. Some of these buried themselves in the ground at the foot of the cliff; some slid along the rubbish of previous debris, grinding it to powder and marking their descent by a line of dust; some bounded along with great velocity and plunged into the river, scattering its waters in spray. A noise like the pealing of artillery accompanied every fall. In the intervals between the slips and when the dust dispersed, the face of the descent was seen to be broken into ravines, or scoured with deep channels, and blackened with moisture. About half-a-mile beyond, and considerably higher than this crumbling mountain, was another whose top was tufted with snow . . . It appeared to me that the melting of the snows on the principal mountain, and the want of a sufficient vent for the water, was the cause of the rapid decay of the hills which surrounded it. For the water which in the summer lodges in the fissures and clefts of the latter, becomes frozen again in winter, and in its expansion tears to pieces the surrounding and superincumbent rocks. Again, melting in the summer, it percolates through the loosened soil, and, undermining projecting portions of the rocks, precipitates them into the valley.

One feels from this account that Moorcroft would have made the charge of the Light Brigade sound like a trot down Rotten Row!

And he has the same reticence when it comes to describing the physical dangers which now almost daily encompassed his expedition. Only very occasionally, lost between statistics on rhubarb and pomegranate planting, do we get a fleeting glimpse of what conditions must have been like.

The river rushed down with great rapidity and noise. A bridge was placed across the rocks which confined the torrent. We crossed at some risk, and one of my followers was thrown into the current by his hill pony; he managed, however, to get out unharmed . . . Many of our people suffered from exposure and fatigue. The sun for a few hours was intensely hot, whilst the wind blew piercingly cold from the snow-clad peaks. I had some pain in my head, my face was stripped of skin, and my lips were shrivelled and cracked. Many people were in the same state, and were attacked with fever . . . As we entered the gorge a sudden gust of wind brought on such a cloud of snow as to conceal the Mullah and a little girl riding on a couple of yaks. When the blast ceased [we] saw the yaks without their riders: they had been blown off their seats, and were buried beneath the snow. After some delay the bodies were found: the girl recovered, but the old man was dead . . . There was much snow on the northern face of the pass, the surface of which was frozen, but the crust was in many places very thin, and gave way beneath the weight of the yaks; they were constantly sinking deep into the bed of uncongealed snow, so that we were five hours in reaching the top of the pass. The descent was still more difficult and dangerous. The snow had been mostly melted, but the frost had glazed the water such as had been thawed during the day; and the mixture of ice in sheets, or in powder, with fragments of rock and loose stones, rendered the footing insecure both for men and animals. An Arab horse of mine, having missed his footing, slid down a sheet of ice for some distance, and recovered himself only by a vigorous effort, on the brink of a preciipice many hundred feet high.

Nor was it only the terrain that was hazardous. In the latter part of his journey we get a hint of other dangers.

Mr Trebeck was fired at from the street. The shot passed through the window and struck the side of the room near a light upon a table at which my young friend had been writing. He had just quitted his chair a few minutes before, or he would have been killed . . . As night fell we made the best arrangements we could against an attack. I ordered my escort to fire several rounds, for the double purpose of intimating our position and of getting their pieces in order.

Reading between the lines one can see that after he left Ladakh, Moorcroft was in constant peril, not only from marauding brigands but from a succession of local rajahs, determined to mulct his expedition of everything possible in return for its temporary safe-conduct.

Before the net closed round him, he was allowed one brief but glorious hour of triumph: his entry into Bukhara the Noble, the greatest and most remote of the emporiums of central Asia. Moorcroft and Trebeck entered the city on 25 February 1825, and the latter compared their joy to that of the Crusaders on entering Jerusalem – 'after a long and laborious journey of more than five years,' he wrote, 'we have a right to hail the domes and minarets with as much pleasure as did Geoffrey de Bouillon.' They had a surprisingly good reception. They were given permission to ride through the city – an unheard-of privilege for a non-Muhammadan – and, what was equally unheard of,

The upper reaches of the Tsangpo (Brahmaputra) River

permission to trade. Gratefully they sold the bulk of their merchandise and bought 100 horses: not as many as Moorcroft wanted, but their performance more than lived up to his expectations. Things seemed to be going well, and one suddenly detects in the old man's diary an optimism which for the previous couple of years had been absent.

In June they left Bukhara, setting out 'in sanguine mood' on the long trek home.

By November it was all over. Moorcroft and Trebeck were dead, and their retinue scattered throughout the valleys of Afghanistan.

What happened will probably never be known. The expedition re-crossed the Oxus early in August. Then, apparently anxious to avoid Kabul where the rajah was known to be unfriendly, they struck out across the deserts west of Balkh. This, Moorcroft had been told, was the home of the finest horses in Asia, and he intended to augment his herd by trading direct with the breeders of the desert oases. He knew the risk. 'The experiment is full of hazard,' he wrote, 'but *le jeu vaut bien la chandelle.*' The candle, alas, had not long to burn. At Andkhui, in the very back of beyond, Moorcroft was taken ill: some say of fever, some say of poison, some say of a bullet lodged in his chest. On 27 August he died. A few weeks later the expedition doctor was also dead, and soon after that, the faithful Trebeck.

It is possible they all succumbed to Kunduz fever – possible but not probable, for it stretches credulity beyond belief that the three leaders of the expedition should die within so short a span of time from natural causes. The odds are that they were murdered by marauding brigands, acting under the orders of a rajah they had antagonized on their outward journey.

So ended the first, and probably the greatest, of the early journeys over the western Himalaya and the Hindu Kush.

Moorcroft was an extraordinary man. In his lifetime he inspired the almost fanatical affection and respect of his subordinates – 15 years after his death his garden in Leh was still being cared for by his faithful Ladakhi servants in the hope that he might one day return – and after his death almost everything he had predicted came to pass. The Punjab became British territory as he had always said was inevitable; Ladakh fell to the Sikhs as he had feared but later came under British protection as he had hoped; Bukhara fell to the Russians as he had warned; there was a Muslim rising against the Chinese in Turkistan as he had predicted. It is no exaggeration to say that the story of the exploration of the western Himalaya is the story of Moorcroft's dreams and fears becoming reality.

Yet history has not been kind to him. It was several decades before his diary was published; lesser men won accolades for 'discovering' regions which he, in fact, had not only visited but mapped; and few people today have even heard of the man who at the very least should be regarded as the father-figure of exploration in the western Himalaya and the Hindu Kush. An untimely death and a convoluted style of prose can blunt even the greatest achievements.

Before the next great explorer, festooned with easels, fishing-rods and rifles, headed into the mountains, two eccentrics, brilliant, unstable and transient as comets, sped briefly across the tableau of the western Himalaya.

Victor Vinceslas Jacquemont was a French botanist. And if the picture that springs to mind is of an earnest man of science diligently collecting specimens, nothing could be further from the truth. When, in 1830, Jacquemont took Calcutta society by storm, he was 28, tall, handsome – 'all grey eyes, cherubic countenance and chestnut curls' – and already the darling of the Paris salons, a friend of Prosper Merimée and Stendhal. He was more dilettante than diligent. From Calcutta he made his way to the remote hill station of Simla, which he hoped would be the springboard for his visit to Kashmir, where he intended to collect flora and fauna for *Le Jardin des Plantes* in Paris.

He spent a year in Simla, in theory waiting for permits and letters of introduction for his trip to Kashmir, in practice having the sort of time that lesser mortals only dream of. He did everything in style. For dinner (over which he never took less than four hours) his Perigord pâté, truffles and Rhine wine had to be brought specially from France – although for 'afters' he was more than content with the local *mocha* coffee and *nautch* girls. His diary reads like an extract from *The Thousand and One Nights*:

> *We dismounted at the gates of a delightful oasis. There were great beds of stocks, irises and roses, and walks bordered by orange trees and jasmine bushes, beside pools in which were playing a multitude of fountains. In the middle of this beautiful garden was a little palace, furnished with the uttermost luxury and elegance. This was my home. Luncheon was awaiting me in my sitting-room, served on solid silver. Dinner was served by torchlight . . . The old roué, my host, then sent for fine young girls from his seraglio, ordered them to sit down in front of me and smilingly asked me what I thought of them. I said in all sincerity that I considered them very pretty, which was not one tenth of what I really thought!*

Tibetan soldiers and yaks

Never can the preparations for an expedition have been more gastronomically and sensuously satisfying!

In March 1831 he crossed the Sutlej, 'with a cart, a couple of camels, three or four servants and my trusted horse' – although the latter was soon discarded in favour of an elephant, 'which I found a great deal more comfortable'.

It is easy to smile at Jacquemont. He was indeed the archetypal *poseur*: vain, self-indulgent, selfish, too determinedly witty to be funny, and too idiosyncratic to be taken seriously. But he was no fool and he was certainly no coward, and if some of his escapades deserve a place in the *Decameron*, others deserve nothing short of the *croix de guerre*. He was also remarkably successful, traversing some of the most hazardous terrain in the world with pomp, circumstance and obvious enjoyment. One incident demonstrates how he did it. At Mirpur, in the foothills of the Pir Panjal, he was taken prisoner by the commandant of a local fort, who reckoned that the flamboyant Frenchman would make

Above: Rongbuk Monastery with
Mount Everest in the distance.
Below: Tibetan woman and child.
Right: Ovis Hodgsoni – the largest
wild sheep of the Himalaya

The Himalchuli range from Borlang

Top: The Hunza Valley, Kashmir.
Above: Band-e-Amir lakes and waterfalls,
Afghanistan

Top left: Bullocks and field terracing, Nepal. Right: The Khyber Pass, Pakistan. Above: Yaks seen on the way to Mount Everest with Kantega in the background

The Maharajah Jung Buhadoor of Nepal, with his wife,
daughter and slave girls, photographed by Dr H.A. Oldfield, 1860

the ideal hostage. How wrong he was! Although Jacquemont's handful of followers were quickly disarmed and easily dispirited, and he himself was jostled by a rabble with lighted matchlocks, he affected a world-weary and devastating unconcern. He refused to speak to his captor until a chair had been brought for him, and a parasol to give him shade erected. He then proceeded to lecture the commander of the fort on the enormity of his crime in even thinking of detaining him. Eventually, with a glance at his watch, he demanded breakfast. When it was explained that none was ready, his outrage was as devastating as his disdain. 'Do you not hear,' he shouted at his nonplussed captors. 'The lord wishes for milk. Send to the neighbouring villages so it may be brought at once.' And when the chastened banditti sheepishly set out in search of milk, he called them back and explained that the milk of a goat or a buffalo would not be good enough; he had to have cow's milk. 'They were,' in Jacquemont's own words, 'crushed by my disdain.' Next morning he left the fort not a penny the poorer, and with a ceremonial escort.

The next four months he spent in Kashmir and Baltistan, in the starkly beautiful jumble of peaks and gorges where the Himalaya converge with the Karakoram. From this little-known mountain fastness he amassed a sizeable collection of flora and fauna: over 400 plants and a smaller number of stuffed birds and preserved fish. These he crated up in musket-cases for *Le Jardin des Plantes*, and headed back for the Sutlej. On his outward journey he had had no more than a cart, a horse and a couple of camels; homeward, he had a retinue of 50 porters to carry his specimens and an escort of 60 cavalry to guard them. Against all the odds, the expedition had been a success.

Sadly, within a few months of returning to Simla, Jacquemont contracted fever which produced an abscess of the liver; he died in Bombay at the age of 31. He may not have been the most dedicated of explorers, but few have travelled with such enjoyment and none with such panache; he also has the distinction of being the first and by no means the least in a long tradition of Himalayan naturalists.

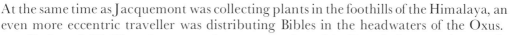

At the same time as Jacquemont was collecting plants in the foothills of the Himalaya, an even more eccentric traveller was distributing Bibles in the headwaters of the Oxus.

Dr Joseph Wolff was born near the upper reaches of the Danube in 1795, the son of a

German-Jewish rabbi. When asked at the age of seven what he wanted to be when he grew up, he replied 'the Pope'. By the time he was 21 he had been converted to Christianity, could speak German, Hebrew, Greek, English, Arabic, Syrian and Persian, and had been granted an audience with the Pope. On the advice of the latter he entered the *Collegio di Propaganda*, where he proved a brilliant but disruptive pupil, born to trouble as surely as sparks fly upward. He encouraged his fellow neophytes to cheat during the auto-flagellation sessions by flogging their leather breeches instead of their bare backs; when ordered to kiss a monk's feet, he bit his toes; he declared that the church should never have burned heretics, and when told that 38 Popes had sanctioned this, he replied tartly, 'Then 38 Popes were wrong.' For this he was thrown out of the Catholic church. He became a Protestant, entered Cambridge University, and at the age of 26 set out on the first of his many journeys as a missionary. In the course of the next 12 years, to quote his own words, he 'laboured among [his] brethren in Palestine, Egypt, Mesopotamia, Persia, Krimea, Georgia and the Ottoman Empire; then in England, Scotland, Ireland, Holland and the Mediterranean. [He] then proceeded to Turkey, Persia, Turkistan, Bokhara, Afghanistan, Cashmeer, Hindustan and the Red Sea.' *Wherever he went*, wrote Wilfrid Blunt in *The Golden Road to Samarkand*,

> he made friends – and enemies; wherever he went he argued. He argued with Christians and Jews, with Hindus and Mohammedans, with Sunnis and Shiahs. He argued about everything: good-humouredly, tirelessly and without any regard whatever for the consequences. He exposed himself fearlessly to dangers of every kind. He had much in common with St. Paul. But whereas Paul followed up his proselytizing by the establishment of churches, Wolff rushed about in a mad wanderlust, from place to place, preaching here (in a dozen different languages), debating there, scattering Bibles everywhere; here today and gone tomorrow, often with a hostile mob at his heels.

In Turkey he was bastinadoed. In Turkistan he was tied to a horse's tail and flogged. In Abyssinia he was horse-whipped by the Wahabites. In the Hindu Kush he was captured and told, 'you must say "there is God and nothing but God and Mahomet is his Prophet" or we will sew you in a dead donkey, burn you alive and make sausages of you,' to which he replied, 'There is God and nothing but God and Jesus Christ is the Son of God.' This so outraged his captors that they decided that to burn him alive would be too quick a death; instead they stripped him naked and left him in the waist-deep snow to die of cold. Wolff, however, was a great survivor; he managed to struggle through to Kabul. A year later he was appointed curate to the quiet little Yorkshire village of High Hoyland. It seemed that at the age of 43 the Wandering Jew had come at last to the end of his travels. Yet his most gallant and quixotic escapade was still to come: his attempt to save Stoddart and Conolly from the death-pit in Bukhara.

Colonel Charles Stoddart was an unlucky pawn in the early moves of the Great Game, the confrontation between the British advancing into the mountain complex from the south and the Russians moving in from the north. In 1838 he was sent to Bukhara to offer the Amir the support of Her Majesty's Government in the event of a Russian attack. Stoddart, however, behaved with such petulance and arrogance that he quickly found himself in the *Siah Chah* ('black well'): a loathsome 20 foot (6 m) deep pit, stocked with specially bred ticks, snakes and reptiles which lived on flesh – human flesh if they were not fed their usual offal. After being hauled, for the better part of a year, in and out of the pit like a yo-yo, Stoddart saw his grave being dug in front of him and was offered the choice of becoming a Muslim or being burned alive. He apostatized, was given a Muslim name, publicly circumcized and restored to a degree of freedom.

At this stage the British government decided to launch a belated and injudicious

Arthur Conolly and Charles Stoddart who were executed in 1842 after imprisonment in the snake pit in Bukhara

rescue operation, led by Captain Arthur Conolly. Unluckily for Conolly, his arrival in Bukhara coincided with the massacre of a British force in the mountains south of Kabul; the Amir and his second-in-command the Nayeb decided that British 'protection' was something they could manage very well without, and Conolly joined Stoddart in the *Siah Chah*. Here they remained month after month, year after year; ragdolls dancing to the tune of a sadistic puppeteer. In March 1842 Conolly wrote a pathetic last note to his brother in England:

> *This is the 83rd day that we have been denied the means of getting a change of linen from the rags and vermin that cover us; when we begged for an amendment in this respect, the Nayeb set his face like flint . . . I did not think to have shed one tear among such cold-hearted men; but yesterday, as I looked upon Stoddart's half-naked and lacerated body, I wept, entreating one of our keepers that he would direct his anger upon me, and not on my poor brother Stoddart who had so suffered so much so meekly for all these years.*

It was to try and negotiate the release of Stoddart and Conolly – a task for which the government had little stomach – that Wolff set out on his second expedition to Bukhara. He made the journey for humanitarian reasons, entirely on his own initiative, and with no official encouragement or support – although a 'Stoddart and Conolly Committee' did raise sufficient funds to pay his expenses, and no less a person than Lady Canning sewed secret documents to the Amir into the lining of his cassock.

Wolff arrived in Trezibond on the southeast coast of the Black Sea towards the end of 1843, and at once set out on his 2000-mile (3200 km) trek to Bukhara, armed only with 'a Clergyman's gown cassock and hood, the mantle of faith, four-dozen Hebrew Bibles, and three-dozen copies of *Robinson Crusoe* in Arabic'. It was a difficult journey, taking him first over the plateaux of Turkey, then across the mountains of Elbruz and finally over the deserts of Iran and Turkmenistan. So bad were some of the mountain tracks that Wolff could only crawl forward on hands and knees a few inches at a time. And more frightening even than the journey itself, was the prospect of what lay at the end of it. For the closer he got to Bukhara the more explicit the warnings became: Stoddart and Conolly had already been ritually executed; if Wolff insisted on entering the city, he would, he was told, suffer the same fate.

Never the man to refuse a challenge, he kept going. He had been warned that as he neared Bukhara he would be met by horsemen carrying baskets in which would be chains to bind him and knives to hack off his head; and when he was a few miles short of the city, horsemen did indeed appear. But to Wolff's astonishment the baskets they were carrying contained not implements for his execution, but offerings of food and drink. He entered the city not in chains but in triumph: to quote from his diary, 'dressed in full canonicals with an open bible in my hand. Shouts from thousands rang upon my ears. It was a most astonishing sight to see people dangling from the roofs of houses, and to hear women screaming "he is the Grand Derveesh of Englestaun." ' He was soon to discover, however, that Bukhara was a great deal easier to get into than out of.

At first, he was by no means badly treated, although it soon became apparent that he was not so much guest as prisoner; nor was it long before the attitude of his captors hardened. No one would tell him what had happened to Stoddart and Conolly. And when he pressed his enquiries, he found himself ushered, politely but firmly, into the same cell as the two officers had occupied overlooking the *Siah Chah*. Soon, ominously, the Nayeb was taunting him with the fate of his fellow countrymen: 'Yes, I had them killed. I know how to treat you Englestauns' – the unfortunate officers had indeed been publicly executed on 17 June 1842, before Wolff had even left England. He realized that he was now likely to share their fate.

Time and again during that summer Wolff was told he would be given permission to leave Bukhara, and time and again the Amir and the Nayeb found excuses to 'delay' his departure. As the months passed their intention became increasingly clear.

One morning, Wolff wrote,

a mulla came to my cell with a message from the Amir: was I prepared to become a Moslem? 'Tell the king NEVER, NEVER, NEVER,' *I replied.*

Next there came the executioner what had put Stoddart and Conolly to death: 'Joseph Wolff' he said, 'to thee it shall happen as it did to Stoddart and Conolly.' And as he spoke he made a sign at my throat with his hand. I prepared for death, and carried opium always with me. But at the last I cast away the opium and prayed.

He wrote a last message to his wife and son. Then, unexpectedly, when he had altogether lost hope, he was released, laden with presents and told that he could go. His change of fortune seems to have been due partly to the good offices of Colonel Butenyov, head of the Russian mission to Bukhara (who, it is pleasant to record, did everything possible to persuade the Amir to release his prisoners), and partly to the Persian ambassador who wrote simply but effectively to the Amir, 'If you do not send back Joseph Wolff I shall become enraged with you.'

So the intrepid clergyman, his wanderlust finally sated, returned to England, where he passed the remainder of his days as the eccentric but well-loved vicar of a Somerset village. He died in 1862, outliving, against all the odds, both the Nayeb – whom the Amir cut in half with an axe in 1847 – and the Amir himself – who died in 1860 having had his five brothers killed and one of his wives stabbed to death as he lay dying.

The Russians meanwhile, as Moorcroft had predicted, annexed both Samarkand and Bukhara. With Russian troops now within a few days' march of both the Pamirs and the Hindu Kush, the British began to fear for the safety of India. There was a sudden proliferation of government agents in the Afghan and Kashmiri valleys: a sudden desire to find out exactly how formidable a barrier the mountains were.

◆

Both Jacquemont and Wolff had been accused by their contemporaries of being British spies. Such an accusation was seldom levelled at our next traveller, yet a spy is what Godfrey Thomas Vigne almost certainly was, and a highly successful one.

He was born in London in 1801, son of a wealthy merchant who supplied gunpowder to the East India Company. He was educated at Harrow and, on leaving school, for several years practised successfully as a solicitor. Then came the first of a series of incidents in his life which do not quite make sense. He abandoned a promising career because, we are told, he was 'too delicate'. Yet law is hardly the most physically demanding of professions; Vigne was subsequently to prove an unusually robust explorer, and one simply cannot accept that he found the physical demands of Lincoln's Inn too great for him. One possibility is that he gave up legal work in order to have more time to indulge his passion for sport – in particular, cricket and hunting – and painting. Another is that he was offered the chance of combining the sporting life he so much enjoyed with work of an exploratory nature, either on behalf of the East India Company or, more likely, the government. Whatever his motive, he turned up in India early in 1834, and to quote his own words, 'ran at once to the cool air of the Himalaya'. After surveying a couple of passes into eastern Tibet, he headed for Kashmir, and almost immediately disappeared into the unknown. There followed five years of continuous travel through some of the most demanding terrain in the world. Can it, one wonders, have been for nothing more than his personal enjoyment?

Vigne himself, in his *Travels in Kashmir, Ladakh, Iskardo etc.*, gives no hint that he was anything other than a sportsman-cum-artist, indulging his hobbies in territory that was ideal for both. And it is certainly true that he regarded hunting as not so much a pastime as a way of life: in the course of his travels, he shot, with impartial enthusiasm, pheasant, partridge, snipe, quail, alligator, antelope, leopard, tiger, panther and 'grey mullet as they rose to the surface'; he coursed with hounds, cheetahs and falcons. He was also a competent botanist and geologist, and a gifted artist. When asked what he did, he replied, 'I can draw.' He certainly could, and many of his sketches and portraits were exhibited at the Royal Academy.

Vigne had one other attribute as a traveller which was perhaps of more use to him than all the others put together: he was a likeable and sensible man, who had the knack of getting on famously with *everyone*. He was on Christian name terms with half the hierarchy of the company and government; he treated his porters with rare consideration, insisting they all had tents to sleep in; and when the local traders tried to cheat him, he regarded it as a huge joke: 'When detected in a fault their excuses are so ready and profuse, and so abound in humour, it is impossible to abstain from laughing.' Of all the early explorers in the Himalaya, he is the one, one feels, with whom it would have been easiest to share a tent.

Yet he had one weakness. Either by accident or design – and how *can* it have been the former? – he was unbelievably vague about dates, distances and itineraries. It is therefore difficult to piece together a chronological account of his wanderings, and impossible to reconstruct a map. For a man who in other respects was so precise and orderly, this was surely out of character. It makes one wonder. One cannot help wondering, too, if he was really no more than an itinerant artist, how he so easily obtained permission to visit both Kashmir and Baltistan, areas taboo to others.

Vigne's reputation is based on his detailed exploration of the Vale of Kashmir, and his discovery of the Karakoram. He spent rather more than three years in the Vale, and he came to know it intimately and love it deeply. He called it *the noblest valley in all the world*, and analysed its charms with perception.

Innumerable villages were scattered over the plains in every direction, distinguishable in the distance by the trees that surrounded them; all was soft and verdant even up to the snow on the mountain tops; and I gazed in surprise, excited by the vast extent and admirably defined limits of the valley and the pefect proportions of height to distance by which its scenery is characterized . . . rendering it not unworthy of the rhyming epithets: Kashmir bi nuzir *(Kashmir without equal),* Kashmir junat puzir *(Kashmir equal to Paradise).*

He reckoned the Vale was ideal for colonization. He saw it, wrote John Keay, 'as a miniature England in Asia . . . a place where the rulers of India, having left the heat in the plains and having dumped the White Man's Burden on the Pir Panjal, could change into their old tweed suits and settle down before a log fire on their own few acres.' 'I wish to heaven,' he wrote, 'that some thousands of our emigrants had a footing here in the heart of Asia.' Time and again his descriptions end with the inference that the one thing the Vale needed to make it the *ne plus ultra* was a touch of Britishification.

> *Above the convent is the celebrated Gut Murg, or mountain of flowers: a lovely spot, flat, green, open and perfumed with flowers; the snowy peaks sloping gently upwards from it, and the valley itself extended beneath it; whilst the scenic disposition of its woods and glades, watered by a stream that winds its whole length, is so highly picturesque that little is wanting but a mansion and a herd of deer to complete its resemblance to the perfect English park . . . I am fearful of wearying my readers by so constantly referring to the beauties of the scenery; but it is impossible to travel among the glades and streams of Kamrej without being delighted with its sylvan aspect. In the plains the apple-orchards are numerous, and the best fruit in the valley is found in Kamrej, which would prove capital cider country.*

As well as exploring the Vale itself, Vigne spent a considerable time in the mountains that surround it. To the south he crossed the Lesser Himalayas five times, on each occasion by a different pass; while to the north he crossed the Greater Himalayas no less than six times, again on most occasions by a different pass. Passes seemed to have a particular fascination for him. And this could be significant, for if Vigne *was* a spy, it would have been the possible invasion routes from north-to-south which he was anxious to study. It was surely not by chance that he visited and mapped some 21 passes leading into and out of the Vale.

However, his most important feats of exploration were carried out beyond Kashmir, in Baltistan, a world of soaring peaks and deep-cut valleys where the chain of the Himalaya converges with the knot of the Karakoram. No European before him had penetrated this spectacular fastness. Vigne visited it on no less than four occasions, probing its passes with tenacity.

His first visit, in 1835, led to some spectacular discoveries and some hair-raising encounters. Towards the end of August he was crossing the Gurais Pass when he stumbled unexpectedly on 'the most awful and the most magnificent sight in all the Himalayas': 23,000 feet (7000 m) of cliff-cum-ice leaping near-sheer from the lifeless gorge of the Indus. *The stupendous peak of Nanga Parbat*, he wrote,

> *burst suddenly upon my sight, rising far above every other around it and entirely cased in snow, except where its scarps were too precipitous. It was partially encircled by a broad belt of cloud, and its finely pointed summit glistening in the full blaze of the morning sun, relieved by the clear blue sky beyond it, presented an appearance of extreme altitude . . . It was a sight that excited even my apathetic servants. 'What sort of mountain is that, Sahib!' exclaimed my Kashmiri tailor.*

Vigne, ever-modest with his estimates, reckoned the summit was 'above 19,000 feet [5800 m]. In fact it is 26,661 feet (8126 m): a great juggernaut of a mountain, which was later to acquire an evil reputation among mountaineers – more lives have been lost on Nanga Parbat than on any other Himalayan peak.

A few days later he had an equally exciting if quite different encounter – with Ahmed Shah, the ruler of Baltistan. A great deal depended on how the two men got on, for although Vigne had been given leave by the British to enter Baltistan, he had no official status. John Keay's description of their meeting is splendidly evocative.

Suddenly out of the silence came a noise like no other on earth, 'the loud, distant and discordant blasts of Tibetan music; the sound grew louder and louder [Vigne tells us] *until we were all on the tiptoe of expectation.' From the darkness emerged a band of fifes, clarinets and six-foot long trumpets. Forty soldiers, 'the wildest looking figures imaginable', followed, and with them their young commander, a son of Ahmed Shah. The Rajah, it transpired, was only a few miles ahead. He had issued forth to intercept a band of robbers, and was now lying in ambush for them just over the pass. Vigne would meet him next day when the action was over . . . The two men met as soon as the robbers had been successfully annihilated. Vigne in his broad-brimmed white cotton hat and white duck-shooting jacket was approached by a tall and imposing figure who doffed his turban and salaamed frequently. The Englishman took his hand, and wrung it vigorously, explaining through the interpreter that such was his native custom. Ahmed Shah was delighted. It was his lifelong ambition to meet a 'Feringhi', and now this had happened on a day when he had already fought a successful action. So far so good, thought Vigne, and after more mutual flattery, he was emboldened to ask leave to sketch his host . . . Given the situation, the result shows a remarkably steady hand.*

For the next three days they travelled together across the bleak Deosai plateau. The altitude was about 12,000 feet [3660 m], and there was a heavy frost at night. The Rajah presented Vigne with a pair of warm Tibetan socks. He returned the compliment with a bottle of brandy. They were getting on famously. When Vigne exhibited his pin-ups, 'engravings of Chalon's beauties', the Rajah gazed in silent admiration. There followed a print of King William IV and his consort, and the Rajah insisted on writing a personal note in the margin sending to His Britannic Majesty respectful salaams and an earnest wish for protection. Vigne declared that he had no political status, though he admits that Ahmed Shah did not appear to believe him. But regardless of [politics] *there developed between them a real and lasting friendship.*

It was soon after this meeting that Vigne got his first glimpse of Baltistan. A little before sunset he and Ahmed Shah were approaching a ridge behind which, the rajah told him, lay the upper reaches of the Indus. Unable to contain his excitement, Vigne galloped on ahead, scrambled to the top of a mini-glacier, and peered eagerly over the edge. *Through a vista of barren peaks*, he wrote,

of savage slopes and various colours – in which the whiteness of gypsum was contrasted with the red tint of iron – I, the first European that had ever beheld them, gazed down upon the sandy plains and green orchards of the [upper] *Indus, with a sense of pride and pleasure of which no one but a traveller can form a just conception . . . To the north, wherever the eye roved, there arose with surpassing grandeur a vast assemblage of enormous summits.*

He had discovered the Karakoram.

The sight of this 'vast assemblage of summits' came as a considerable surprise to Vigne, for it had been thought that beyond the Himalaya lay only the comparatively level plateau of Tibet. The discovery of this farther and even more formidable range gave the world its first indication of the true enormity of the complex.

Vigne spent much of the next four years probing the Karakoram: not a continuous probe, but four summer expeditions in which he explored the area around Gilgit, several of the major passes and the magnificent Hispar-Biafo glacier. He was a brave and determined traveller but no mountaineer, and no one other than a mountaineer could hope to cross the highest mountain system on earth. Vigne suffered from frost-bite, snowblindness and hypothermia; he was trapped in snowdrifts; he fell into crevasses; he spent nights on the ice covered in only a single frozen-solid blanket. He tried again and again to find a way through. He failed. However, his very failure constituted an important success. For what he was surely looking for was a north-to-south invasion route: a pass through which the Russians might flood into India. After four years he was able to assure the powers-that-be that no such pass existed: that the western Himalaya and the Karakoram formed a barrier which was inviolate. Having accomplished his mission, he disappeared from India and never returned.

Almost as important as Vigne's discovery of the Karakoram was his attitude towards his discovery. He loved the mountains. *I shall never forget*, he wrote on his last visit to Baltistan,

> *the glorious view that presented itself from the top of the path. Mountain seemed piled upon mountain in a most stupendous confusion of mist and glacier, glistening with the dazzling and reciprocated brightness of snow and sunbeam. The outlines, bold, precipitous and majestic, were rendered more so by being discernible for an instant only, then hidden by the rapidly driven clouds. I feel sure that had Mont Blanc been placed beside it, it would have been disregarded on account of its insignificance and tameness.*

He was the first European to see the mountains as we see them today: not as an inanimate barrier, but as a manifestation of nature at its most magnificent.

G.W. Hayward in Indian attire, c. 1870

With the western Himalaya and the Karakoram now seen to be an effective bastion against Russian invasion, interest again became centred on the Hindu Kush.

The Hindu Kush straddles Afghanistan, a country whose politics in the mid-nineteenth century were characterized by a series of internecine quarrels, assassinations, set battles and palace revolutions. A synopsis reads like the plot of a soap opera. Kabul was ruled by Dost Muhammed, the youngest of about 20 brothers belonging to a branch of the ruling Durrani family. Another branch of the family ruled in Kandahar, bitterly jealous of their younger brother's success. Others used to rule in Peshawar, but had been ousted by Ranjit Singh, who was not a Durrani but a Sikh. Shah Shuga, the ex-ruler of Kabul, was being championed by the British as 'King of all the Afghans', while his brother in Herat was being groomed for the same job by the Russians. In the west, the Persians were settling old scores and annexing the occasional slice of disputed territory. In the east, the Chinese were painting enormous rock-murals of Europeans, so that itinerant 'Feringhies' could be recognized, apprehended and put to death.

Across this troubled tableau moved a succession of travellers, some of whom were genuine surveyors (men like Strachey and Johnson), some political agents (like Burnes and Hayward), and some eccentric loners (like Gardiner and Wolff). Most of them came to a violent end: Burnes knifed to death in Kabul, Johnson poisoned in Ladakh, Hayward ritually beheaded in the Darket valley. Those who survived only managed to do so by the skin of their teeth. Gardiner, for example, suffered the agony of seeing his young wife and son hacked to pieces, while he himself suffered '14 terrible wounds', including one in his throat, so that for the rest of his life whenever he drank he had to clamp-tight his gullet with a pair of steel pincers.

All these explorers contributed to the unveiling of the Hindu Kush. But the man who, in pure geographical terms, made one of the most important discoveries was, improbably, a modest naval lieutenant.

John Wood was the first man to take a steamboat up the lower reaches of the Indus, no mean achievement on a river notorious for its constantly shifting sandbars and dangerous rapids. A year after his ascent of the river, he was chosen to go on a political mission to Kunduz, which lies north of the Hindu Kush, in a marshy and insalubrious valley almost 1000 miles (1600 km) from the sea. And if one wonders why a naval lieutenant should have been sent to so unlikely a locale, Wood himself provides the answer with characteristic simplicity. 'The object of my thoughts by day,' he wrote, 'and my dreams by night had for some time been the discovery of the source of the River Oxus . . . and I had hopes that Murad Beg [the rajah of Kunduz] would concede his permission for me to trace the course of this river.'

Murad Beg was a warlord: the shrewd and unscrupulous commander of some 15,000 predatory horsemen who for several decades had been terrorizing the Afghan–Turkestan border; Wood describes him very aptly as 'the head of an organized banditti'. For most of his life Murad had refused to have anything to do with the British. Then, in his old age, he unexpectedly sought their help, for a surprising reason: his brother was going blind. Having great faith in the powers of healing of the 'Feringhies', he decided to invite them to Kunduz.

From the British point of view, the invitation could hardly have come at a more opportune moment. Alexander Burnes, a political agent-cum-explorer-cum-scholar whose ability was matched only by his self-assurance, was devoting his very considerable energy to stemming Russian expansion into southern Asia; an ally on the Turkestan border seemed like the answer to his prayers. Percival Lord, a political agent and doctor, and John Wood, an acknowledged authority on rivers, were sent to Kunduz.

They left Karachi, on the delta of the Indus, in December 1836. It took them nearly a year to ascend the river and cross the mountains into the plains of central Asia. Wood's comments on the Indus are worth recording.

Just as Livingstone in Africa hoped to bring prosperity to the continent by opening up its rivers, so Burnes in Asia hoped to develop the Indus into a trade route which would carry British goods and British influence deep into the heart of Asia. Wood's report disillusioned him. 'There is no known river in either hemisphere,' wrote the practical lieutenant, 'discharging even half the same quantity of water which is not superior for navigational purposes to this far-famed stream.' And he supported his opinion with a number of accurate if long-winded descriptions of sandbars, whirlpools and rapids.

At 7 a.m. we passed through the Dubber Mountains, a range that here extends on both sides of the river. The acute turnings among the steep bluffs caused by these mountains gave rise to numerous violent eddies, over which, had the boat's beam been less, she could not have safely ridden. In these eddies we were often completely drenched by the surging waves, which flew up in jets when the boat came in contact with the whirling current . . . What a contrast does the Indus in this part of its course present to the shoaled and wide-spread river of the plains! Here it gushes down a valley varying from one-hundred to four-hundred yards [90–365 m] wide, between precipitous banks from seventy to seven-hundred feet [21–215 m] high. Its character is not that of a brawling stream, but as if conscious of its own magnitude and strength, it pursues its course in silence. The country through which this ceaseless tide is rolled is a moderately elevated tableland extending from Attock to the Great Salt Range. The banks of the river throughout the whole of this distance are formed by hills that rise immediately from its waters in bold bluffs or steep slopes. Compressed by its rocky banks the great stream glides smoothly onward. But where its surface is broken by opposing rocks, the angry spirit of the river is roused, and then the turmoil is dreadful. The enormous body of water, crushed against the obstruction, becomes white with spray and foam. If it be a rocky ledge in mid-river, the water, rising up its face, rolls off in huge waves that extend to both banks, forming dangerous eddies; to keep clear from these tumultuous vortices requires both nerve and skill.

A few miles above Attock, Lord and Wood left the Indus and headed into the Hindu Kush. From now on the perils of the river were superseded by the perils of the mountains, with potential marauders ever hovering in the wings. Wood's published diary, *A Journey to the Source of the River Oxus*, evokes both the dangers and pleasures of Afghan travel.

Late in the evening we arrived, weary and somewhat disheartened, at the bottom of a deep dell along which was scattered the village of Sambala. Its male inhabitants, armed to the teeth, kept hovering about our encampment, wistfully eyeing the baggage, but restrained from any act of violence by the knowledge that we were guests of both Kabul and Kunduz. Nothing but this kept them from considering our property a lawful prize . . . Next morning we were astir early, anxious to quit a dangerous neighbourhood. [soon] we reached a shallow ravine, on the opposite bank of which stood a tower, commanding the ascent. On approaching the foot of this tower, we saw that it was full of armed men. Others put in an appearance from all quarters, and we were soon surrounded. Three men came out of the tower; a parley was held, and we were given to understand that we must pay certain taxes before we would be permitted to pass . . .

– a story to be repeated many times in the months ahead after many such confrontations. There were, however, more pleasant moments.

We passed the night [Wood wrote] under the roof of a Hazara family. The house was of stone, low, flat-roofed and contained a considerable number of small apartments, in one of which the females slept, and in another the men of the family and ourselves. The fire-place in the kitchen or sitting-room was merely a hole scooped in the earthern floor, while the smoke found a vent through two apertures in the roof. On top of the house was piled, in bundles, the winter's store of fuel. An Hazara house, with a cheerful fire on its hearth, is a snug berth, and one that evoked in me that glow at the heart which cannot be described: a calmness of spirit, a willingness to be satisfied and pleased with everything around me.

Wood might have got on well, one feels, with that lone traveller of our own age, Eric Shipton, for both had the same ability to be calm and comfortable in any circumstances, the same curiosity to know what lay beyond the horizon and the same knack of transforming the rigours of high-altitude exploration into a worthwhile adventure.

The two travellers arrived in Kunduz early in December 1837, and Lord at once examined his patient. His diagnosis was not encouraging. Murad Beg's brother was suffering from trachoma; one eye was already blind, the other was failing and there was not much hope of saving it.

Lord prescribed what remedial measures he could, and then suggested that, since treatment was likely to be a lengthy business, his colleague might be allowed, while waiting, to explore the Oxus. The rajah consented. And within a week of his arrival in the capital, Wood was given the opportunity he had hoped for.

Seldom can so important a journey have been embarked on with such insouciance.

Monday the 11th December [Wood wrote] *was fortunately a market-day in Kunduz; so that the articles required for our expedition were at once obtained, and lest Murad Beg might recall the permission he had given, we started the same evening for the Oxus. We adopted the costume of the country, as a measure calculated to smooth our intercourse with a strange people, and we had little baggage to excite cupidity or suspicion. Coarse clothes to barter for food were our sole stock in trade; and my chronometers and other instruments the only articles of value I took with me. Dr Lord accompanied us for the first few miles, then parted from us with cordial wishes for the success of our expedition.*

It is roughly 600 miles (965 km) from Kunduz to the source of the Oxus: first through terrain that is bleak and sparsely populated, then through terrain which in those days was *terra incognita* and virtually uninhabited. The journey was made at the height of winter, and conditions were always difficult and frequently appalling. Here, one feels, were the ingredients of high adventure; yet Wood's narrative is curiously unexciting. As a travel-writer he is almost obsessively diffident, and constantly underplays his hand. It is only by reading between the lines, by noting the throw-away references to arms lost through frost-bite and pack-animals crashing through the ice, that one realizes what a feat of tenacity and endurance his journey must have been.

At first the going was not too arduous as Wood and his seven Hazara followers, all mounted, traversed the jumble of hills between the Pamirs and the Hindu Kush. His diary for 16 December describes a typical morning.

A cloudy dawn ushered in a gloomy day. Clouds floated low about the mountain-sides, and the course of the river far ahead could be traced by the heavy masses of fog that hung over its surface. These, put in motion by an easterly wind, came rolling down the valley like clouds of smoke from the muzzle of some enormous gun. For the first ten miles we followed the bank of the river upon a road slippery from yesterday's rain . . . Then, leaving the river to our right, we proceeded for four miles through low rounded hills which in this neighbourhood rise only some 200 feet [60 m] above the river; all of them are grassy. The bulk of Koh Umber towers 2500 feet [760 m] above the hills, a large portion of it encased in snow.

The main excitement on this part of their journey was provided first by an earthquake, and then by meeting a group of slave-traders. Wood was appalled to find 'this degrading traffic in souls' flourishing in the heart of Asia.

As the cavalcade headed east, the rain and mist of Kunduz gave gradual way to the snow and bitter winds of the foothills of the Pamirs. When they reached Jerm in late December the temperature was $-25°F$ ($-32°C$). For the next five weeks blizzards closed in, and Wood was unable to move. Ever practical, he spent his enforced leisure learning Badakshi.

At the end of January he was told that a group of travellers had forced their way down the Oxus from Whakan. They had had a terrible journey, half of them being swept by an avalanche into the river and drowned, but the survivors had won through. It says much for Wood's determination that he regarded this as a good not a bad augury, and next day set out for Whakan. The temperature was now $6°F$ ($-14°C$), the wind gusting to over 50 knots, and snow was sweeping down from the Pamirs in great near-horizontal sheets. As they struggled up the 10,000-foot (3050 m) pass that led to Ishkashim, Wood and his party met a solitary traveller clad from head to foot in the skin of a horse; unable to ride his animal through the deepening snow, he had killed it, skinned it and struggled on on foot, encased against the cold in its hide. This, too, Wood regarded as a good sign. He pressed on. And coming at last to the top of the pass, he stood staring down on what he presumed to be the upper reaches of the Oxus: an unending snowscape, bounded to the south by the rugged peaks of the Hindu Kush, and to the north by the rounded domes of the Pamirs. All was as motionless and silent as the face of the moon. Of the river there was no sign; like everything else, it lay hidden under the snow.

Descending into the valley, they followed the Oxus for several days, forcing their way through groves of willows bowed low with snow. It was, the laconic Wood tells us, 'a hard, cold march, with the temperature sunk to the 6th degree above zero, and the effect of the wind to be dreaded . . . Eagles soared high above us, but even at their highest they were below the summits of the great mountains lining the valley.'

At Ishkashim they were obliged to cross from the south bank of the river to the north. The Oxus here was not much more than 30 yards (27 m) wide, but crossing it was no easy matter. In mid-winter – when the river was at its lowest – it had been frozen solid; but now, swollen by the New Year snows, it had 'burst its winter fetters', and had become a churning morass of great slabs of broken ice and swift-running water, festooned with bridges of snow. They crossed by the snow-bridges, losing one of their pack-animals as the precarious footing gave way beneath them.

Another problem faced them some 50 miles (80 km) up river at Qala Panja. The Oxus divided, and Wood was uncertain which branch to follow. The southern branch *looked* the larger, but in the northern the current was faster and the water colder. Cold water, Wood reckoned, indicated a higher and therefore a more distant source. He followed the northern branch.

He arrived at his decision carefully, conscientiously and sensibly – he was that sort of man – and even today it is difficult to be sure if the branch he followed was the major or the minor feeder, for the true source of a river depends on many and often conflicting factors. What *is* certain is that whether Wood was right or wrong, his judgement was certain to be challenged by both geographers and politicians; for the Oxus was about to become a line of demarcation, the boundary between Russia and Afghanistan, and for more than half a century its source and hence its course was a matter of weighty debate in the corridors of London and St Petersburg.

Wood, of course, knew nothing of this as he probed ever deeper into the Pamirs. He had, in any case, more than enough on his plate for the present without worrying about the future, for his Hazara companions had now come to the end of their tether. Tough as they were, they had had enough; they refused to go a step farther. Wood, however, was not the sort to give up, and he turned for help to a band of nomadic Kirghiz who happened to be camped nearby. The Kirghiz had a bad reputation; they would, he was told, 'cut off my ears if not my head'. But he went boldly into their black-domed tents and asked for help, and the next day a party of 14 men, mounted on yaks, set out for the Bam-i-Duniah, the 'roof of the world', where according to Kirghiz legend, the Oxus had its source in a lake encircled by eternally snow-covered mountains.

It was a nightmare journey.

It is rather more than 50 miles (80 km) from Qala Panja to the source of the Oxus, and the route involves a climb from 12,000 feet (3660 m) to close on 16,000 (4880 m). It was so cold that February that the mercury disappeared into the bulb at the bottom of Wood's thermometer. He had no tents – for shelter he and the Kirghiz built walls with frozen blocks of snow. In the waist-deep drifts, it sometimes took them two hours to struggle a couple of hundred yards, and when they left the snow fields and tried to follow the river, their animals crashed through the ice. On their first night, three men were so badly frostbitten they had to return. More of the Kirghiz gave up on the second night, and more again on the third. But Wood, who must surely be among the physically toughest of explorers, ploughed doggedly on, until he came at last to his desideratum.

After quitting the surface of the river we travelled about an hour along its right bank, then ascended a low hill which bounded the valley to the eastward. On surmounting this, at five o'clock on the afternoon of 19th February 1838, we stood, to use a native expression, upon the Bam-i-Duniah, or Roof of the World, while before us stretched a noble frozen sheet of water, from whose western end issued the infant river of the Oxus. On three sides the lake is bordered by swelling hills about 500 feet [150 m] high, whilst along its southern flank they rise into mountains 3500 feet [1065 m] above the lake or 19,000 feet [5795 m] above the sea, and covered with perpetual snow, from which never-failing source the lake is supplied.

Wood was tempted to christen his discovery Lake Victoria, but thought better of it, 'deeming it proper it should retain the name Sir-i-kol, the appellation given to it by our guides'. In this he was less parochially minded than Speke, who insisted on the lake *he* discovered – the source of the Nile – being named after the Queen.

It was too late that evening to study the lake. But first thing next morning Wood and half a dozen of the Kirghiz made their way to its centre, armed with pickaxes and 100 fathoms of rope, determined to take soundings. The ice, however, proved recalcitrant; at a height of 16,000 feet (4880 m), even the slightest physical effort led to breathlessness and sickness, and the first hole they made proved too small and produced only a fountain of water which soaked them to the skin. Panting with exhaustion and festooned with icicles, they tried again. This time they succeeded, and soon Wood was paying out his rope in the best naval tradition. But for nine feet (2.7 m) only. Then he struck bottom.

The depth of the Sir-i-kol may have been something of an anti-climax; but its setting seems to have made a deep impression on Wood. In about the only purple passage in the whole of his diary, he extolled its desolation:

Wherever the eye fell one dazzling sheet of snow carpeted the ground, while the sky everywhere was of a dark angry hue. Clouds would have been a relief to the eye; but they were wanting. Not a breath moved along the surface of the lake; not a beast, not even a bird, was visible. The sound of the human voice would have been music to my ear, but no-one thinks of invading these gelid domains. Silence reigned – silence so profound that it oppressed the heart, and as I contemplated the summits of the everlasting mountains, where human foot had never trod and where lay piled the snow of ages, my own dear country and all it contains passed across my mind with a vividness of recollection I had never felt before. It is all very well for men in crowded cities to talk of the delights of solitude. Let them pass but twenty-four hours on the banks of the Sir-i-kol, and it will do more to make them contented with their lot than a thousand arguments.

A month later he was back in Kunduz. Things had not gone well in his absence. Mohammed Beg's eye was worse rather than better, and Wood noted in his diary: 'Our reception was less cordial than it had formerly been, and I could gather from the altered manner of our host that our influence at court was on the wane.' That spring he and Lord withdrew to Kabul. This, however, proved tantamount to leaping from frying pan to fire, for it was not only in Kunduz that British influence was now on the wane; it was happening throughout Afghanistan. One reason was the vacillation of the Governor-

General, Lord Auckland, who found it difficult to make up his mind which of the ever-warring rajahs to support. Another reason was the growing influence of the Russians, whose agents offered the various rulers large sums of money to attack one another, taking care always to finance the winners the most generously. In an attempt to restore order, the British sent the Army of the Indus into the Hindu Kush, but it was ambushed and massacred, literally to the last man. The British garrison in Kabul suffered the same fate, and agents like Burnes and Lord not only saw their dreams turned to dust, but lost their heads into the bargain.

One of the very few to survive was John Wood. Disagreeing with the vacillations of Auckland's policy, he had resigned from the East India Company and returned to England. Here he became something of a recluse, not bothering to turn up even to receive that most coveted of explorers' accolades, the Gold Medal of the Royal Geographical Society. One gets the impression that he was never quite forgiven by the establishment for not forfeiting his head in the Afghan rising; for when, years later, the commander-in-chief in India particularly asked for him to be attached to his staff, the Company's board of directors refused to sanction the appointment.

The Afghan massacres have been described as 'the worst defeat ever suffered by the British army in Asia'. The immediate consequence was that Afghanistan became as taboo to travellers as Bhutan, Nepal and Tibet, and from that day to this the territory north of the Khyber Pass has been treated with the greatest circumspection.

With access denied to both the eastern Himalaya and the Hindu Kush, the exploration of the mountain complex from the south came to a virtual halt. It was a very different story in the north, for the low-ebb of British exploration coincided with the floodtide of Russian.

<hr />

The Russian advance into the mountains had the inevitability of a tide submerging the flats of an estuary. Over the previous three centuries Russia had been adding to her territory at an average rate of more than 75 square miles a day, her total acquisition being some seven million square miles. By the middle of the nineteenth century she was expanding so rapidly that exploration was lagging behind acquisition, and vast areas of desert mountain and steppe, in the neighbourhood of the Alai, Pamirs and Tien Shan, had been claimed but were still unmapped and virtually unknown.

One of the earliest and certainly one of the greatest explorers of this bleakly beautiful heart of Asia was Petr Petrovich Semenov-Tyan-Shanskiy (usually known outside the USSR as Peter Semyonov, the title 'Tyan-Shanskiy', awarded him by the Tsar, meaning simply 'of the Tien Shan'). Semyonov was born in 1827. His parents expected him, like most of his contemporaries in the landed gentry, to make a career for himself in the army, but after three years at a military academy, Semyonov decided to study geography, and took his degree at St Petersburg University. At the age of 22, he joined the recently formed Russian Geographical Society, and was given the mammoth task of translating the works of those fathers of modern geography, Ritter and Von Humboldt. Both Ritter and Von Humboldt believed that the mountains of central Asia would prove volcanic in origin, and it was partly to put this theory to the test that Semyonov embarked on his expedition to the Tien Shan.

He prepared himself with the dedication of a modern athlete. First he went to Germany, and studied in Berlin under Ritter. Then he went to Switzerland, where the delights of mountaineering were being savoured for the first time by a cosmopolitan élite, and took part in some of the earliest climbs in the Bernese Alps. And finally he went to

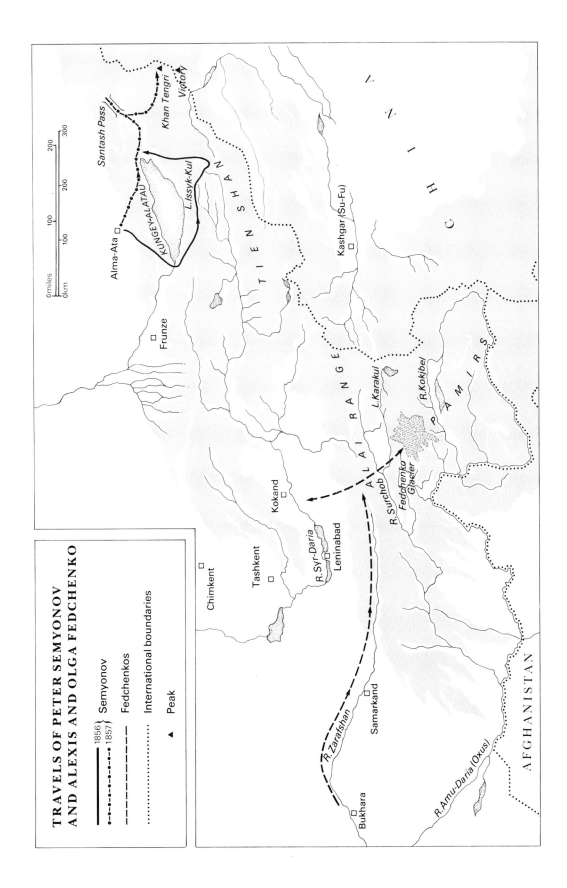

TRAVELS OF PETER SEMYONOV
AND ALEXIS AND OLGA FEDCHENKO

1856 } Semyonov
1857 }
        Fedchenkos
        International boundaries
▲   Peak

0miles
0km
100   100
200   200
300

Italy; here, since he expected the Tien Shan to be volcanic, he studied Vesuvius, 'climbing the volcano,' his biographer tells us, '17 times from all sides, on several occasions descending into the crater when it was full of smoke'. In 1856, backed by a grant from the Geographical Society and provided with an escort of 50 Cossacks, he arrived in Alma-Ata, now a modern industrial city with nearly a million inhabitants, then a frontier post with only a few hundred.

It was known that to the south of Alma-Ata lay a great lake, the Issyk-kul, and it was believed that the southern shore of this lake was bordered by a chain of snow-clad peaks, the Celestial Mountains of mythology. Few people, however, had set eyes on these mountains, and fewer still had set foot on them; nobody had attempted to survey them or study them. Semyonov hoped to do both. In this he was one of the first of the truly modern explorers: a seeker-after-truth, who was not content merely to visit a place, but who wanted to know it scientifically, to analyse its rocks, to classify its flora and fauna. We are told that he had a particularly keen eye for trees and plants – the latter he listed in solid blocks a hundred at a time in footnotes; but he also recorded many other things, from the predatory habits of the Kirghiz to the alcohol problems of officials in the far-flung outposts of empire. Like his mentor Ritter, he was a monumental amasser of facts.

In the summer of 1856 he embarked on a preliminary reconnaissance, leading his mini-army of Cossacks into the Kungey-Alatau, a spur of the Tien Shan which borders the northwest shore of Lake Issyk-kul. Reaching the crest of this range, he was able to look across to the great peaks on the far side of the lake. 'Today,' he wrote in his diary, 'I saw for the first time, on the distant horizon and glinting in the sun's rays, what for many years had been the object of my thoughts and aspirations – the unbroken snowy chain of the Tien Shan.' It was, however, to be some time before he set foot in the mountains; and on this first sortie he contented himself with making a sizeable collection of plants, flowers, grasses and rock samples, and 'showing the flag' in the foothills.

'Showing the flag' was an important part of Semyonov's work. His expedition may have been part-scientific, but it was also part-military – hence the strength of his escort – and his diary is full of references to the hostility and terror with which his troops were regarded by the mountain people.

We chose as our camp-site a copse of willows in the bed of a deep valley, the walls of which consisted of dark-purple rocks rising near-sheer to 2500 feet [760 m] above the river. In this confined space it was difficult to find room for our tents, our baggage, and upwards of 50 men and 70 animals. The wind, increasing to gale force, had by midnight cleared the sky, of which we could catch no more than a glimpse because of the narrowness of the defile. The night was cold, and my wet tent, stretched hurriedly between two willows, soon froze solid. We didn't dare light fires because of the proximity of the Kara Kirghizes; but I posted lookouts among the rocks. At 1 a.m. one of these gave the pre-arranged signal for danger, and we all jumped to our feet in silence, grasping our weapons. For a moment the only sound was the cocking of guns, as we prepared to face an attack. When I asked the lookout the cause of the danger, he pointed in silence to a small ledge halfway up the face of the cliff; from this ledge came the occasional whistle, and a number of small stones and loose shingle raining down upon us. Soon we could make out in the moonlight a line of men and animals passing along the ledge some thousand feet above us. We felt sure they must be the Kara Kirghizes, who had come across us unintentionally and were now endangering their lives by scaling the cliff-face in an effort to avoid us. For almost an hour we listened to the sounds high above us, as in single file the men led their horses along the ledge. At last all was still. Our fear was that the Kirghizes would alert their countrymen, who, warned of our approach, would next day give us a hostile reception.

No attack developed, either that night or the following morning. But in the afternoon,

Top: Dr Sven Hedin on a Kirghiz camel

*Above: Olga Fedchenko's sketch of the
Chtchovrovskik Glacier*

Semyonov related,

climbing a small ridge we came unexpectedly on a cluster of Kirghiz yourtas [tents]. Six women and perhaps as many children ran to meet us, and threw themselves at our feet imploring mercy. Never before had I seen such terror, such deathlike pallor, on human faces. For the women recognized us as those Russians with whom their fathers and husbands had recently fought, and they considered themselves lost. It was a long time before I was able to convince these wretched people that neither their lives nor their property were in danger; but after receiving presents of multicoloured handkerchiefs and silver coins their fears were at last allayed. The men of the village, they told us, had at our approach jumped on to their horses and fled into the hills; all except one old fellow who, having no horse, had made off on a cow. We found the animal no more than a couple of hundred yards from the village, grazing behind some rocks. We couldn't at first see its rider; then we spotted him in a deep cleft in the ground, out of which, so great was his terror, we could hardly drag him.

That autumn Semyonov returned to Alma-Ata, and began to classify his collection of flora and write up his diary. The next spring, as soon as the snow in the foothills had melted, he set off again, determined this time to penetrate to the very heart of the Tien Shan.

It is difficult to piece together a readable narrative of his travels, for he had no fixed objective, and there was therefore no climax to his expedition. Instead, we have a succession of long, arduous and richly rewarding treks through a virgin range, through whose precipitous valleys he struggled with difficulty, whose beauties he described in evocative prose, and whose flora, fauna, rocks, climate and orography he recorded in meticulous detail.

He approached his objective this time via the northeast shore of Lake Issyk-kul, leading his mini-army – 25 men, 30 horses and 16 camels – up the Santash Pass, 'the pass of the counted stones'. *Here*, he wrote,

we found an enormous pile of stones, raised by human hands. According to legend, Tamerlane, on his march westward, passed this spot with his troops. Wishing to ascertain the strength of his host, he directed each warrior to take a stone and drop it on the same spot; thus a colossal mound was formed. Years later the victorious but decimated army returned by the same route. This time Tamerlane ordered each warrior to remove a stone from the heap. The resulting pile enabled him to estimate his losses, and served also as a memorial to those who had fallen.

From the far side of this pass opened up a magnificent vista of lake and mountain.

It would be difficult to imagine a more splendid sight. The sapphire-like colour of the Issyk-kul bears comparison to the equally blue surface of the Lake of Geneva, but its expanse (5 times that of the latter) and its magnificent background impart to it a grandeur which the Swiss lake can not claim. For in place of the comparatively low cluster of the Savoy Alps, the entire southern shore of the Issyk-kul is bordered for more than 200 miles [320 km] by the towering, unbroken and snow-covered chain of the Celestial Mountains. The stark outline of its spurs and the dark furrows of its lower valleys are softened by the transluscent canopy of mist which most of the time clings to the surface of the lake: mist which serves to heighten the white peaks as they rise above it into the clear-blue sky . . . The landscape, however, is far less beautiful than that surrounding the Swiss Lake; for instead of gardens, prosperous villages and romantic castles, there is nothing here but a barren desert-shore, devoid of everything which civilized man might implant: unfruitful, rocky, covered with pebbles and virtually devoid of trees – it is only along the banks of the impetuous mountain torrents that one finds a few stunted willows or the occasional cluster of Hippophae rhomnoides *with silvery leaves and bright red fruit. Very occasionally, nestling among the trees, one may see the encampments of the Kirghiz herdsmen, with their white felt yourtas and long-necked camels.*

By the end of May, Semyonov was heading into the main chain of the mountains: a world of vast slopes of granite and schist, split by spectacular, steep-sided valleys. The higher his men climbed the more precipitous the mountain tracks became. The vegetation grew thinner; so did the air. Before long they were suffering from altitude sickness and exhaustion, and from June onwards Semyonov's diary is an almost continuous recitation of hazards and near-disasters.

Our ascent became steeper and steeper. So long as we followed the stream our route was more difficult than dangerous; but when we were forced to climb a steep granite ridge our progress became perilous indeed. We were compelled to abandon a camel and three horses which had been badly injured by falls from the snow-covered rocks . . . We commenced a descent by a winding path between the most stupendous rocks. The path had been cut with great difficulty out of granite, and was only passable at hazard to life. As usual the horses had to be led . . . Continuing the ascent for about three miles we emerged unexpectedly on to the shore of a beautiful alpine lake of emerald green. Around the lake were piled in wild confusion steep escarpments of rock, rising to a height of more than 1000 feet [305 m]: rock which was layered with strata of green schist and striated by cascading streams falling in clouds of spray to the lake beneath. Beyond the lake, the rocks formed a gigantic barrier across the valley: a barrier through which there wound a single narrow zigzag path, overhung by one of the huge spurs of the Tien Shan. It was a place of flood, avalanche and death – everywhere we looked were strewn the carcasses of camels, horses, sheep and goats: a picture in keeping with the sublime but fearful character of the scenery. We were now only a short distance from the Zauku Pass, but the most difficult part of the journey still lay ahead. Soon we were enveloped in a blizzard, and our horses, trembling with fear, were continually stumbling over the icy rocks and shying in terror at the sight of every carcass that we passed. We were obliged to dismount and lead them; but even so, there were accidents. The artist's horse missed its footing and fell on top of him, injuring his leg. My own horse fell and cut itself so severely that it bled to death. Eventually some men and animals became so utterly exhausted they could proceed no farther. I was therefore obliged to divide my party, pressing on with only one guide who told me that the difficulty of breathing at the top of the pass would be so great that it would be impossible to spend more than half-an-hour there. At last we attained our objective, the highest point of the pass, and stood gazing on the scene of unexpected beauty which lay ahead of us: a vast plain, dotted with green ice-encrusted lakes, and of so great an elevation that the mountain tops which rose from it appeared no larger than hillocks. We continued our journey for a further 5 miles [8 km] across this plain, passing many icy lakes, one of which is the source of the Nargn, the principal feeder of the Syr-Daria. It was at this moment in our journey that I found myself in the very heart of Asia, nearer to Delhi than to Omsk, nearer to the Indian Ocean than to the Arctic, and midway between the Pacific and the Black Sea. At an elevation of more than 15,000 feet [4575 m] the fire which we tried to kindle crackled fitfully and gave off little heat. Yet all around us, peeping out from the newly-fallen snow, were Alpine flowers of the most brilliant colours it would be possible to imagine.

It is typical of Semyonov's attention to detail that he listed them: '*Ranunculus fraternus, Oxygraphis glacialis, Dracocephalum altaicum, Draba,* and a few *Chrysosplenium glaciale* and *Hegemone liliacina.*'

He would have liked to continue his exploration by descending the southern slopes of the Tien Shan, but, to quote his own worlds, 'decided to abandon the idea, fearing to jeopardize the safety of my men and incur the moral responsibility for any disaster that might befall them.' He recrossed the pass, rejoined his Cossack escort, and within minutes saw his expedition come within a hair's-breadth of obliteration: 'I had scarcely rejoined my companions, when a terrible rolling-and-booming noise, like successive peals of thunder, resounded above us, causing our Kirghiz guides to flee in all directions.

A huge avalanche came crashing down very nearly on top of us, strewing its debris only a few yards to the side of our camp.'

It was now past mid-summer, and Semyonov headed east through the mountains towards the Chinese border, his objective being that part of the Tien Shan which could not be seen from Lake Issyk-kul. On 26 June 1857, he came suddenly on a cluster of magnificent peaks, the highest in the range, no fewer than 30 snow-capped giants of over 20,000 feet (6100 m), with Khan Tengri ('Lord of the Spirits') at 23,616 feet (7203 m) and the recently rechristened Victory Peak at 24,406 feet (7444 m) towering above the others. It was the fitting climax to a major journey of exploration.

In the autumn Semyonov headed back for Alma-Ata. As he neared the lake, he turned for a last glimpse of the mountains he loved: 'It was almost dark. A full moon was rising into the cloudless sky. In one of the gorges a pall of smoke indicated a forest fire. Mist was forming a transparent haze along the feet of the mountains, and above this haze

Inhabitants of the banks of the Amir,
1866

the summits glowed roseate and seemingly far away although they were perfectly clear. Sorrowfully, I cast a last glance at the snowy peaks which for so many years had been my desideratum.'

Semyonov never set foot in central Asia again. Returning to St Petersburg he settled down to the life of scholar and administrator, becoming vice-president of the Russian Geographical Society, a post he held for 41 years until his death in 1914.

His achievements were of the greatest importance. Not only was he the first European to explore the Tien Shan, he was also the first to classify their flora and fauna, and to study their geological structure – establishing beyond doubt that Ritter and Von Humboldt were wrong, and that the range was *not* volcanic in origin. Flowers and grasses, animals and insects, mountains and glaciers were named after him. He was a great explorer. It is fair to say that he added the Tien Shan to the map of Russia.

◆

What Semyonov did for the Tien Shan, the Fedchenkos were also to do for the Trans-

Alai and the Pamirs.

Alexis Pavlovich Fedchenko was born in Irkutsk in 1844. He appears to have been an unusually talented and likeable young man, who, by the time he was 25 was a competent geologist, a qualified naturalist and married to a girl who was a more than competent artist. Olga Fedchenko accompanied her husband wherever he went, even on the most hazardous of his travels, and her sketch, 'The Summer Remnants of a Pamirs Glacier' shows the quality of her work. In the late 1860s the Fedchenkos explored the valley of the Zarafshan, on whose banks stand the great cities of Bukhara, Samarkand and present-day Leninabad. They paid particular attention to the upper reaches of the river in the Trans-Alai Mountains, an area claimed by Russia but as yet unexplored.

The Trans-Alai is a region of scenic and ethnic paradox: vast, desolate hillsides split by the occasional small and fertile valley; fiercely independent, often nomadic peoples (Kirghiz, Uzbek, Tajik and Mongols) ever feuding, yet ever bound by the comradeship of those whose lives are a continuous struggle against their environment. The Fedchenkos wouldn't have survived for long in this forbidding territory if they had not had the protection of the local rajah, the Khan of Kokand. The Khan gave them an imposing guarantee of safe conduct:

> To the governors, amirs, serkars and other authorities of the districts of Marghilan, Andijan, Shaler-Khan, Aravan and Bulak-bashi, be it known that six Russians, including one woman, with seven attendants, are travelling to see the mountain countries, wherefore we command they be received as guests in every district and place, that no nomads or Sarts lay hands upon them, and that the said Russians be permitted to perform their journey pleasantly and with ease. This must be obeyed without demur.

> Seid Muhamed Hudoyar Khan

Armed with this document and provided with guides, Olga and Alexis headed into the unknown. Only 24 hours out of Kokand there was an incident which might well have deterred less dedicated travellers.

> I was informed [wrote Alexis Fedchenko] that a local rising had recently been suppressed, and that only yesterday the last of the captured insurgents had been executed. He was put to death in a most barbarous manner. On one bridge he had his nose chopped off; he was then led to another bridge where his ears were cut off; on a third bridge his hands were lopped off, and on a fourth his head was severed from his body.

The Trans-Alai, like the Hindu Kush, was no place for the faint-hearted.

As explorers, the Fedchenkos have not the same standing as Peter Semyonov. The territory they passed through was less spectacular, and more populous, and their collection of flora – although far from negligible – was less comprehensive. Their importance lies in the fact that they were the first people to explore a potentially valuable frontier area over which Russia was claiming suzerainty. They were pathfinders: travellers who, like Semyonov, had no specific objective, but who explored an area hitherto unknown to Europeans, recording the bleak grandeur of its scenery and the agricultural expertise of its inhabitants. Their diaries have few highlights; the entry for one day reads very like the next.

They had endless trouble with their guides. *Our mehtar*, wrote Alexis while he and Olga were still in Kokand,

> gave me a most gloomy account of the difficulties and dangers of the mountain paths. I thanked him for his solicitude on our behalf, but told him that my wife and I were well accustomed to the mountains, and that where he could lead we could follow. I could see this didn't please him . . . Next

day we set out for the pass, which was about five miles distant. When we had proceeded about two miles our guides dismounted and pointed out the pass, telling us that nothing would induce them to come farther. To prove their point they lay down on the ground and refused to get up! . . . Our guide had a superstitious terror of the mountains. Between Varukh and Sokh, in the Karokul defile, he behaved in a most extraordinary manner, continually muttering prayers, and looking up with fear and trembling at the overhanging rocks. At last he flung himself to the ground and refused to go a step farther. I began to despair of our ever reaching the Trans-Alai!

Alexis attributes their guides' recalcitrance to laziness. 'They were inclined,' he wrote, 'to pass no more time than they had to in the mountains because of the discomfort and inconvenience.' This may have been the truth, but it was not the whole truth, for if Olga and Alexis had failed to return from their travels, their guides would almost certainly have forfeited their noses, ears, hands and heads.

Two particularly interesting features of the Russians' diaries are their descriptions of glaciers and their accounts of the agricultural expertise of the people of the mountain valleys.

They were the first Europeans to set foot in the great valleys of ice which are so spectacular a feature of the north face of the Pamirs; in particular, they discovered the enormous glacier which is named after them, and which until recently was thought to be the largest in the world outside the Arctic and Antarctic.

In order to study this glacier [wrote Alexis] I walked about 2 miles [3.2 km] along the slope of the mountain, then climbed down on to the ice. Its upper reaches consist of a vast bowl of frozen snow nestling beneath the peaks of the main range; this bowl is about 3¼ miles [5.2 km] in width, and is surrounded by 9 great peaks all of them between 18,000 and 19,000 feet [5490–5795 m], the lowest depression between the peaks being not less than 14,000 feet [4270 m]. From the troughs between these summits the most stupendous rivers of ice, each with its line of lateral moraine, are squeezed down into the principal glacier. From where I stood (at about 12,000 feet [3660 m]) I could see 7 lines of moraine working their way down through the ice. The surface of the glacier was also littered with stones, some of which, shading the ice beneath them from the sun, were poised on little columns of ice, looking for all the world like so many tables. The insect Podura was found in great abundance under these stones . . . . The glacier ends at approximately 10,000 feet [3050 m]. It must at one time have descended even lower; for its terminal moraine, a great semi-circular rampart, lies 175 feet [53 m] below its present extremity. That this terminal moraine has been long detached from the glacier may be deduced from the great number of plants growing among the stones. We collected specimens, both of these and of the host of alpine flowers flourishing between 10,000 and 12,000 feet [3050–3660 m].

This would have been of interest to geologists and naturalists; but of greater interest to the Russian authorities must have been the Fedchenkos' comments on the prosperity of some of the regions through which they passed.

In the mid-nineteenth century it was generally thought that the upper reaches of the Amu-Daria, Zarafshan and Syr-Daria would be barren and sparsely populated. It was the Fedchenkos who first revealed that the arid hills of this part of central Asia were in fact split by the occasional valley which was both intensely cultivated and populous. 'Here,' wrote Alexis, 'every particle of soil is put to good use. The whole valley is under the most careful cultivation, and consists of a mosaic of fields, sown with cotton, wheat, barley and millet, divided by hedgerows: all watered by numerous *aryks* [irrigation canals] of various sizes and dimensions – we followed one along the side of the valley for no fewer than 47 miles [76 km].' They were also the first people to note the totally different life styles of those who lived in the valleys and those who lived in the hills:

In this part of central Asia, animal husbandry and crop growing do not go hand in hand. Where much attention is paid to the soil, and where in consequence field and garden yield abundant produce, there are no herds of animals, and the people lead static lives. But where the cultivated zone merges with the steppe and there is a scarcity of water, one finds huge herds of oxen, sheep and horses; here the people lead nomadic lives, occupying their villages only in winter; the rest of the year they are away in the hills, driving their herds from pasture to pasture over the trackless steppe.

The Fedchenkos also noted the presence of coal, oil, iron, gold, limestone and marble. It is not therefore surprising that their travels triggered off a full-scale Russian military expedition into the area, complete with naturalist, topographer, geodesist and Cossack guard: an expedition which penetrated to that *ultima Thule* of travellers, Lake Karakul.

In 1865, at the start of their travels, the Fedchenkos had lamented that 'more is known about the moon than about the Pamirs'. Within 25 years the regions through which they travelled had come under Russian suzerainty. But by then Alexis was dead, killed in a climbing accident on Mont Blanc at the age of only 29; a tragic end to a gifted explorer and a likeable man.

◆

Semyonov and the Fedchenkos did their exploring in territory which was (or was about to become) Russian. Nicholas Mikhailovich Przhevalski did his in territory which was predominantly Chinese – the Gobi desert and the northern plateau of Tibet.

When in September 1870 he left the Siberian frontier town of Kiakhta at the head of the obligatory escort of Cossacks, Przhevalski's objective was Lhasa via Peking. There was, however, a great deal more to his expedition than an attempt to reach the Forbidden City. In the preface to his book, *Mongolia, the Tangut Country and the Solitudes of Northern Tibet*, he explains very clearly the purpose of his mission:

The whole vast plateau of central Asia, between the mountains of Siberia to the north and the Himalayas of India to the south, is terra incognita: of its geology, climate, flora and fauna we are almost totally ignorant. This, it seemed to me, would be a most rewarding area for research – although I was soon to discover that its scientific attractions were counterbalanced by the appalling difficulty of its terrain – wind-lashed deserts devoid of water and temperatures alternating between burning heat and searing cold, not to mention a suspicious and barbarous population.

Przhevalski, it soon becomes clear from his diary, liked neither the country through which he travelled nor its inhabitants.

His journey took him first to the Gobi desert, which he crossed by a more direct route than his predecessor Hsuan Tsang. The Russian's published diary evokes both its bleakness and its monotony.

The Gobi is undulating rather than flat, although you do sometimes come across tracts of level plain, particularly near the centre. There is no running water between the Tola River to the west and the Chinese border to the east [i.e. for more than 600 miles: 960 km]; the summer rains, it is true, do form temporary lakes in the hollows, but these soon dry up in the extreme heat. The soil is a coarse red gravel, interspersed with ridges of black rock, and drifts of yellow sand. Vegetation can find little sustenance here, and the Gobi produces only a grass tough as wire and the occasional scrub wormwood. Of trees and bushes there are none. Indeed how could there be in a region where the winds of winter and spring rage with such violence that they uproot even the humble wormwood, roll it into bundles and send it spinning over the plain . . . The barrenness and monotony produce in the traveller a sense of depression. For weeks on end the same objects appear ever before one's eyes: cheerless plains, covered with yellow withered grass. With measured tread our camels advance for tens, hundreds, it seems like thousands of miles; but the scene remains sombre and unattractive as ever. The sun sets; darkness descends; the cloudless sky glitters with a myriad stars as our caravan halts for the night. The camels show unmistakable satisfaction, and lie down beside the tents of their drivers. Within the hour men and beasts are asleep, and all around reigns the silence of the desert: absolute: deathlike: as though outside of our encampment no living creature existed in all the world.

It must have been a welcome relief, at the eastern extremity of the desert, to pass through the Great Wall of China and into the cultivated and populous plains around Peking. This was one of the few parts of China which Przhevalski seems to have liked, and he commends its soil, its climate, the multiplicity of its birds and the beauty of its landscape.

There was a temporary hold-up in Peking – due probably to the fact that there had been a Muhammadan uprising that winter in the northwest border provinces – and for some time the Russians were refused exit permits, and had to content themselves with minor excursions into the neighbouring hills. But they at last managed to obtain the necessary letters of introduction, guides, camels and provisions, and by the spring of 1871 were heading west along a little-used caravan trail in the direction of Tibet.

They were to spend the next two years exploring the barren wilderness between the Yellow River and the Gobi desert: a region of arid hills and saline plains. Even an expedition which was well-equipped and had sufficient money to buy provisions would have found the exploration of this bleak and sparsely populated area an arduous task. Przhevalski's expedition was neither well-equipped nor wealthy. His clothing and tents were inadequate against the rigours of the Tibetan winter, and he was so short of funds that, on more than one occasion, he had to sell his rifles in order to buy food.

The wonder is not that he failed to reach Lhasa, but that he managed to push as far into Tibet as he did: some 400 miles (640 km) beyond Lake Koko-Nor.

His diary records his mounting disenchantment with the terrain through which he struggled, and the gradual deterioration of his expedition's vigour and health. Of the foothills of the Ala Shan he wrote:

The heat in the valleys was intense. The yellow-grey soil, overlaid with a veneer of salt, was peculiarly unattractive. Not a blade of green could be seen. The wind was for ever whipping up whirling columns of saline dust, which blinded and choked us. There were no animals. No birds. Over the whole area reigned a deathlike silence . . . Of the Tingeri Sands: *Hillocks, most of them 50 to 60 feet [15–18 m] in height and composed of fine yellow sand, stretched from horizon to horizon. This sand, heated by a blazing sun, is forever being carried by the wind from one hillock to another. Our camels sank deep into it with every stride. This is a terrible place in which to be caught by a whirlwind, for at such times the tops of the hillocks are whipped clean away, and the sun is obscured by driving clouds of sand . . .* Of the upper reaches of the Yellow River: *The thermometer dropped to −26° Fahrenheit [−32 °C] and once we stopped to make camp the severity of the cold was felt by all. The sun set in a purple haze, and the dry-as-dust snow around our* yurta *turned blue as ice. At our wits' end for fuel, we were obliged to cut up and burn a saddle in order to make ourselves a little tea, which was all we had that evening to eat or drink.'*

Not until the autumn of 1872 did they manage to struggle through to the Koko-Nor ('the blue sea'), the largest of the many magnificent lakes which lie scattered across the Tibetan plateau. Przhevalski's description shows that he could, when given the chance, delight in the beauty of his surroundings.

The Koko-Nor [he wrote] *lies a little to the west of Si-ing, at a height of some 10,500 feet [3200 m] above sea level. In shape it is an ellipse, with its longer axis running east-and-west. It is between 200 and 230 miles [320–370 km] in diameter – the natives telling us they could travel round it in a fortnight on foot or in seven days on horseback. Its shores are flat and shelving, its waters saline and undrinkable. This salt, however, imparts to its surface the most exquisite dark blue colour – which the Mongols aptly compare to blue silk. When the sun is shining this blue lake, framed by its ring of low snow-covered hills, is indeed the most beautiful of sights.*

Winter was not far distant, and Przhevalski must by now have had fears that Lhasa was beyond his reach. However, he struggled on, determined to explore as much of the plateau as he could before cold, exhaustion and lack of funds forced him to give up. It was a terrible journey.

The climate and natural character of these Tibetan deserts are beyond belief. The soil is clay, mixed with sand or shingle, and almost devoid of vegetation. Here and there a tuft of grass or a patch of lichen may cover a few square feet: but in most places the soil is coated with a layer of salt, white as driven snow. The grass is all of one species – Graminaea *– so parched by the wind that as one steps on it, it crackles like straw and disintegrates. The high altitude affected even the strongest of us; and even a short march or the climbing of a modest slope, tended to induce languor, giddiness and vomiting. Because of the lack of oxygen in the air it was difficult to light a fire, and difficult to breathe.*

*Houses and artefacts of the people of the Amir, from
a Russian album for travellers to the Amir*

About the only thing they did not lack that winter was food, for the plateau abounded with game, and in particular with yak. 'Had we not seen them with our own eyes,' wrote Przhevalski, 'we should never have believed that such vast herds could exist in these sterile conditions. Yet by wandering from place to place they manage to find nourishment.' He went on to give a detailed description of the yak and its habits, followed by a long dissertation on the pleasures of hunting it. In this he was in the tradition of many great nineteenth-century explorers – men such as Speke, Baker and Vigne – to whom love of the chase was an essential adjunct to their love of travel. The part played by bloodsports in the history of exploration may not, to some people's way of thinking, be edifying, but its influence should not be under-estimated: several of Livingstone's great journeys were made in the company of elephant hunters; and if it had not been for Przhevalski's prowess with a breech-loader, his expedition would have survived that winter for days rather than months.

However, there came a time when even a plentiful supply of yak-meat was not enough to keep them going.

> *The next two months [December 1872 to February 1873] were the most arduous of the whole expedition. Winter had set in with severe frosts and storms, and the want of even the bare necessities of life had so reduced our strength, that only a consciousness of the scientific importance of our labours enabled us to keep going . . . Each morning we rose two hours before sunrise, lit our argols and boiled our brick tea, which, mixed with barley-meal, was the only breakfast we could afford. At dawn we prepared for the march, dismantling our yurta and packing it with our other baggage on to the camels. This took more than an hour; and often by the time we were ready to start, we already felt exhausted. On the march it was usually too cold to ride, and most of us preferred to walk. Our clothing by now was so worn after two years' use that it afforded little protection against the cold. Our fur coats and trousers were in tatters. We had no boots, and had to resort to sewing bits of yak hide to our leggings. Often by midday the wind had increased to the violence of a hurricane, filling the air with sand-dust-and-salt, so that we were obliged to halt.*

There follows a description of dismantling their *yurta*, breaking ice for water, and hunting for and cooking their evening meal.

> *One would have thought that after all these exertions we would have slept soundly. But this wasn't so. For our fatigue was not of the ordinary kind; it was more like a running-down of our whole bodily system; while the rarified air made our throats so parched that we were constantly half-choking, and sleep for much of the night was denied us.*

On 22 January 1873 they reached the banks of the Yellow River, midway between Lake Koko-Nor and Lhasa. It was the end of the road. Both men and animals were by this time totally exhausted, and the expedition funds had been reduced to no more than one pound sterling. They had no option but to turn back.

Their return to Lake Koko-Nor was a harrowing experience. So too was their recrossing of the Gobi. But at last, on 1 October 1873, they struggled back over the Russian border to Kiakhta.

The bare facts of their journey make the mind boggle. They had been away for more than three years. They had travelled over 7000 miles (11,265 km). They had traversed some of the bleakest terrain on earth where no Europeans had set foot before them. In the course of their wanderings they had collected over 4000 plant specimens (of which 102 were previously unknown) and over 1000 bird specimens (again including many species that were new); they also brought back 37 large mammals and 90 small, 70 reptiles, 11 fish and over 3000 insects. And what is perhaps even more meritorious, for every day they were on the move they kept a continuous route survey and a continuous meteorological record. Seldom before or since has an expedition been so long in the field and brought back so impressive a collection of scientific data.

Between 1873 and 1888 he led three other major expeditions, ranging far and wide over the mountains and deserts of central Asia, and was the first man to explore the eastern reaches of the Tien Shan. In 1888, while preparing for a fifth expedition, he unexpectedly collapsed and died. He was buried – at his request – in his explorer's kit on the shore of Lake Issyk-kul, looking out over the tableland of central Asia where he had spent the better part of his life.

*Members of Przhevalski's expedition to
Central Asia, 1885*

Two other travellers who made major journeys through central Asia were Thomas Atkinson and Ney Elias. Hardly anyone has heard of the former, and hardly anyone has been able to understand the latter, yet both, in their very different ways, were great explorers.

'Thomas Witlam Atkinson,' to quote the then President of the Royal Geographical Society who wrote his obituary, 'was born of humble parents in the little village of Cawthorne in Yorkshire on 6th March 1799. His only education was at the village school. At the age of eight he was following the plough, and at the age of nine was earning his own living first in a quarry and then in the yard of a stonemason.' In 1819 he moved to Barnsley where he was employed as a mason rebuilding the Church of St Mary. His work in carving and sculpture was of outstanding artistic merit, and it was due to his skill as a mason that he eventually found himself in Russia. In 1842, while in charge of restoring the church of St Nicholas in Hamburg, he met Von Humboldt who, in Atkinson's own words, 'advised me to go and see the Creator's most magnificent edifices in rock and stone which were in central Asia'. He managed to obtain an audience with the Tsar, who was so impressed with his character and ability that he gave him the unprecedented privilege of a pass to travel as his guest throughout the length and breadth of Russia. Armed with this, an artist's easel and paints, and little else, Atkinson and his wife set out in 1859 on a little known saga of exploration.

In the preface to his book, *Oriental and Western Siberia*, he wrote: 'The sole objective of my travels was to sketch the scenery of Siberia – scarcely known to Europeans. In all, I travelled some 39,500 miles [63,555 km] in seven years, visiting regions unknown to Marco Polo or the Jesuit priests. I managed to produce 560 sketches (faithful representations without taking any artistic liberties) executed in the moist colours of Winsor and Newton.' As well as these excellent sketches, he and his wife produced three books about their travels: all good, entertaining reading, with enough human drama, danger, excitement and exotic settings to form the basis of a dozen film scripts. Why, one wonders, are they not better known?

The answer, I think, lies largely in Atkinson's 'humble' birth. In those days most explorers were either government officials, serving officers or scientists, which meant they were members of the upper-middle or middle class; a working-class explorer was almost unheard of. It also told against Atkinson that he saw the country he traversed not as a scientist or a politician, but as an artist. When he looked at a landscape, he was interested not in its scientific composition but its beauty; when he met a person he saw him not as a pawn in the restructuring of frontiers, but as an individual. In addition, his writing was too popular in style to be taken seriously. Eyebrows were raised at his hilarious bouts of vodka drinking, his dramatic fights with eagles, his being pursued half-naked over the steppe by Chinese convicts. As for Mrs Atkinson deliberately humiliating the male-chauvinist Kirghiz by offering tea to the women but not to the men! Could it all be true?

Atkinson's narrative is certainly over-indulgent in places, his names and distances are sometimes inaccurate and his maps often at fault; but what he wrote has the ring of first-hand observation and can be verified. The contemporary view of him is summed up by Semyonov:

> Atkinson, the English artist, in his book of travels published in 1858 gives an account of his journey from the River Kunchun in the Southern Alai, across the Black Irtysh to Lake Ubsa-nór; thence south to the Chinese town of Barkul at the base of the Tien Shan, travelling then parallel to this chain as far as the meridian of the Bogdo-Ola Mountain, finally proceeding to Lake Ala-kul in Russian territory. It is to be regretted that so extraordinary a journey, unprecedented in the history of the exploration of Asia, has had no beneficial scientific results.

History, up to now, has endorsed Semyonov's judgement, and it is doubtful today if one person in a million has heard of Thomas Atkinson. Yet scientific achievement is surely not the only yardstick by which an explorer should be judged. Atkinson and his wife were the first Europeans to visit vast reaches of central Asia; their travels were characterized by considerable powers of endurance, great courage, human warmth and a very real love for the country through which they travelled and the people they met. There are obvious affinities between their story and that of Samuel and Florence Baker; and it could well be argued that the lovers on the steppe deserve a niche in history alongside the better-known lovers on the Nile.

Whatever faults Atkinson may have had as an explorer, one fact about him stands out clearly: he thoroughly enjoyed his travels. He was forever encouraging the wives of his hosts to drink vodka, ever going into rhapsodies over the wonders of nature, ever struggling to the top of some impossible crag with his easel.

Enjoyment does not seem to have been a word in the vocabulary of Ney Elias.

He was born in 1844, the son of well-to-do Jewish parents who were apostates – a psychiatrist might see in their renunciation the seeds of their son's lifelong introspection. Ney was a clever, meticulous and conscientious child, who matured into a shy, self-effacing man who became arguably the most dedicated explorer the world has ever known, for he spent virtually the whole of his adult life crossing and re-crossing the deserts and steppe, often by routes never before attempted and often alone. A great many of his journeys read like a gazetteer of Central Asia. In 1868 he surveyed the delta of the Yellow River. In 1872 he journeyed from Peking to Moscow via the Gobi desert (a marathon for which he was awarded the gold medal of the Royal Geographical Society). In 1875 he pioneered a route from Burma to western China. In 1877 he crossed the Karakoram from Ladakh to Turkestan. In 1880 he crossed both the Karakoram and the Pamirs. In the course of the next ten years, he crossed and re-crossed the mountains again and again, serving on a number of political missions and boundary commissions. Invariably he kept a meticulous topographical, meteorological and ethnological record of his travels. Yet no matter how much he achieved, Elias seemed never to be satisfied; for he was a perfectionist, who set himself such impossibly high standards it was inevitable that he would fall short of them. To quote Francis Younghusband:

Sir Ugyen Wang Chuk and Tongsa Penlop,
rulers of Bhutan, with Younghusband

I always thought him the best traveller there has ever been in central Asia, because he was not only so extraordinarily determined in completing his travels but he brought back such truthful and accurate accounts. His only fault was that he invariably began his reports in a way which made people in offices think his mission must have been a failure. He had such a high idea of what he ought to have done, that, considering he had not come up to his own standards, he wrote as if the whole thing had been a failure.

It has been suggested there was a streak of masochism in his nature. This may be so; but to the handful of people who got close to knowing him, Elias was a kind, gentle and unbelievably modest man. The story goes that he once attended a dinner given in honour of a traveller who had just returned from Turkestan. This traveller was making much of his achievement in crossing a certain pass, when the man sitting next to Elias whispered: 'Didn't *you* cross that pass more than once?'

'Yes,' said Elias, 'eighteen times.'

Although little known in his own country, Elias has always been regarded by the Russians as one of the truly great explorers of Asia, 'in merit second only to the giant Przhevalski'. But perhaps the tribute which he himself would have valued most was his brief obituary in an Indian paper: 'Few of the Queen's servants in Asia have done so much and talked so little about what they have done.'

◆

The influx of Russian explorers, followed by Russian troops, into the north-facing slopes of the mountains fanned the flames of the Russophobia which was latent in the wake of the Crimean War. Just as today many people see a Communist under every bed, so in those days many people saw a Tsarist political agent behind every rock in the Khyber Pass. The British in India began to look with renewed anxiety at their northwest frontier, and decided that the farther they extended their territory into the mountains the better. The frontier, in other words, became a prize – arguably the ultimate prize – in the Great Game, that power struggle in central Asia between Great Britain and Russia which lasted throughout the second half of the nineteenth century. 'Frontiers,' wrote Lord

Curzon, president of the Royal Geographical Society and himself no mean explorer of the mountains of Asia, 'are the razor's edge on which hang suspended the issue of war or peace and the life of nations.' From the middle of the century onwards, pushing back the northwest frontier became work not only for explorers but for patriots.

One stumbling block to any extension of British territory was the hostility of the hill tribes, and, in particular, the Sikhs. This was resolved by the Sikh Wars of 1845 and 1848 which led to the conquest of Sind (and the sending of what is surely the most succinct military communiqué of all time: 'Peccavi' – I have sinned) and this in turn led to the acquisition of the whole of the Punjab.

Another stumbling block was that the frontier area was very imperfectly known. A handful of travellers – Moorcroft and Vigne, Gardiner and Wood, Burnes and Thomson – had, it is true, brought back surveys of various parts of it, but no general map was available. No one knew, for example, where the Himalaya ended and the Hindu Kush began, how high were the great peaks of the Karakoram, how vast the lonely reaches of the Pamirs.

All this was about to change. For by 1850 the Great Trigonometrical Survey of India was pushing into the foothills of the Himalaya.

Few projects have demanded such prolonged and meticulous labour as this survey. It had been initiated by William Lambton in the early years of the nineteenth century, then expanded into a project of international importance by Sir George Everest from the 1820s to the '40s; now, in the 1850s and '60s it was about to be completed by Sir Andrew Waugh. In his book, *Abode of Snow*, Kenneth Mason, himself a surveyor of repute, wrote:

> *Sir George Everest, with very few assistants, measured the great meridional arc* [or great circle] *passing from Cape Comorin in the south, through the centre of India, to the Himalaya. This arc forms the foundation on which was calculated the mathematical spheroid . . . of India. The positions and heights of the Himalayan mountains, indeed of all places in India, are calculated on this spheroid. On completion of his arc and the network of triangulation associated with it, it became possible to add by observation a framework of triangulation covering the Himalaya, and to fix with accuracy the positions and heights of the summits without actually setting foot on them.*

Everest's survey was the basis for mapping the whole continent of Asia, and has been described with justification as 'perhaps the greatest geographical achievement on any continent in any age'.

Right: Col. Sir George Everest, Surveyor-General of India, and, below, with stick on far right, supervising the erection of a survey mark

From the British point of view, it was a happy coincidence that the arrival of Waugh's surveyors in the foothills coincided with the acquisition of a vast new territory immediately to the north, and with the most pressing political need for this territory to be mapped. Within a couple of decades Waugh and his assistants had mapped it, having triangulated virtually the whole of the Himalaya, the Hindu Kush and the Karakoram, and part of the Pamirs and Kun Lun. What is more, they did their triangulation with such accuracy that the positions and heights they accorded the peaks are still accepted today as the most reliable ever made. It is interesting to note that this mapping was carried out by British officers working in perfect harmony with native Khalasis during the decade of the Indian Mutiny.

Throughout the 1850s and '60s little groups of these highly skilled and utterly dedicated men, armed with plane-tables and theodolites, pushed deeper and ever deeper into the mountains. The difficulties facing them were enormous. Their equipment was both delicate and cumbersome, and whereas ordinary travellers were able to seek out the easiest routes, via valley and pass, Waugh's surveyors had to be forever seeking the highest vantage-point, forever climbing from peak to peak. And once they had climbed a peak, they had to construct, on its exact summit, an observation post: a solid stone platform to support their theodolite, a hut for their lampmen and a cache for their food. In his diary for April 1855, one of the surveyors, Thomas Montgomerie, described setting up such a post on Muli, a comparatively minor peak in the Pir Panjal.

It was necessary to stay on the peak for several days (i.e. to reside well above the snowline at a height of more than 15,000 feet [4575 m]). Wood and provisions had to be sent on ahead, and sufficient labourers had to accompany the party to clear away the snow, then build the platform and masonry pillar, and construct a hut for the lamp-party . . . After a severe uphill march over the snow, ascending no less than 7000 feet [2135 m] on the last day, we reached the summit. Mr Johnson, in choosing a site for the station, naturally selected the highest part of the snow. It was found, however, that this was not the highest part of the mountain, for even after removing an enormous quantity of snow, no rock or solid ground could be perceived. Another part of the summit was then tried; and here, fortunately, rock was found within 11 feet [3.35 m] of the surface of the snow. Here building was commenced . . . The working party, however, were soon surrounded with a thin cloud, so charged with electricity that their hair and clothing crackled and emitted sparks. This electricity, added to snow-blindness, headaches and cold, made [work difficult]. But after much labour a platform and pillar were finished, and a hut constructed. After several days' residence on the peak, during which he was much hindered by cloud and snow-storms, Mr Johnson took the necessary observations and descended safely.

This was a scene to be repeated many hundreds of times on many hundreds of even higher peaks in the years to come; only not always with so happy an outcome. Writing in 1955, Kenneth Mason described how, revisiting an observation post in the Karakoram, he 'found the original raised platform, 14 feet [4.3 m] square, still intact, with the surveyor's finely chiselled marking-stone firmly in position. Nearby was a ruined stone shelter, in the corner of which was a human skeleton.' It will never be known how many dedicated surveyors – Khalasis employed by the survey on a salary of no more than six rupees (about 60 British pence) a month – died of cold, starvation or exposure on some isolated peak. It is not known how many peaks they climbed, nor which of these peaks was the highest – although Mason suggests that the Khalasi who in 1860 struggled with a 14-inch theodolite to the summit of Shilla (23,050 ft, 7030 m) may hold the record.

It is a humbling thought that these dedicated men, untrained in the techniques of mountaineering, were regularly climbing peaks which were more difficult and a full

10,000 feet (3050 m) higher than the European summits which were defeating contemporary alpinists in Europe.

It may be invidious to single out individuals from what was essentially a departmental triumph, but the contributions of two men were outstanding: Johnson in the field, and Montgomerie in the Surveyor-General's office.

Most of William Henry Johnson's colleagues were officers in the Bengal Engineers; he, however, joined the Himalayan Service which was a government department. At the age of 17, he was surveying in the upper reaches of the Sutlej, and by the time he was 22, he was a seasoned campaigner, well qualified to help open up the vast new territory which had recently come under British jurisdiction. Colonel Walker, who was in charge of the day-to-day running of the Surveyor-General's office, gives us an indication of the task facing Johnson and his colleagues:

> *In 1854, when the survey party was about to enter Kashmir, many parts of this territory were imperfectly known. There were many valleys which had not been traversed, and many peaks whose heights and positions were undetermined. In particular our information as to the mountain region north of Ladakh was very scanty indeed, being dependent on data provided by early travellers which was in many instances incorrect – Nanga Parbat, for example, was supposed to be only 'about 19,000 feet [5795 m]', whereas it turned out to be 26,620 [8119 m]. A few sportsmen had brought down reports of the curious customs of the Buddhists, and the wonderful animals – wild sheep as big as ponies, and wild cattle with bushy tails and fur-covered flanks – but there was little data for forming even a general idea of the topography. All was new ground, and suspected of being of the most interesting character, since within it were believed to lie some of the largest glaciers on the globe, huge valleys as high as the summit of Mont Blanc, and prodigious mountain chains with peaks of 26,000 [7930 m] and even possibly 28,000 feet [8540 m].*

It was, to quote Johnson, 'quite a challenge!'

To start with, his work took him no farther north than the Pir Panjal, but by 1857 the survey was progressing into the unknown mountains beyond the headwaters of the Indus. *Here*, we are told by Walker,

> *Mr Johnson selected and built stations on the high peaks above the plains of Deosai. This elevated and uninhabited tract of country is bordered by immense snowy mountains and deep valleys. In the course of his work Mr Johnson ascended many peaks with an average height of 17,500 feet [5340 m], and frequently had to remain on them lodged in his tent for several days detained by a succession of snow storms. He spared no effort to render the undertaking a success.*

Montgomerie's report on Johnson's work is even more evocative of hazard.

> *These plains were a great obstacle, there being no habitation within 7 or 8 days' march, and the people unwilling to enter the area from Kashmir. On the plains themselves the only firewood is got by digging up juniper roots and stunted willows. In the mountains there is no firewood at all. The stations established were all between 16,000 and 18,000 feet [4880–5490 m], and it was often necessary to reside in them for several days because of the clouds. Only with the greatest difficulty were the signalmen fed, and on two occasions they were starved out and had to retreat. Stations of this height are always unpleasant to man, although there is slight compensation when the upper level of the cloud falls, leaving the observation post, as it were, on an island surrounded by a sea of cloud from which other peaks stand out like other islands. In good weather the views were magnificent, the atmosphere being wonderfully clear. It was across these plains of Deosai that I took the first observation to K2 (28,287 feet [8628 m]) at a distance of 136 miles [219 km] . . . Notwithstanding the difficulties, triangulation was successfully carried out without relaxing any of the rigorous rules . . . For this a great deal of the credit must go to Mr. Johnson.*

Top: Watercolour by Dr H.A. Oldfield of shrine to Vishnu's wife, Bhadgaon, 1853. Above; George Stubbs' painting of one of the two yaks Warren Hastings had sent home to England, only one of which survived the voyage.

*Top: Pony-trekking in the Himalayan
foothills and, above, inside a tribesman's
yurt*

The felt yurts of the Turko-Mongols

Top: 'The town of Keerung on the eastern bank of the Boori-Gundee River'
and, above, 'Bhootiyas from Lhasa', both painted by Dr. H.A. Oldfield

For the next five years Johnson worked almost literally night and day extending the survey northwards. In 1862 he triangulated the area between Leh and the Chinese border. 'High as were the stations in the Upper Indus Valley,' wrote Colonel Walker, 'they were surpassed in elevation by the peaks observed from by Mr Johnson in the course of this survey. The average height of the posts attained on this series was 19,877 feet [6062 m], two of the stations being well over 20,000 feet [6100 m]. While working in this area – as might have been expected – the party underwent great hardships.'

Next year Johnson pushed even farther north, and even higher.

On arrival in the Changchenmo Valley [wrote Montgomerie] *it was found that the plains towards Tartary were still covered with snow, even at the end of July. Since the country to be surveyed proved more difficult than had been anticipated, Mr Johnson took with him nothing but the bare necessities of life, and reduced his party to the lowest possible number . . . Finding there was no route via the Sheok River, he climbed right over the mountains till he struck the road to Yarkand. Having reached this road, he then traversed the Karakoram Pass, and descended by a march of three days into Eastern Turkestan. Only then, having more than completed the work allotted him, did he return to Leh. The above will give you but a faint idea of the terrible hardships encountered. The country traversed was utterly desolate; all fuel and food had to be carried; for more than a month Mr Johnson was at an elevation of over 15,000 feet [4575 m]; several of the posts he established were at a height of over 21,000 feet [6405 m]; once he climbed to 22,300 feet [6800 m] . . . I think he deserves very great credit for this work, and I hope his services will meet with favourable recognition.*

A few weeks after he wrote this, Montgomerie, who had been in charge of the Kashmir/Ladakh/Baltistan survey since its inception, went on extended leave to England. Without doubt Johnson ought, on merit, to have been appointed his successor. For years he had been Montgomerie's trusted second-in-command; his commitment to the Survey was total, his skill as a triangulator unquestioned, his courage as a mountaineer unsurpassed; he was loved by his Khalasis, and respected and trusted by the people of Kashmir, Ladakh and Baltistan. Yet for the third or fourth time in his career, Johnson was passed over, and saw the Survey to which he had devoted the best years of his life put in the hands of a junior officer only recently arrived from England. For Johnson's background, like Atkinson's, was not quite 'right'. He was not an officer, and some hinted darkly that he was not a gentleman either, for he had been educated 'not at Sandhurst but at Mussoorie, a place where parents who are too poor to send their children home, send them'.

So instead of the 'favourable recognition' which he undoubtedly deserved, the unfortunate Johnson was given a not very exciting desk job. It looked as though a brilliant career had been brought to a premature end, when, at the suggestion of his friend Montgomerie, he was given the chance of making a final survey of the area along the Ladakhi–Chinese border.

He set out in July 1865 on a journey which was to become a *cause célèbre*; for once again he crossed the frontier without permission and penetrated deep into Chinese territory; in addition, the survey he brought back was inaccurate.

Crossing the frontier may have been reprehensible, but it was understandable. Johnson had always been a man of enormous enthusiasm: one of the seekers of the world, anxious to

> *Go always a little father: it may be*
> *Beyond that last blue mountain barred with snow,*
> *Across that angry or that glimmering sea.*

He may not have had written permission to cross the frontier, but he believed he had tacit approval; he also had a personal invitation from the Khan of Khotan to visit him in his capital. It is therefore hardly surprising that he seized this unique opportunity to survey unknown territory. Within a month of leaving Leh, he was climbing the Kun Lun, the coldest and least-known mountains on earth. He climbed three of the highest peaks, hoping to look down on the country around Khotan and Yarkand. He was disappointed, and realized that he was standing not on the summit of some simple ridge, but on the outpost of yet another vast and complex system, a jumble of peaks spread out beneath him like a featureless sea from horizon to horizon. No one knew precisely where the frontier was, but it must have been obvious that it lay behind rather than ahead, and a more prudent man would have turned back. Johnson, however, accepted the offer of the guides who had been sent by his friend the Khan, and plunged boldly into the mountains. On 2 October he entered Khotan, where only two Europeans (Marco Polo and De Goes) had preceded him.

He spent three weeks there, behaving, it seems, with circumspection and acquiring a great deal of useful information. Then he headed back for Leh, which he reached only after a journey of unbelievable difficulty – for more than a week neither the warmth of the sun nor the warmth of his fire was sufficient to melt the icicles congealed to his mane-like beard.

This was a major feat of exploration. Johnson, however, was met not with praise, but with the official reprimand that he 'ought not to have crossed the frontier without the permission of the government'. He might have accepted this. What he was not prepared to accept was the Survey's criticism of his work.

It is generally agreed that Johnson's surveying on this last journey was not up to his usual high standard; in particular, his claim to have climbed E61 (23,890 ft, 7285 m), a peak a little to the south of Khotan, was erroneous. Even Montgomerie commented that his friend 'seemed to have got in a coil with his plane-table', while Walker was scathing: 'His report contained more errors than I would have believed possible; it had to be entirely re-written and his map recast.'

One wonders what went wrong? It has been suggested that after working for ten years among the highest mountains in the world, Johnson was suffering from cumulative altitude sickness, and that his brain had deteriorated. In view of subsequent events, this seems unlikely, and I believe there is a much simpler explanation. In his previous surveys Johnson had worked in the open, with the help of the local inhabitants. On his journey to Khotan he was obliged to work in secret and without co-operation. 'The Khan,' he wrote, 'opposed my taking astronomical observations; for his courtiers considered this might be a preliminary to the country being taken possession of by the British. After leaving Ilchi I was not able to observe for latitude at any place except Sanju. Here I was put up in a house with a large hole in the roof, and after locking the door, this admitted my observing with the eight-inch theodolite.' Under these conditions it is hardly surprising his work was not 100 per cent accurate.

Over the next few years, Johnson and Walker indulged in a bitter personal vendetta. Johnson accused his superior of deliberately inserting errors into his reports in the Surveyor-General's office in order to denigrate his journey – surely one of the most preposterous charges ever laid against a well-run government department. Walker wrote of his subordinate that he had 'neither the benefit of a liberal education, nor the ability to rise above the disadvantage of his position' – surely one of the most priggish and malicious gibes ever levelled at a major explorer. Mountaineers, both in India and in England, sprang to Johnson's defence; the Royal Geographical Society elected him an honorary fellow and awarded him a gold watch, and there was a widespread feeling that he had been hard done by – as indeed he had.

Not surprisingly, Johnson resigned from the Survey. It is, however, pleasant to record that the Maharajah of Ladakh quickly appointed him as his *wazir* (or governor), a position a great deal more prestigious and lucrative than working for a government department.

He made a good *wazir*. His rule, we are told, was 'enlightened and just'; he maintained friendly relations with the British government; and he seems to have been not only respected by the Ladakhi people but genuinely loved – although his detractors point out that contemporary sources say he 'took a great interest in *nautches* and *tamashas*' (dancing girls and orgies). He was certainly a man who lived life to the full.

He died – almost certainly poisoned – in 1892. His family were treated a great deal more generously by the Maharajah of Ladakh than by the British government, for the Maharajah not only gave his widow a generous pension, but cared with real affection for his 13 children and innumerable grandchildren – one of his daughters, Ada, lived in a 'grace and favour' house on the outskirts of Srinagar for more than 60 years until her death in 1943.

A man who seldom failed to support Johnson was his immediate superior, Thomas George Montgomerie, the brain behind the operators in the field. He arrived in India in 1851, with a degree in mathematics, spherical trigonometry, differential and integral calculus and astronomy. He was attached to the Bengal Engineers, whose officers provided the core of those working on the Survey, and such was the quality of his work that within four years, at the age of only 25, he was put in charge of the triangulation of Kashmir. It has been claimed he was 'a desk man, who rose to fame on the shoulders of his surveyors'. This, however, does him less than justice, for in his early days Montgomerie experienced his fair share of difficulties and dangers in the field. Witness his diary:

> *The ascent of Ahertatopa was easy, but I had to make up a portable lightning conductor to protect the theodolite; no iron being available, I spliced together the mining tools, crowbars etc., and pitched the conductor in the snow close to the observatory tent . . . We had hardly got the tent up than a severe storm came on, first a strong wind threatening to blow us down the ridge, then a fall of heavy hailstones. About 4 p.m. snow began to fall, and at 5 p.m. the lightning and thunder seemed to be centred on the peak itself. The iron stove in my tent began to crackle, the hair of my dog crackled too, and in the dark sparks were clearly visible . . . Our tent was in sloping snow and connected to the observation platform by only a very narrow ridge, giving just enough foothold; on either side was a precipice; communication therefore was not easy, especially at night when the snow was frozen and slippery.*

His diary also records those moments of satisfaction which can be savoured only by those who work in the field:

> *It was here that I first saw the heliotropes shining down from the peaks of the Pir Panjal. The snow extended so many thousand feet below the summits that it was not easy to visualize men were residing there, the only indication of life being the pinheads of light shining from the apex of the noble cones with that intense brightness peculiar to a well-tended heliotrope: a sight not easily forgotten.*

In 1864, with his survey to all intents and purposes completed, Montgomerie returned to England on sick leave, and one might have thought his greatest achievement lay behind him. In fact it was about to begin: his training of the Pundit explorers.

The British had two reasons for wanting to know what lay beyond their borders with China, Tibet, Bhutan and Nepal: first, a genuine desire to put *terra incognita* literally on the map, and second, a wish to find out exactly what sort of a barrier the mountains provided for the defence of India. The Johnson furore underlined the fact that territory beyond the frontier could not be surveyed by British explorers. Montgomerie, however, had a high opinion of native explorers – without the work of his Khalasis his survey would never have got off the ground. And he now hit on the idea of training Indians as surveyors, equipping them with the basic tools of their trade, disguising them as pilgrims with prayer wheels and rosaries, and sending them to make route surveys of the area beyond the frontier.

To say the work was both difficult and dangerous would be an understatement: difficult because of the desolation, isolation and extreme height of the ground to be explored; dangerous because the authorities in the border states imprisoned, tortured and frequently put to death foreigners caught in their territory. Montgomerie's Pundits (as his native explorers were called) risked their lives with every step they took. And how many steps this frequently was! They were trained to walk at a uniform 2000 paces to the miles, to count every pace they took, and after 100 paces to drop a bead from their rosaries into their prayer wheels. When the Pundit Nain Singh made his epic journey from Sikkim to Lhasa, he covered 1580 miles (2540 km): that is, he took 3,160,000 paces, every one of which he meticulously counted. The mind boggles at such devotion to duty.

In a paper read to the Royal Geographical Society, Montgomerie described the Pundits' equipment and the subterfuges they adopted to avoid detection.

I had noticed the frequent use made by Tibetans of the rosary and the prayer wheel, and consequently recommended Pundits to carry both with them, especially as it was thought these ritualistic instruments could, with a little adaptation, form useful adjuncts in carrying out a route survey.

It was necessary that Pundits should be able to take their compass bearings unobserved, and that when counting their paces they should not be interrupted. Nain Singh found the best way of effecting this was to march with his servant separately, either behind or in front of the rest of the party. When people did come up to him, the sight of his prayer wheel was generally sufficient to prevent them from addressing him. For when he saw anyone approaching, he at once began to whirl his wheel round; and as all good Buddhists doing this are supposed to be absorbed in religious contemplation, he was seldom disturbed. The prayer wheel used was an ordinary hand one; but instead of the usual Buddhist prayer Om mani padme hum *('Hail, oh jewel in the lotus') were slips of paper for recording bearings, etc. Their rosaries, instead of the usual 108 beads, had 100, every tenth bead being larger than the others. The small beads were made of red composition to imitate coral, the large ones were seeds of the udras plant. This rosary was carried in the left sleeve; at every 100th pace a bead was dropped. Each large bead to fall therefore represented 1000 paces or half-a-mile.*

Observations of latitude were difficult. They were usually taken with an Elliot sextant of 6" radius, reading to ten seconds. Artificial horizons of dark glass were provided; but the use of quicksilver was found more satisfactory. Nain Singh invested in a wooden bowl, such as is carried at the waist by all Bhotiyas for drinking purposes; and he found this answered capitally for his quicksilver, since its deep sides prevented the wind from acting on the surface. Quicksilver is a difficult thing to carry; but he managed to conceal his by putting some in a cocoa-nut, and by carrying his reserve in cowrie shells sealed with wax.

Of all the tasks that Montgomerie set his Pundits, two were particularly dear to his heart: to triangulate the forbidden city of Lhasa, and to trace the course of the Brahmaputra River.

The Pundit Nain Singh accomplished the first; and in his great journey of 1865/6 he not only accurately fixed the position of Lhasa, but he also brought back the most succinct and informative description of the city that had so far been written. In his report to Montgomerie are found in abundance all the facts and anecdotes which were denied us by the austere Grueber and the neurotic Manning. Of the Dalai Lama he said:

This Lama is the chief Guru of all Tibet. He does not, however, interfere with state business, but is regarded as a Guardian Divinity who is supposed never to die. The people believe that on his death he transmigrates instantly to another body, being privileged to do this 13 times – the present Lama is in his thirteenth transmigration. Buddhists believe that no sooner is the Lama born again than he is able to speak, and all withered plants and trees about his birthplace immediately bear green leaves. As soon as the news of such an occurrence reaches the court at Lhasa, four ministers repair to the site of the miraculous birth. They take with them all manner of articles which are placed before the child, who is asked which of them belonged to the recently deceased Lama. Should he identify all the articles correctly, he is pronounced no imposter but the true reincarnation, and is forthwith taken to the fort Po-ta-la and placed upon the throne.

Mohammedans, however, told me another story. They say that from the day of a Lama's death, all male births in Lhasa are recorded. The four ministers are told the names of the children born, and they proceed to teach one of them all that he needs to know. When they think he has come to years of discretion, the previously narrated ceremony of choosing articles is conducted, and the Lama 'found'. It is said that the Tibetans have need of such a Lama in order to prevent the government of their country falling completely into the hands of the Chinese.

Not much of what went on in Lhasa escaped the observant Nain Singh, whose report contains information on such varied subjects as housing, the composition of the Tibetan Army, crop production and imports and exports, together with descriptions of religious ceremonies, festivals and dances. Many lesser travellers have had their exploits preserved in handsome volumes. It is sad that Nain Singh's are preserved only in the dry-as-dust and little-read *Records of the Survey of India*. However, on a happier note he was, on his retirement, given a generous pension, and honoured by the Royal Geographical Society, who in 1877 awarded him their gold medal, 'thus publicly marking [their] appreciation of the noble qualities of loyalty, courage and endurance, by the display of which he added so largely to our knowledge of Asia'.

These same qualities – loyalty, courage and endurance – were much in evidence in the work of the Pundits who traced the course of the Brahmaputra.

Montgomerie suspected that the Brahmaputra which came pouring down from the mountains of Assam might be the same river as the Tsangpo which, over 1000 miles (600 km) away, flowed east from the mountains around Kailas; but the junction between the two rivers had never been proved. There was an unexplored area between Dhemu Chamnak, where the Tsangpo cascaded off the Tibetan plateau, and Sadiya, where the Brahmaputra debouched into the Indo-Ganetic plains. It is not much more than 120 miles (193 km) from Dhemu Chamnak to Sadiya, yet in that comparatively short distance, the river – if indeed it *was* the same river – dropped from 10,000 feet (3050 m) to close to sea-level and doubled its discharge. Did it drop spectacularly in what could be the world's most awesome falls, or did it descend through a series of rapids? Was its flow augmented by other great feeders, or merely by the world's heaviest rainfall? These were questions which no explorer, European or Pundit, had been able to answer. For so impassable was the river gorge, and so hostile the tribes whose longhouses commanded the surrounding hills, that although many had tried to follow the river's course, none had succeeded.

In the 1870s Captain Harman of the Royal Engineers came up with an idea for proving whether or not the rivers were one and the same. He suggested that a number of specially marked logs be thrown into the Tsangpo at Dhemu Chamnak, and a watch kept for these logs at Sadiya on the Brahmaputra. The Pundit Kinthup (his first name is unknown), a native of Sikkim, was given the task of making his way to the lowest possible point in the Tsangpo and secretly throwing in the logs.

The events of the next four years have been aptly described as an odyssey. Kinthup set out on 7 August 1880, travelling as the servant of a Mongolian lama visiting relatives in Lhasa. The early stages of their journey were uneventful, and they had no difficulty in reaching the Tibetan capital, where the lama at any rate seems to have much enjoyed himself, 'feasting non-stop for six days in the Ser-ra monastery with his former colleagues'. By mid-September they were following the Tsangpo as it wound its way over the barren highlands of Tibet. Their first and not very serious delay occurred at Tsetang, where the lama was taken ill and confined to his bed for three weeks. 'During this time,' we are told, 'Kinthup had to cut grass for the lama's horse, and was badly treated; however, he bore his misfortunes with patience, fearing his position would become worse if he showed resentment.' Throughout October the two travellers followed the river, spending some nights in monasteries, some in *jikkyops* (huts specially built by the government for pilgrims and traders) and some in caves. They had a hard time crossing the Kongbu Nga La Pass: 'the ascent is steep and dangerous, and the pass all the year round covered in snow. In this neighbourhood are many barbarians and many herds of wild sheep. The winds are violent.'

From now on the Tsangpo became increasingly difficult to follow, cascading in rapids through a succession of dark and precipitous gorges. It was not, however, the river which finally brought them to a halt but the lama. At a place called Thun Tsung 'he fell in love with the wife of his host, and could in no way be persuaded to continue the journey.' What the host had to say about this is not known, except that 'after four months Kinthup, with great difficulty, arranged for the sum of 25 rupees to be paid to the husband in compensation, and the travellers moved on.' They were now destitute – thanks presumably to the lama's *amours* – and had to spend much of the time begging for food. A further difficulty was that they were forced to cross the Tsangpo frequently, and at each crossing had to show passes and pay bribes.

At Tongjuk Dzong they had a setback. *Here*, wrote the not very literate or coherent Colonel Tanner who subsequently pieced together Kinthup's report,

a bridge is built over the stream and an old man checks that persons passing over it have official permission. So the lama went to get this permission, while Kinthup stayed at the bridge, hiding his compasses and pistol. After four days the lama returned with the permission, and they crossed the bridge and went to the official's house, where they were given quarters with the servants and furnished with flour, meat and tea. Next morning a servant of the official came to Kinthup and said; 'Now, my friend, my master orders you to give him the things that you promised.' Kinthup replied that he had promised nothing, whereupon the servant got angry and said, 'Your duty is not to contradict but to obey.' And he took the pistol and one compass and gave them to his master.

Worse was to follow. Reading between the lines, it is clear that the lama was by this time heartily sick of the hazardous enterprise on which he had been persuaded to embark. He told Kinthup he would be away for a few days, ordered him not to leave the official's house, and rode off on a horse he had somehow found the money to purchase. The Pundit never saw him again. It was only gradually that the truth dawned on him: he had been sold into slavery in exchange for a horse.

The details of his servitude are not known, although it would seem that he was none too well treated and spent much of his time stitching clothes and cutting grass. All we are

Top: *Bridge across a river, Tibet,*
photographed by Capt. C.G. Rawling 1903–5

Above: *Lake Manasbal, Kashmir*

told is that after seven months of drudgery he was able to escape – 'saying that he was going on an errand, he crossed the bridge and ran off at his utmost speed.'

A less dedicated man would surely have run for home, but Kinthup, determined to fulfil his mission, struggled south down the Tsangpo. It was a journey of extreme hazard. Time and again he was forced to leave the river and traverse the sodden Abors and Mishmis hills, where the rainfall is over 300 inches (760 cm) a year. Fearing pursuit, he avoided monasteries and villages and slept wherever he could in caves or fissures in the rocks; but inevitably there were times when he had no option but to cross the river, and at one such checkpoint – Marpung – his pursuers caught up with him. There was a monastery at Marpung, where '15 nuns and 30 priests are allowed to live together,' and here Kinthup sought sanctuary. Throwing himself at the feet of the head lama, he explained that he was a humble pilgrim who had lost both his parents and had been sold treacherously into slavery; he begged the lama not to hand him over to his pursuers. After ten days' bargaining, during which the Pundit's life hung in the balance, the lama agreed to purchase him from his owner for 50 rupees – although whether this was out of compassion or because he reckoned him cheap at the price is not clear.

For the next four and a half months Kinthup served his new master; then he was given leave, ostensibly to go on a pilgrimage. However, instead of journeying to the holy places, he made his way down the Tsangpo to a lonely reach of the river. Here he hid his things in the jungle, and went in pretended search of salt. But instead of digging salt, he cut logs. In five days he cut 500 logs, all one foot long. Having marked these as instructed by Captain Harman, he carried them into a deep cave and hid them. He then returned to the lama.

He returned to the lama because he had a problem. It was now more than 18 months since he had left Sikkim, and long past the time when he should have thrown his logs into the river. He therefore needed to get a message back to Captain Harman, advising him of a new time of launching the logs; for he knew that after so long a delay a continuous watch for them was unlikely to be maintained at Sadiya. So he served the lama for a further two months, before asking permission to go on another pilgrimage. Impressed by such piety, the lama again granted him leave. 'So Kinthup left the monastery a second time. But instead of going to the holy mountain of Tsari where he said he was going, he made his way to Lhasa.'

One can only regret that there is not a better account of Kinthup's travels than that provided by Colonel Tanner. The colonel was no writer, and seems to have had no idea that he had in his hands the ingredients of a minor epic of exploration. Here is a typical entry: 'Shinging (Singging) which is the next place he visited is a village of about 60 houses. From the top of the hill above Shinging (Singging) there is a short cut to Rikar (Puging). On his way from Angi (Arging) he crossed a stream by a stone bridge from the right-hand side. The stream flows towards the south.' Faced with page after page of this not very inspiring itinerary, the reader has to rely on the occasional aside to realize what the journey must have been like.

Ascending the pass, he slept the night on flat open ground. The ground was covered with snow . . . Between Ani Pasam and Pankangkingma there are no shelters except for caves. The road is bad, and so steep that no four-legged animal, not even a mule, can use it . . . For several days there was neither house nor shelter. No trees. Nothing but a big lake. In all directions the ground was barren and covered with snow.

By the time he struggled through to Lhasa, Kinthup had been in slavery for 15 months, and trekking through some of the bleakest terrain in the world for another 15 months. It would have been understandable if he had given up and returned to India; but instead he sought help from a Sikkimese official who was visiting one of the monasteries. He gave this official a letter, addressed to the Surveyor-General, and begged him to see it was delivered to the authorities in Darjeeling.

Sir – the Lama who was sent with me sold me to an official as a slave, and himself fled away with the Government things that were in his charge. On account of this the journey proved a bad one. However, I, Kinthup, have prepared the 500 logs according to the orders of Captain Harman, and am preparing to throw 50 logs per day into the Tsang-po at Bipung, from the 5th to the 15th of the tenth Tibetan month of the year called Chkuluk.

Having done what he could to ensure this letter would be delivered, he set out on his return journey to the monastery at Marpung.

Tanner dismisses the next nine months in one paragraph.

Crossing the Tsang-po, he reached Chemna and retraced his route to Pemako, where the road to Lhasa and Gyada join. From this place he originally went to Lhasa, and now on his return he went back to the Lama who rescued him from the official, and again served under him for 9 months. At the end of 9 months the Lama set him free, saying, 'I am glad to see you visiting the sacred places, so from today I give you leave to go anywhere you like.' Kinthup bowed thrice before him, and bid him good-bye thankfully. After a month he made his way to Bipung where he stayed 10 days and threw the 500 logs into the Tsang-po; then returning he spent one month longer in order to earn money sufficient to buy food for his journey back to India.

In all of Tanner's report there is no mention of the two aspects of Kinthup's journey which cry out for comment. There was the ever-present danger that the Pundit had to live with every day of every month of every year, for if at any time during his travels or his servitude his true identity had been discovered, he would have forfeited his life. And there was his unswerving devotion to duty over a span of more than four years, for not until September 1884 did he struggle back at last to his home near Darjeeling.

One wishes his story could have had a happy ending, but Kinthup, alas, appears to have been a born loser. Nothing ever went right for him. Arriving home, he found that his mother had died during his wanderings, 'so he stayed in his village [Tanner reported] for 2½ months performing her funeral rites.' On reaching Darjeeling he found that his letter had never got through to the Surveyor-General; no watch had been kept; and his logs had drifted unsighted into the Bay of Bengal. Worse still, Captain Harman had died, and Kinthup's report of his adventures was received with incredulity. Many years were to pass before it was realized that every scrap of the information he brought back was the plain, unvarnished truth. By then he had disappeared.

Kinthup was the archetypal Pundit, the epitome of those unselfish, unrewarded men – so anonymous that in many cases they were known only by their initials – who risked their lives for a cause they did not wholly understand and for a country other than their own. Even today and even in India and Pakistan their exploits are little known, yet in the history of exploration there have been few finer achievements.

◆

By the end of the nineteenth century, little scope remained in the mountains for exploration *per se*. All the ranges had been traversed, most of the major peaks had been triangulated, most of the frontiers defined.

One of the last frontiers to be defined – not *the* last, for the Soviet–Chinese frontier is still in dispute to this day – was the one which for 50 years had turned the Hindu Kush and the Pamirs into a chessboard for moves in the Great Game: the border between Russia and Afghanistan. The way this was finally delineated is ironic.

For 50 years the British had struggled north through the mountains, subduing the people of this valley, allying themselves with the people of the next, establishing hill forts, killing and being killed: all for the sake of pushing the frontier north and keeping the Bear at arm's length. Yet when, in 1895, the border was finally settled, the British officer in charge of its demarcation could write: 'It is a matter of indifference to all exactly where the line is drawn.' While of the Russians, who for half a century had been such bogeymen, he could write: 'They are grand chaps . . . I cannot conclude without acknowledging both the excellence of their mapping and the warmth of their hospitality . . . I have nothing but the most pleasant memories of our alliance in the field.' It is certainly pleasant to record that when the players in the Great Game at last met face to face, they became the best of friends.

The object of the Commission was, to quote its commander in the field Colonel T. H. Holdich, two-fold: 'Firstly, to make topographical maps of the country adjoining the boundary in order to assist the Commission to a conclusion as to its final position; and secondly, to effect such a junction with the Russian survey system as would ensure a common basis for the mapping of both sides in future.' What was needed therefore was a survey team-cum-diplomatic mission. This was a major undertaking, and in June 1895 the better part of 100 men assembled at Bandipur in Kashmir – five European officers, 18 native surveyors, an escort of 19 NCOs and sepoys, more than 40 native followers, and 200 Kashmiri ponies, with a further 600 ponies as a back-up force to keep the entourage supplied with fuel and food while it was on the move.

It has been said 'it is more blessed to travel than to arrive,' and certainly many lovers of the Himalaya have found the approaches to the great peaks as deeply satisfying as the peaks themselves. Certainly that summer the road to the Pamirs seemed touched with magic. *We came to Yasin*, Holdich wrote,

> *in July; and for many miles the track leading from village to village ran through close-set lanes bordered with hedges of wild rose, clematis and passion flower. Cornflower and poppy were in bloom in the fields, and the little orchards with their soft green turf sloping to the river edge presented to us a picture of England at its most beautiful.* [A sentiment of which Vigne would surely have approved.] *Darkot, two marches beyond Yasin, is particularly picturesque. For here are the colour and luxuriance of well-cultivated fields and orchards enclosed in a mighty surrounding wall of granite and limestone cliffs, up whose rugged sides wind the grandest glacial staircases the world has to show. One of these glaciers leads to the Darkot pass, and this we now ascended . . . In deep snow at the summit of the pass our surveyors made their first observations to carry the Indian triangulation over the Hindu Kush.*

During the first three weeks of July the expedition pushed steadily north through the Hindu Kush and the Pamirs, until on 22 July they found themselves approaching the Russian encampment on the shore of Lake Sir-i-kol, Wood's controversial source of the Oxus. 'About two miles from this lake,' wrote Holdich, 'we were met by a detachment of Cossacks, bearing torches at the end of their lances to light us into their camp.' The senior British officers, in the best tradition of the day, had intended changing for dinner. 'But the Russian Commissioner would accept no excuse for delay, insisting that our dusty party ride on to the Russian camp at once. Here we were received with the most courteous hospitality, and the foundation there and then laid for that feeling of good fellowship between the two camps which never afterwards was broken.' A great deal of vodka was drunk that night. The senior British officer proposed that the range dividing the Greater Pamir from the Lesser should be known as Range Nicolas in honour of the Tsar; the senior Russian officer proposed that the Sir-i-kol should be known as Lake Victoria in honour of the Queen; both agreed that their line of demarcation should be called 'La Concorde'. And the fact that none of these suggestions was in the end accepted by cartographers matters a great deal less than the fact that they were made.

During the next six weeks, the Commissions completed their survey work independently, ironing out any differences between them on the spot. The weather was against them: 'day after day of heavy sleet, with cloud settled low over the ranges.' The terrain was against them, too: 'featureless valleys bordered by wide ridges, their watersheds hidden amid eternal snows and glaciers, and offering no peaks for recognition.' Yet at the end of their calculations, the British and Russian teams produced maps which were in near-miraculous agreement. The British survey had started 2000 miles away in Madras, the Russians' 3000 miles away in St Petersburg. At the end of their triangulation they found themselves 'standing together on the roof of the world with practically no difference between us to eliminate . . . surely a cause for mutual congratulation.'

On 7 September the position of the final pillar in the frontier was determined, 'at that point where a rugged spur of the Sarikol carries the boundary into the perpetual ice and snow of the main range. Here, in a solitary wilderness 20,000 feet [6100 m] above sea-level, at a spot inaccessible to man, the three great Empires meet. No more fitting trijunction could be imagined.' A few days later there was a farewell party.

Nothing [Holdich continued] *could exceed the enthusiasm with which the toast of* 'Entente cordiale' *between our countries was received. The scene after dinner was one which will be long remembered. Wood had been collected from valleys south of the Hindu Kush and brought with us as a provision against a winter in the Pamirs. All this wood was now stacked into such a bonfire as the Pamirs will never see again, and round about it various dances were conducted with much energy and spirit. The night was still, and as cold as 25° of frost could make it, and the moonlight glinting on the freezing surface of river and marsh added not a little to the fantastic effect of the scene.*

A month later the British were back in Bandipur after one of the most successful and rewarding missions ever to penetrate the mountains. Not a man had been lost, not a day had passed without valuable survey work being carried out, and a frontier which had been in dispute for 50 years had been most amicably delineated.

The Pamir Boundary Commission marked a very welcome rapport between Great Britain and Russia. But amid all the bonhomie and congratulations there was one not so happy note. The Commission had included representatives, not only from Great Britain and Russia, but also from Afghanistan. Sadar Ghulam Mohiuddin Khan and Maulvi Ashur Muhummed Khan were the Afghan representatives, and they, it was reported, observed the work of the surveyors 'with a regret they took no particular pains to conceal'. Which is not surprising; for it was, after all, their country which the Lion and the Bear were carving up between them.

With the demarcation of this much disputed frontier, men's thoughts turned from exploration to exploitation. There was, in the generally accepted terms of wealth, little to exploit in the mountain complex: few minerals, few surplus crops, fewer artefacts. But the great ranges could boast one asset which was unique: the mountains themselves. They were, quite simply, the most magnificent on earth. What a challenge these magnificent peaks presented to mountaineers, whose love affair with the European Alps was drawing to its close and who were now looking for fresh fields to conquer.

CHAPTER FIVE

THE CLIMBERS

MOUNTAINEERING is a modern pastime. Until a couple of hundred years ago, nobody climbed for pleasure. This is probably because our ancestors regarded mountains as outlandish and dangerous territory, unfit for crop growing or habitation. Being useless, they were unknown; being unknown, they were feared. This fear was in many instances nurtured by the Church. Early Christians thought of mountains as the homes of demons and dragons, while later Christians regarded them as the symbolic bastions of Satan:

> *Through many a dark and dreary vale*
> *They passed, and many a region dolorous,*
> *O'er many a Frozen, many a Fiery Alp.*
> *Rocks, caves, lakes, fens, bogs, dens and shades of death,*
> *A Universe of death, which God by curse*
> *Created evil.*

On a more practical level, they were said to 'harbour outlaws, obstruct prospects and make difficult communications.' They were best avoided.

Two factors helped to change this attitude: the romantic movement in the arts, and the birth of a more scientific approach to geography.

At about the time of the French Revolution, romantic philosophers like Rousseau began to extol the wonders of the natural world and the virtues of the 'noble savage', while at the same time romantic poets such as Wordsworth began to eulogize not only the gentle face of Nature – its daffodils and violets – but also its 'noble rocks and mist-encompassed heights'. Writers such as Wordsworth, Byron and Shelley were, to their generation, cult figures, read far more avidly than any poet is read today, and their work helped people to look at the mountains with new eyes.

Almost simultaneously there emerged, under the influence of Ritter and Von Humboldt, a new school of geographers: men who were anxious, above all, to amass scientific facts. To these men the mountains were a challenge. Which rocks, they wanted to know, were they composed of? What forces had raised them; what was their climate, flora, fauna and geomorphology? Men began to climb mountains in order to learn about them – the acquisition of knowledge was a major factor, for example, in the expeditions of Semyonov and Przhevalski; and from the middle of the nineteenth century onwards, many major climbs had a dual objective: to conquer some virgin peak, *and* to add to the cornucopia of knowledge.

In view of this background it is not surprising that mountaineering was conceived and nurtured in the European Alps, which are unique among the great ranges of the world in lying at the heart of a dense and sophisticated population.

The peasant farmers who lived in the mountains of Europe, Rousseau's 'children of nature', took little interest in land above pasture-level, and the impulse to explore the peaks came almost entirely from educated town folk. One such man, Horace de Saussure (in his day reputedly the richest banker in Geneva) offered a reward to the first person to climb Mont Blanc; and in 1786 the reward was claimed by Michel-Gabriel Paccard, a modest Chamonix doctor who perhaps more than any other man deserves the title 'father of mountaineering'. Paccard's climb inaugurated a century of great activity in the Alps: huts were built; clubs were founded; the employment of guides became standard practice; equipment (boots, ice-axes, ropes and crampons) grew increasingly sophisticated; and mountaineering became accepted as a respectable middle-class sport – a typical climber of those days would have been a don, barrister, clergyman or doctor. By the middle of the century, a spate of books, lectures and magic lantern shows was giving thousands of city-bound people the chance of savouring vicariously the delights of the peaks. As for the peaks themselves, they fell one by one to the assault of tweed-jacketed *aficionados*: Monte Rosa in 1842, the Eiger in 1858 and the Matterhorn in 1865.

With the climbing of the Matterhorn, which for many years had been considered inviolate, the thoughts of mountaineers turned to more distant heights to conquer; and in the last quarter of the nineteenth century almost every major range in the world saw the arrival of mountaineers, who climbed its most formidable peaks with comparative ease – Elbruz (19,350 ft, 5900 m), the highest of the Caucasus, was climbed in 1874; Chimborazo (20,563 ft, 6272 m) in the Andes in 1880; Mount Cook (12,349 ft, 3766 m) in the New Zealand Alps in 1894; and Mount Kenya (17,058 ft, 5203 m) in 1899. Soon there were only three places in the world where the peaks remained inviolate: Alaska, Antarctica and Central Asia. Of these, the mountains of Central Asia presented the ultimate challenge, and in the 1880s men started coming to the Himalaya to climb for pleasure.

◆

These late-nineteenth-century climbers were not, however, the first people to set foot in the upper reaches of the mountains. In many instances they were preceded by hunters.

Hunting, wrote Colonel Kinloch of the Kings' Royal Rifles in 1867,

> *is an instinct prompted by a healthy nature, and there are few who question the advantages to be derived from field sports . . . There is [he admits] a limited school who talk of immorality and cruelty; but it will be found that the professors of such doctrines have very peculiar views on other subjects. If they had their way men would become effeminate, and women lose much of the charm of their sex.*

This logic may seem, at best, questionable today; but in the mid-nineteenth century it was widely accepted. Boar-sticking was the favourite pastime of every mess in India, and it was usual practice for officers to spend at least part of their leave in the hills in search of 'heads'. The gallant colonel's trophies for a couple of seasons include tiger, panther, lynx, Indian wolf, Tibetan wolf, wild dog, snow bear, black bear, elephant, rhinoceros, wild boar, yak, gazelle, Tibetan antelope, Indian antelope, serow, gooral, tahr, markhoor (spiral and straight horned), ibex, burrell, sambur and three species of deer.

A glance through the memoirs of these sportsmen reveal that, by and large, they had little rapport with their native *shikari* (gun bearers), and were utterly insensitive to the trail of carnage and suffering they left in their wake. *The bear is uncouth*, wrote Kinloch,

> *and I for one can never watch him without laughing at his absurd appearance; he is peculiarly stupid and loutish . . . I put six bullets into the mother bear, but she managed to get away, leaving a good deal of blood behind her. As I was reloading I spotted her cub, and told my coolie to catch it. He did*

*Top: 'He stood up on his hind legs', from 'In and Beyond the
Himalayas' by S.J. Stone, 1896*

*Above: Bag made in 1864–1865, used as frontispiece to Col. Kinloch's
'Large Game Shooting in Tibet and Northern India', 1885*

so, but the little brute was so savage, the stupid fellow let it go. The Kashmiri are a lazy, lying race, the men deficient in pluck and most troublesome as coolies.

The memoirs of Inspector-General of Police S. J. Stone reflect the same attitude:

The descent was steep and covered with snow, and the coolies lagged. I was hungry. Strong measures were called for. So I birched the men on the legs with thin stinging twigs from the trees. The effect was stimulating: and lasting! . . . My shot turned the yak, and I felt certain he had been hit. As he made up the hill I had time to put in four more shots. One broke his right hind leg below the knee. This crippled him; but nevertheless he made a bolt round the steep and stony hillside. We ran to cut him off, and Paljour [the shikari] got above me. The bull sighted him and charged him furiously, straight downhill. Paljour fled towards me at his best pace, screaming at me to fire; but I could not, for the stupid fellow was directly in line with the bull. I shouted to him to get out of the way, but he was too flustered. Fortunately a small rock jutted out of the hillside, and Paljour squeezed under it. The infuriated beast stood pawing the rock above him, only a few feet from the man: the one mad with rage, the other off his head with funk. I put a .500 into the beast's chest, and down he came straight for me. I backed away, and fell into a stony hole, cutting my legs pretty severely. But in the hole I was out of sight of the furious animal which thundered past me, only a few feet away. I had just time to twist myself into a sitting position, and deliver my second barrel into his shoulder as he rushed by. That finished him. He fell twenty yards below me, sprawling on his belly with his legs splayed out. His head was raised, and he was bleeding copiously from the mouth. After we had recovered somewhat, we went down to the yak which was still alive, and I was debating whether to spend another cartridge on him, when Paljour shouted at him – abusingly, I suppose – in Tibetan. The sound of the human voice so roused the savage brute's fury that he tried to rise. But it was his last effort. He collapsed, and rolled over and over down the hillside, bringing up on a hard bit at the bottom, flat on his back, dead. We pitched camp beside his carcase.

In between such passages, it comes as a surprise to find both Stone and Kinloch extolling the beauties of the Himalaya with real feeling: an ambivalence caught with precision in the memoirs of another hunter, Colonel Bairnsfather of the Bengal Lancers:

Each season in the Himalaya has its own particular charm. In spring the snows are still low down, and as we reach the top of some high pass, there bursts on our view a wondrous scene of purest white, reaching away, billow on billow, as far as the eye can see, the higher peaks flushed in the rose of the morning sun . . . In autumn mist hides the lowlands, giving to the higher peaks the effect of little islands standing in an ocean of snow. Little by little these wraiths are dispersed by the morning sun, revealing, feature by feature, all the loveliness of the land, till soon the only mist is that which comes from scattered villages nestling among autumn-tinted woods. The sky is bright blue, the air still and crisp. But come, let us be sportsmen! A pipe smokes the better while watching our men skin some bear or ibex after a good day's shoot!

The hunters were not good ambassadors for the European way of life – what, one wonders, did the gentle Buddhists of Ladakh, Baltistan and Nepal, to whom the killing of even a fly is taboo, think of the wholesale decimation of animals whom many of them regarded as kindred spirits? Nor, initially, were the climbers either liked or understood.

Of the latter, first on the scene was W. W. Graham, who arrived in Kathmandu early in 1883, to quote his own words, 'purely to climb and purely for sport and adventure'.

Accompanied by a Swiss guide, Joseph Inboden, Graham succeeded in climbing an unnamed 20,000-foot (6100 m) peak in the vicinity of Kangchenjunga. Later in the same season, with another guide, Ulrich Kauffmann, he attempted Nanda Devi and Dunajiri, possibly reaching 22,700 feet (6925 m) on the latter before being forced down

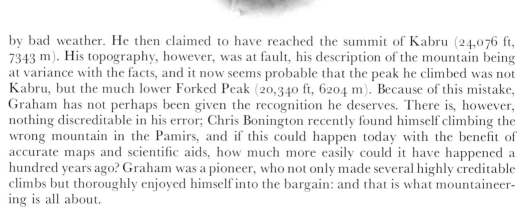

W.W. Graham: probably the first European to climb in the Himalaya 'purely for pleasure'

by bad weather. He then claimed to have reached the summit of Kabru (24,076 ft, 7343 m). His topography, however, was at fault, his description of the mountain being at variance with the facts, and it now seems probable that the peak he climbed was not Kabru, but the much lower Forked Peak (20,340 ft, 6204 m). Because of this mistake, Graham has not perhaps been given the recognition he deserves. There is, however, nothing discreditable in his error; Chris Bonington recently found himself climbing the wrong mountain in the Pamirs, and if this could happen today with the benefit of accurate maps and scientific aids, how much more easily could it have happened a hundred years ago? Graham was a pioneer, who not only made several highly creditable climbs but thoroughly enjoyed himself into the bargain: and that is what mountaineering is all about.

Graham's reports were studied with interest not only by alpinists but by scientists. One organization which read them with particular care was the Royal Geographical Society of London. This society, which had been founded in 1830, had as its broad objective 'the promotion of geography'. In the past it had fathered explorers such as Ross, Franklin, Eyre, Livingstone, Burton and Speke; in the future, it was to beget Scott, Shackleton, Fuchs, and Hunt, Hillary and Tenzing. Now it decided that mountaineering might, under certain conditions, be a branch of geography to which it could extend patronage, and in 1892 it sponsored a major expedition to the Karakoram.

The expedition was led by Martin Conway, an experienced alpinist, and included an artist, A. D. McCormick, several Swiss guides, and Lieutenant Bruce of the 5th Gurkhas, a man who over the next 40 years probably did more than anyone to promote mountaineering in the Himalaya. The Society's *Journal* described their progress:

> *On February 6th, 1892 the members of a mountaineering and scientific expedition sailed for Karachi, whence they will proceed to the mountains of Baltistan. Their object is to make a thorough exploration of the glacial area of the Karakoram. They propose to make their main centre the great Baltoro Glacier, believed to be the largest in the world outside the Arctic and Antarctic. Here they will make scientific observations of glacial phenomena. It is also their intention to make a determined attempt on one of the loftiest peaks, with a view to discovering the limit to which qualified mountaineers can climb without being stopped by the rarity of the air –*

a combination of scientific research and straight mountaineering of which the Society approved.

Even before they left Kashmir it was obvious that porters were going to be a problem. Lieutenant Bruce had brought with him four Gurkhas, on loan from his regiment, and they proved, according to expedition leader Conway, 'a tower of strength

Bhotia Tenzing Norkey on the summit of Everest, 1953

*Top: Summit ridge of Ogre with Karakoram range
in the background. Above: Pete Boardman (right)
and Joe Tasker on the summit of Kangchenjunga*

Camp II (22,000 ft, 6,705 m) on the first ascent of Ogre; Hispar Pass can be seen at the head of the glacier

Top: Changabang and, below,
Dougal Haston on the summit of
Everest, 1975

. . . I cannot speak too highly of them.' The local men, on the other hand, he described as 'a rotten lot, always wanting to lay down their packs and run' – although it is interesting to note that Bruce eventually gained their confidence, and that by the end of the trip they were ready to follow him anywhere.

Another problem was the weather, which Conway described in a letter to the Society: 'Conditions have been dreadful: daily snow, and such huge and terrible avalanches. The peaks are difficult in their lower parts, but the regions above 17,000 feet [5185 m] look easy' – a popular misconception among nearly all the early climbers.

I devoted the best part of a month to the Bagrot Valley, but constant clouds made surveying and climbing difficult. We climbed one 15,000-foot [4575 m] peak, and one of 17,000 [5185 m]. We also made a desperate assault on a 23,000-footer [7015 m], but were driven down from our high camp (15,600 ft [4755 m]) by a terrible storm which lasted a week! Avalanches of huge size fell all around us. One brought down four ibex; another nearly took off two Gourkhas [sic] who had gone to look for the dead ibex. A huge dust avalanche enveloped us completely, but did us no harm.

An English hunter and his Tartar gun bearers,
photographed by Capt. Mockler-Ferryman, 1890

Having digested this, the Society saw to it that future expeditions avoided the summer monsoon.

After retreating briefly to Gilgit, Conway pushed on towards his main objective, the Baltoro Glacier. Their problem now was the rivers, swollen by monsoon rain.

On August 1st we came to a stream which is usually only two yards wide, but which had so waxed in volume that our endeavours to cross it were for a long time fruitless. Eventually McCormick and a Gourkha succeeded in crossing with a climbing-rope. With this fastened from bank to bank, and the Gourkhas and Bruce standing thigh-deep in the icy stream to help, we at last succeeded in conveying the coolies over. The stream was rising steadily all the time, and the last to cross were buried up to their chests in the swift torrent. Bruce was here, there and everywhere, manifesting his usual abundance of energy; he himself carried over almost half the sheep, taking them one by one under his right arm, while with his left he grasped the rope . . . Thenceforward we advanced towards the foot of the great glacier. It took us a day and a half of most laborious travelling to reach the foot of the ice. The whole way we had to traverse a steep stony valley bare of vegetation, while the sun blazed down on us with fury. Above us was a precipitous rock-face, below us the raging torrent. We had to find a

*The Baltoro Glacier in the Karakoram, from
the Duke of Spoleto's expedition, 1929*

*precarious way between the two, sometimes descending to the very verge of the water, sometimes
scrambling across the face of precipitous rocks. At last the foot of the Baltoro Glacier came in sight,
and we pitched camp close to an ice cave from which the river rushed out in mighty volume.*

During the next few days, as they made their way up the glacier, peak after magnificent
peak revealed itself in what many mountaineers consider one of the most awe-inspiring
vistas in the world. 'On the first day Gusherbrum [26,470 ft, 8073 m], disclosed his giant
tower right ahead of us, uncompromisingly inaccessible . . . The evening of the second
day revealed the glorious Masherbrum [25,660 ft, 7826 m], his summit golden in the
sunlight and his grand skirts of snow sweeping down to the glacier beneath.' While on 10
August there rose up at the head of the valley 'an enormous mountain, not marked on
any map. It was throne-like in form, and auriferous veins seemed to permeate its mass;
we therefore named it the Golden Throne [Baltoro Kangri, 23,390 ft, 7134 m]. And as
we gazed at this most beautiful mountain, revealed in the mixed light of moon and
dawn, we cried, "That is the peak for us! That one we will climb, and no other." '

Conway, however, was soon to be disillusioned in his belief that the upper reaches of
the Karakoram were 'easy'.

He managed to climb the Crystal Peak (19,400 ft, 5917 m) after 'a glorious ascent in
which all the Goorkhas [sic] went well, and we were not unduly inconvenienced by the
rarity of the air.' However, he never got even close to the summit of Baltoro Kangri.

Throughout the second half of August – from the 13th to the 28th – his expedition
laid siege to the mountain in what was to become the approved Himalayan style. A base
camp (Junction Camp at 12,000 ft, 3660 m) was established on the glacier moraine;
Camp 1 (Footstool Camp at 16,500 ft, 5033 m) was set up 'in a magnificent position at
the foot of the precipices of the Golden Throne, with a peak of over 25,000 feet [7625 m]
on either side'; Camp 2 (Serac Camp at 18,000 ft, 5490 m) was laboriously stocked with
provisions. Then their difficulties began: 'Dawn on the 21st broke lurid and threatening.
An ominous orange glow rested on the higher peaks, and illuminated the wild clouds
that swirled about them; it was obvious the weather was about to break.' Next, Bruce

and one of the Gurkhas succumbed to altitude sickness and had to descend to Camp 1. And, finally, the supposedly 'easy' approach to the summit turned out to be fiendishly difficult, and not to lead to the summit at all!

> *Beyond the col, the slope presented a very steep face of mingled ice and rock, which had to be surmounted before we came to the main* arête. *We had a tough scramble of it for a quarter of an hour, then expected better things. But, to our horror, we found that the ridge leading to the summit was not of snow but of hard blue ice. Every step we took had to be cut.* Zurbrigger [*one of the Swiss* guides] *found the work of step-cutting – severe at any time – far more fatiguing than at the Swiss levels . . . The rest of the ascent was monotonous. The white ridge led straight up in front of us, and had to be followed. It was of ice, and here again every step had to be cut; also the ridge was heavily corniced to our left, so we were forced to keep to the right-hand slope, and were ignorant of the view on the other side. Our advance was slow, and the heat which the burning rays of the sun poured upon us did nothing to add to its rapidity. It was as though we were in the midst of an area of utter aerial stagnation, which made life intolerable. I heard the click-click of Zurbrigger's axe making steps, and struggled mechanically from one to another, only dimly conscious of the vast depths below us filled with tortured glacier and gaping schrunds. Then the slope became less steep. A few more steps, and at 2.45 p.m. we stood on the summit.*
>
> *But here a most unwelcome surprise awaited us. The summit of the Golden Throne was still some 1300 feet [395 m] above us, and the peak on which we stood was absolutely cut off from it by a deep depression, of whose existence we had been till now in ignorance. We had climbed another mountain!*

'There was,' Conway added, 'no debate about what we should do next. Nothing remained for us but downward and homeward.'

They stayed on the summit – which they named Pioneer Peak and whose height they calculated at 22,600 feet (6893 m) – for more than an hour: sketching, taking photographs, and taking observations for triangulation. Taking observations, too, of their pulse rates, and discovering that 'our hearts were being sorely tried, mine in particular being in a bad state.' Then they very prudently descended. A few months later Conway was back in England.

It had been a successful expedition: the longest glacier in the world outside the Arctic and Antarctic had been surveyed; several major peaks had been discovered, triangulated and climbed; and a great deal of scientific data had been brought back. What attracted most attention at the time was Conway's conquest of Pioneer Peak, 'the greatest proven altitude that anyone has yet attained' – Graham's claim to have reached 22,700 feet (6925 m) on Dunajiri not being considered proven. However, at a talk given to the Royal Geographical Society, a future president, Douglas Freshfield, paid tribute to an even greater achievement. 'Few travellers,' he said, 'can ever have brought back more fruitful results. I say fruitful because I am sure that his exploits will have the effect of interesting Indians in mountaineering, and that Mr Bruce's Ghurkhas [*sic*] will solve many problems. For if we can teach these people to act as mountain guides, then we shall have solved the problem of the exploration of the Himalayas,' – a prophesy which was to reach fulfillment 60 years later as Hillary and Tenzing stood on the summit of Everest.

◆

At about the time that Conway was taking observations from Pioneer Peak, Fanny Bullock Workman was riding her bicycle through the alleys of Algiers, brandishing a steel-cored riding-crop at the dogs and a revolver at the bazaar-tenders. She was a formidable traveller. In 1898 she and her husband descended on India, with the intention of bicycling from Cape Comorin to the Himalaya.

This was a journey which many people today would find beyond them; but Fanny (who was then rising 40) and her husband William (who was over 50) were not the sort to be defeated by dirt, discomfort and native apathy. With their bicycles festooned with baggage, including a kettle from which Fanny refused to be parted, they covered anything up to 80 miles (130 km) and mended anything up to 40 punctures a day; the nights they usually spent in railway waiting rooms, 'sitting upright in uncomfortable straight-backed chairs'. The book in which they described their journey, *Through Town and Jungle: 14,000 miles awheel among the temples and peoples of the Indian Plain*, is remarkable more for what it omits than for what it contains; for while the Workmans went to extraordinary lengths to inspect and record every temple, mosque and shrine on their route, they seem to have been totally unmoved by the splendours and miseries of the land through which they travelled. They made no mention of what Dorothy Middleton so aptly describes as India's captivating glamour and appalling poverty. One passage in

Above: Fanny Bullock Workman crossing the Rose Glacier and, left, holding a 'Votes for Women' placard on the Silver Throne Plateau, East Karakoram, at 21,000 ft (6,400 m)

particular from Dr Workman's diary, gives us the clue to their character: 'It causes me the greatest annoyance,' he wrote, 'to be forever importuned for medicine by the halt, lame and blind, malformed children, adults inflicted with incurable diseases, and the aged staggering under the burden of senile degenerative processes.' The Workmans obviously did not love their fellow-men.

They did, however, love the mountains, and were to spend the next 15 years in the Himalaya and Karakoram.

Fanny and William were Americans, rich and indefatigable. They employed top-class alpine guides, used the most up-to-date equipment, and organized their climbs with great efficiency; they were observant, opinionated, and led no fewer than eight

*Top: The Bullock Workmans and their porters
climbing in the Hoh Lumba and, above, on the
Col des Aiguilles, Kashmir, 1903*

major expeditions into the mountains, climbing, discovering, surveying and scandaliz-
ing the Old Guard of India by the vigour of their researches and the confidence of their
claims. British writers have tended to play down their achievements. Mason was
particularly scathing – 'a great deal of the ground they traversed had been visited and
described before, though the Workmans often lacked the grace to acknowledge this . . .
they were carping and controversial . . . they lacked a sense of topography . . . they
rarely tried to understand the mentality of their porters and never got the best out of
them': criticisms of which only the last is wholly justified.

Relations between the Workmans and their porters – or 'coolies' as they insisted on
calling them – might be best described as a running battle. They seem to have regarded
the mountain people as less than human. To quote from their *Call of the Snowy Hispar*:

> *The villagers were an odd lot; it was only after considerable persuasion that they could be induced to*
> *work for us . . . When we got to the snowline, they inflicted wounds on their feet and feigned illness.*
> *When we wanted them, they hid themselves and were not to be found. I have never known their equal*
> *for malingering, shirking work, deserting, demanding double rations, looting and mutinying.*

A few pages later, a 'mutiny' is described:

> *We began a zig-zag up the slope, which in places had a gradient of upwards of 60°. The snow had*
> *become softened by the heat of the sun, and Savoye* [the guide] *was kept busy treading out steps to*
> *facilitate the advance of the coolies. But when they arrived at the base of the slope, they all sat down,*
> *and the bearer called up weakly that they were tired and could go no farther.*
>
> *We answered, 'Tell them they must!'*
>
> *On hearing this they began to remonstrate in angry tones. The lambardar* [head-man of
> their village] *then harangued them, and ended with a vigorous use of his stick upon the most*
> *vociferous. At this, they started up the slope, but after a short distance again stopped in a determined*
> *manner . . . and nothing could persuade the recalcitrants to move. Savoye, becoming impatient,*
> *threw off his rucksack, muttering, 'Je descends!'*
>
> *He talked for some time to the lambardar, who did his best to explain matters to the coolies, but*
> *made no impression, for they only became more excited. Suddenly three of them attacked Savoye with*
> *their spiked sticks. He in self-defence, struck the strongest of them over the back with his ice-axe,*
> *felling him to the snow. That settled the issue. That argument they understood. They fell into line,*
> *and began to file slowly upward . . .*

a pattern repeated many times on many mountains.

But if the Workmans' faults are patently obvious, so too are their achievements.
Never before and seldom since have climbers returned again and again to the mountains
with such energy, persistence and enthusiasm. Of the eight major expeditions which they
led into the Himalaya and the Karakoram, four deserve more than a passing mention.

In 1898/9 they explored the area surrounding the Hispar-Biafo Glacier, 'climbing
the Siegfried Horn (18,600 ft [5673 m]), Mount Bullock Workman (19,450 ft [5932 m])
and the Koser Gunge (21,000 ft [6405 m])'. It is true that these peaks were subsequently
re-named and proved to be marginally lower than the Workmans estimated, but for a
middle-aged couple with little mountaineering experience to have climbed them was an
heroic achievement. Fanny disappeared up to her neck in soft snow, losing her topi
'which bounded with lightning speed over a 1000-foot precipice', and was dragged
head-first through a glacial stream at the bottom of a crevasse. 'Is that *really* the
mem'sahib?' asked an awestruck porter, as a tiny figure appeared at the highest point of
the range. It was. And photographs prove it: the indomitable Fanny posed always a little
above lesser mortals, such as her husband, and often disdaining to be roped!

In 1906/7 they explored the Nun Kun massif to the west of Leh. 'The rugged and savage beauty of this group,' wrote Fanny, 'and the evident complexity of its formation, proclaimed it a most alluring field for investigation . . . And this time we decided to employ Italian porters. For we have had more than enough, in the past, of sitting on cold snow-slopes, awaiting the snail-like approach of unwilling coolies, and hearing their wailing complaints and refusals to march.' The highlight of this expedition was their climbing of Pinnacle Peak – 'the highest point in the massif, by the ascent of which Mrs Bullock Workman not only broke her last record-ascent for women, but won a place with Mr Workman in that small band of mountaineers who have reached heights of over 23,000 feet [7015 m].' This last sentence from *Peaks and Glaciers of the Nun Kun* is the sort of fuel which stokes the flames of the Workmans' critics; for as Mason points out, Pinnacle Peak is *not* the highest point in the massif (it is 440 feet lower than Kun) and it is *not* over 23,000 feet but 22,810. 'Also the Workmans' map,' he adds scathingly, 'is faulty in so many respects that it could not be accepted by the Survey of India.' Mason is right, but one feels he might have tempered his criticism by giving Fanny some credit, at the age of almost 50, for having climbed higher than any woman in the world and very nearly as high as any man.

The Workmans had intended to make their Nun Kun expedition their last, but, to quote Fanny, 'we had breathed the atmosphere of the mountain-world, had drunk the waters of its glaciers and feasted our eyes on the majesty of its peaks, and as time passed its siren strains called us to return again to those regions whose grandeur so satisfies one's sense of the beautiful and the sublime.' They went on this occasion to the west Karakoram, and here the pattern of previous expeditions was repeated: endless trouble with their porters, a succession of highly commendable climbs, and a spate of basically true but slightly exaggerated claims. The highlight of this expedition was Fanny's ascent of Watershed Peak (21,350 ft, 6512 m): no mean achievement, as can be seen from her account:

At about 6.30 a.m. we reached the base of a difficult snow-wall leading to the south arête. *This was an exhausting piece of climbing. It might appear that we had only to scramble up the shoulder and walk to the summit. This, however, was not the case. Apart from anything else there was a dizzy turning to make, which brought the snow-wall just ascended into full focus, and such declivities are more agreeable behind one than in front! Also some sharp snow pinnacles had to be climbed over, there being no way round them . . . Savoye cut two steps on to the* arête *directly above my head, drew the rope taut and remarked: 'Don't be surprised, Madame, at the precipices. Just turn quickly.' Taking two long strides, I stood behind him on the* arête. *And what an* arête *it was! A foot and a half wide at the most, and completely ice-glazed. To the right the snow-slope fell away at an angle of some sixty degrees. To the left it sank into a much deeper, steeper and seemingly endless precipice. Giving only a glance at the demoniac chasm we moved slowly but sharply heavenward. Step-cutting now began in earnest . . . After about an hour we came to bare rock. We had a drink of tea and some chocolate, then tackled the jagged intruders, which were disintegrated and rotten. Beyond the rock-zone came an easier slope, topped by a blue ice-wall above which the* arête *continued, a long glistening white shoulder, steeper and ever steeper towards the summit. We stopped for a few minutes to photograph; but not for long, for the weather looked threatening. Far away, apparently suspended between earth and sky, hung the grey massif of K2.*

We attacked the ice wall, anxious to reach the top before mist and cloud cut off the view. This was a nasty few feet. For with the sun melting the ice, steps were hard to cut clean and soon filled with water. We edged sideways, each foot only half-in a step. Beneath us, exposed to our full view, lay half the mountain, its precipitous depths inviting instant death should head or feet fail . . . I have often felt on snow-slopes what I call the tremor of the snow: the contraction of the outer surface under

*pressure. It always got on my nerves. And now, on this last tremendous slant leading skyward, when
I felt the snow give and crack, I felt chilled to the very bone.*

*But suddenly the top was only a few minutes above us. We climbed past another narrow
gruesome shoulder, and thence straight up to a small rounded cone, which as we had expected turned
over to the north in a cornice: the summit . . . The view from the top was the most comprehensive and
beautiful I have ever seen. For the single pyramid of Watershed Peak stands alone, with no near
higher summits to mar the view. To the east, five or six thousand feet [1500–1800 m] beneath us, lay
Snow Lake, its glacial branches spread out like white fans. Beyond, swept a great glacier, unbroken
by crevasses, and beyond the glacier the great peak Kailasa rose like a colossal medieval castle in
turrets of ice and snow. Watershed Peak offered us from its summit a panorama of one of the most
magnificent mountain-landscapes in the world. I felt I had seen wonders not of this earth, the
memory of which will cling while life lasts.*

They had been on the summit only a few minustes when 'a fluffy mist entwined itself
around our cornice and half the mountain-world was lost in a sea of cloud. Doctor
Workman, who had just completed the ascent of a lower peak, recorded what a striking
picture we presented – three black figures encircled by a wreath of cloud, seemingly not
standing on a peak at all but hung high in a heaven of oncoming mist and storm.' The
descent, most of it carried out in cloud, was hair-raising. At one point Fanny fell: 'When
the ice-wall was reached, while treading backwards, I slithered, for the steps had melted,
and both feet shot free. But the rope tightened around my waist; in a second my foot
swung into the next step; and turning face-forward, I risked a leap which landed me safe
on the *arête* . . . At last, plodding half-way up to our knees in wet snow, we arrived back
at camp, where the others, although they didn't say so, were greatly relieved to see us.'

They named the peak Biafo Hispar Watershed, and calculated its height as 21,350
feet (6512 m). Savoye was disappointed that it had not turned out to be another 23,000-
footer, but Fanny rebuked him: 'We didn't come to the Hispar to make records.'

The Workmans' last expedition was their greatest, and gave rise to the only one of
their plethora of books which has stood the test of time, *Two Summers in the Ice Fields of the
Eastern Karakoram*, which is now regarded as a minor classic. Twelve years in the
mountains had mellowed the Workmans. There is less abrasiveness about their last
venture, a better relationship with their porters, and more emphasis on research. The
Royal Geographical Society provided them with instruments; the Survey of India
provided them with the services of two more-than-competent surveyors (Grant Peterkin
and Sarjan Singh); and Fanny, as always, provided a wealth of first-class photographs,
including a classic of herself on the Siachan Glacier carrying a placard demanding
'Votes for Women'! There have been greater mountaineers, but none more combative.
And she loved the mountains. Let that be her epitaph.

◆

Fanny's exploits underline the rapidity with which the winds of change were now
gusting over the ranges of central Asia. Before 1880 no one since the dawn of history had
thought of climbing the mountains for pleasure. Now, within the span of a single
generation, mountaineers from a dozen countries had climbed literally hundreds of the
major peaks, and half-a-dozen peaks of over 20,000 feet (6100 m) had been climbed by a
middle-aged woman.

And what had happened to the mountains was about to happen to the mountain
people. For in 1904 the British invaded Tibet.

'Invasion' is not the word usually used to describe Younghusband's 'diplomatic mission' to Lhasa; yet the dictionary definition – 'make hostile inroad into' – describes very well what took place. The mission was an archetypal Suez, nicely summed up by Peter Fleming: 'Its outward aspect was swashbuckling, romantic and clear-cut; its inner history ambigious and confused; its aftermath unedifying. Over it there hangs, as over some indiscretion, an air of apology and embarrassment.'

The idea of sending troops into Tibet stemmed from the 'forward' policy of Lord Curzon, a man whose ability was equalled only by his arrogance. Curzon had a brilliant career, yet in each office he held, be became involved in bitter and acrimonious controversy. As a distinguished explorer and scholar, he was elected president of the Royal Geographical Society – and his offensive comments on Amundsen's use of dogs on his journey to the Pole triggered off the one serious dispute the Society has ever had with a major explorer. As one of the more skilled and aggressive players of the Great Game, he was appointed Viceroy of India – and his instigation of the Younghusband mission sparked off a campaign which may, in military terms, have been a success, but was, in

*Tibetans with the Union Jack, photographed by Capt.
C.G. Rawling on the Younghusband 'mission', 1903–5*

political terms, a fiasco, for in his anxiety to exclude the Russians, who were not at this time a serious threat to Tibet, Curzon opened the door to the Chinese.

The excuse drummed up to launch the British invasion would have taxed credulity in a comic opera. On 3 November 1903 Curzon, then Viceroy of India, sent a telegram to the government complaining that 'an overt act of hostility has taken place, Tibetan troops having attacked Nepalese yaks on the frontier and carried off many of them.' Soon, to redress this grievous wrong, a column of some 1100 troops and almost 11,000 baggage carriers – mules, ponies, bullocks, camels, yaks and porters – was following the Union Jack into the Jelap La Pass which leads from Sikkim to Tibet. Their objective was to negotiate with the country's rulers a treaty of friendship: a treaty which, it was hoped, would ensure that Tibet remained an independent state and was not absorbed into Russia's ever-expanding empire. It is not the motive that sticks in one's gullet, but the method of achieving it.

The military leader of the expedition, Brigadier-General Macdonald, has been variously described as 'inexperienced', 'incompetent', 'inordinately cautious', 'vacillating' and 'childishly pre-occupied with rank and prerogative'. On a mission which one would have expected to be led by a fire-eater, he was to prove an exceedingly damp squib.

The diplomatic leader, Francis Younghusband, was the fire-eater; he was also a more complex and interesting character. As a junior officer in the King's Dragoon Guards he had won the reputation of being a 'thruster', not in the military field but the exploratory. Before he was 25 he had undertaken several important reconnaissance missions beyond the frontier including a remarkable journey through Mongolia and Sinkiang, had discovered a major new pass through the Karakoram, and had been politely expelled from Russian territory in the Pamirs; before he was 30 he had been appointed British Political Agent in Chitral, proving himself a more than competent player of the Great Game. In 1903 Curzon reckoned he was the ideal man to be given joint command of the mission to Lhasa. There was, however, an unexpected side to Younghusband's character. He was a mystic, an Asian Gordon of Khartoum, a man who was drawn strongly to the spiritual life and who founded the Congress of Faiths, an organization which strove, and indeed is still striving, to break down the barriers between the world's religions. He and Macdonald did their best to work together, but it would be difficult to imagine a more ill-matched pair.

In an address to the Royal Geographical Society, Younghusband gave a frank account of the expedition's dubious origins, military and geographical achievements, and moral dilemma.

He began – and this is significant – with his departure from Darjeeling, as early as June 1903: 'The monsoon had just burst, the rain was coming down in cataracts, and all was shrouded in mist. Few knew of the enterprise upon which I was embarking, but a little knot of people who had assembled in the porch of the hotel got an inkling, and shouted "good luck!" as I rode off into the mist.' Evidence, if any were needed, that the mission was premeditated; for the affair of the yaks was not to take place for another five months. He spent the late summer and autumn encamped on the frontier,

enjoying perhaps the most beautiful panorama in all the world: the unbroken chain of the Himalaya. As I looked out of my tent each morning, while all below was still wrapped in grey, in the distance the first streaks of dawn would be gilding the snowy summit of Mount Everest. By degrees the whole great range would be illuminated, and would shine out in dazzling, unsullied whiteness. Throughout the day it would be bathed in ever-varying hues of blue and purple, until the setting sun clothed it in a final intensity of glory, and left one hungering for daylight to appear again . . . On December 6th, after months of arguing with a people very nearly as obstinate as ourselves, we realised that our political objective would never be attained until we advanced into the country. A move on to Gyantse was accordingly ordered, and a considerable body of troops under the command of General Macdonald escorted us over the Jelap La Pass and into the Chumbi valley.

The Jelap La Pass is 14,390 feet (4389 m) above sea-level, and for a force of several thousand men to cross it in mid-winter was no mean achievement. Luckily it was undefended. Beyond the pass, however, the Tibetans had built a wall which traders were prohibited to cross, and this *was* defended. Younghusband arranged a parley with the general in charge of its defence, and explained his reasons for wanting to enter Tibet:

Next morning, as we debouched from the pine forest in which we had encamped for the night, we could see the wall built right across the road and high up the mountain-side on either hand. Whether we should have to fight our way through, or whether the general would respond to my arguments, had yet to be proved, and Macdonald took every military precaution. But to our enormous relief we saw the door in the tower standing open, and were soon passing peaceably through.

Younghusband, like Bogle more than 100 years before him, was greatly impressed by the fertility of the country and the friendliness of the people. *The idea has grown up*, he told the Society,

> *that Tibet is a wretched place, barren and uncultivated. This may be true of the northern two-thirds, but the southern third is fully as rich as Kashmir or Nepal. Its valleys are up to 10 miles broad, covered with good soil, well-irrigated and richly cultivated. The people were well-to-do, and decidedly well disposed towards us; they soon showed themselves to be keen traders . . .*
>
> *The mission remained three weeks in the lower Chumbi valley, while military preparations for a further advance were completed. Then in the very depths of winter, on January 8th we crossed the Tang-la Pass (15,200 ft, 4636 m) into the Tibetan plateau. Never shall I forget that day. Reveille sounded at the first streak of dawn, and as I looked out of my tent the very spirit of Frost seemed to have settled on the scene. The stars were shooting out sharp clear rays from a steely sky. Behind the great peak of Chumalhari the first beams of dawn were showing, but with no force yet to cheer or warm, and only sufficient light to make the cold more apparent. Water was frozen solid; the remains of last night's dinner was a hard mass. The poor Sikhs were crawling out of their tents so shrivelled with cold it looked as though, if they shrivelled any more, there would be nothing left of them. The temperature stood at 18° below zero [−28°C] or 50° of frost, and though this is not considered much in Canada or Siberia, and I dare say those who have just returned from the Antarctic would consider it pleasantly warm, I should remind you that 50° of frost at 15,000 feet [4575 m] is a very different thing from 50° at sea-level. At 15,000 feet, where the effort of breathing is a continued drain on one's strength, the mere weight of the clothes one has to wear is a strain in itself; any additional effort exhausts one immediately. And if it tries us Europeans, who are more or less inured to cold, how much more distressing must it be to the natives of India. That they were able to march 15 miles [24 km] that day across the pass, and spend the rest of the winter on the other side of it at a height of but little under 15,000 feet, is a striking testimony to their powers of endurance and the high spirit which prevails among them.*

The Tang-la Pass was the scene of the first major disagreement between Younghusband and Macdonald. Younghusband had promised the Tibetan generals that the British would take no hostile action so long as the Tibetans took none. The Tibetans, withdrawing from walls and forts, had scrupulously kept their side of the bargain; in particular, they had left a near-impregnable fortress at the approach to Phari undefended. Macdonald, 'thinking it impossible the Tibetans would be such fools as not to hold the place,' sent troops to occupy it. Younghusband was furious. His sense of chivalry was outraged. He felt Macdonald had involved him in a breach of faith. 'I was very angry,' he wrote. 'And I have never spoken to any man as severely as I spoke to Macdonald.'

Crossing the pass, the mission came to a halt at Tuna, 'a place of no importance' on the Tibetan plateau. No one (then or now) seems to have the slightest idea why Younghusband was ordered to spend the cruellest months of winter in a village which was devoid of material comfort, strategic importance or political significance. Certainly the choice was not Macdonald's. The general took one look at Tuna and refused to stay, pleading that there was insufficient forage, and that his troops would be unable to stand the cold. Younghusband had more guts. Realizing it would be disastrous both strategically and politically to retreat, he accepted full responsibility for the decision to remain at Tuna with a skeleton force, while Macdonald and the bulk of his troops withdrew to the comparative shelter of the lower Chumbi valley.

The next three months were a time of endless blizzard and fruitless negotiation.

> *Almost every morning* [Younghusband wrote] *at ten or eleven o'clock a terrific wind would arise*

Left: Cartoon from 'Punch' and, right,
Tibetan seals permitting entry to
Younghusband's diplomatic mission, 1903

and blow with fury for the rest of the day. Mighty masses of cloud would come sweeping up from India, snow would fall, and for days together we would be the sport of the blizzard. The mountains would be hidden, and nothing would be visible but dull masses of fiercely driven snow, fine and dry as dust and penetrating everywhere. Our camp would be the very picture of desolation. It seemed impossible that the poor sentries at night could stand against the howling storm and the penetrating snow, let alone resist any attack by the Tibetans. Then one morning we would find the snow-clouds had passed away, and the great peak Chumalhari would be standing calm and irresistible out of the mass of cloud still tossing about its base.

In the brief spells of fine weather, Younghusband did everything he could to bring about a diplomatic settlement. But the Tibetans did not want to negotiate; they wanted the British to leave, an impasse nicely reflected in the *Punch* cartoon of November 1903. Eventually, tired of procrastination and eager to 'get a move on' – an Americanism of which he thoroughly approved – Younghusband rode unarmed and unheralded into the Tibetan army's camp: a move of great courage but doubtful wisdom. He was well received by the generals, but not so well received by the lamas, who 'with scowls on their faces remained seated on the ground, showing not the slightest civility, and instigating the generals to detain me'. After the ritual serving of tea, discussion got under way, but with the British refusing to leave the country, and the Tibetans refusing to negotiate until they had gone, it is hardly surprising that little progress was made. Eventually Younghusband was reduced to repeating over and over again that all the British wanted was to establish friendly relations and to promote trade, while the lamas were reduced to repeating over and over again that in order to preserve their religion they were obliged to ban all foreigners from their country. Younghusband did not think much of the lamas' argument, and formed the opinion that they were more concerned with preserving their priestly privileges than with the sanctity of their religion.

He was probably right. The idea that Tibetan lamas formed the élite of a civilized theocracy owes more to *Lost Horizon* than to reality. Many of them entered monasteries through economic necessity, not religious vocation, and were custodians not only of religion but also of a feudal system which was stultifyingly opposed to change. Foreigners, they realized, were instruments of change: they saw them going by night into the forests, and not being molested by demons; they saw them climbing mountains without lighting sacrificial fires, and not being overwhelmed; they saw new skills and new ideas dispersing the superstition of millennia, and tried (with the despair of those who champion a lost cause) to hold back time. In his book *Lhasa and Its Mysteries* Austine Waddell describes the lengths they were prepared to go in order to preserve the status quo. There was, he tells us, a kind-hearted old lama of high position 'who was rash enough to allow an Indian friend to spend a few days with him in the Forbidden City. When this was discovered, the lama was dragged to the market-place and beaten to death; his reincarnation was eternally banned (thus ensuring the death of his soul as well as his body); his estates were confiscated; his wife and family were condemned to life imprisonment; and his servants' hands and feet were cut off, their eyes were gouged out, and they were strung up in public and left to a lingering death.

It was lamas of this persuasion who now, 'looking black as devils', told Younghusband that he was no better than a common brigand and, as he rose to leave, shouted at the generals to seize him. Trumpets sounded, and troops surrounded the house where the parley was taking place. It was, to quote Younghusband, 'a damned ticklish situation', but he kept his nerve, pretended the whole affair was an enormous joke, and managed to bluff his way out of trouble and back to Tuna.

A month later, at the approach of spring, his expedition (about 150 British troops and 900 Indian) was advancing on Lhasa. Almost at once they came face to face with the Tibetan army of more than 3000 troops, entrenched at Guru behind a barricade thrown up across what had once been a bottleneck between hills and lake.

Nothing shows the Tibetan mentality more clearly than their decision to make a stand at this particular spot. It had in the past been a splendid position; it had in the past been the scene of a famous Tibetan victory. But the waters of the lake had, over the centuries, receded, so what had once been a redoubt was now a death trap. Times had changed; but the Tibetans had not changed with them.

There are two views about the tragedy which followed. Some say that fighting was inevitable, and if it had not erupted that day at Guru it would soon have erupted somewhere else; others say that only an unlucky last-minute incident robbed Younghusband of a spectacular and bloodless victory. What happened is this: after a last-minute and abortive parley, the two armies for some time stood facing one another. Twice Macdonald begged Younghusband to let him attack, and twice Younghusband refused to be the first to shed blood. Eventually the British column, under an ash-grey sky and a biting wind, moved slowly forward, straight up to the barricade, without firing a shot. These were quixotic, indeed almost suicidal tactics, the troops being required to walk calmly up to a wall with upward of 1000 muskets trained on them from point-blank range. If the Tibetans opened fire, even with their ancient matchlocks, the British would have been decimated. But not a shot was fired. And eventually the troops circled round the lakeward end of the barricade, and took up position in the Tibetans' rear.

At this point it looked as though the impossible had happened, for the British had marched clean through the Tibetan defences, and the road to Lhasa lay open. A dispatch rider galloped to the telegraph-line to cable news of a famous victory.

The Tibetans, however, still outnumbered the British, and although they were surrounded and in an impossible position tactically, they did not appreciate this; they refused to move away from their wall. The expedition could not with safety by-pass them as though they were a puddle in the road, and Macdonald decided – with some justification in military terms – that they ought to be disarmed. This was the spark that triggered off the holocaust. No troops like laying down their arms, and the Tibetans had a particular aversion to doing so, for their matchlocks were often their own property and were needed for hunting, while their swords were often heirlooms which had been handed down from generation to generation. As the Gurkhas and Sikhs began peremptorily to take away these weapons, many resisted. Tussles broke out. Tension mounted. Stones were thrown. Blows were exchanged. Shouting angrily, the Tibetan general urged his pony into the mêlée. A Sikh tried to grab hold of his bridle, and the general shot away half his face.

There was a moment – perhaps three or four seconds – of absolute silence. Then, probably as a result of some still-continuing tussle, a rifle went off. The Tibetans, thinking they were about to be attacked, drew their swords and flung themselves on the column. The troops opened fire, and from two sides of a square, volley after volley, at point-blank range, thudded into the phalanx of human bodies. It was not a battle, it was a massacre. Within minutes over 600 Tibetans lay dead or dying. They did not flee. They simply turned their backs to the wall and *walked* through the hail of bullets. 'They walked slowly.' wrote Edmund Chandler of the *Daily Mail* – who himself received 17 sword wounds and lost a hand in the mêlée – 'slowly and with bowed heads, as if disillusioned in their gods.' 'It was an awful sight,' wrote a young officer to his mother, 'and I hope I shall never again have to shoot down men who are *walking* away.' It was, to quote Younghusband, 'a terrible and ghastly business'.

The blame for the massacre at Guru is usually apportioned between Younghusband, Macdonald and the Tibetan general who fired the first shot. But most culpable of all was Curzon.

In the weeks that followed, the expedition advanced steadily on Lhasa. Younghusband hoped that the incident at Guru would at least show the Tibetans the futility of further resistance, but in this he was disappointed. They made another stand at Red Idol Gorge, but were dislodged by the Gurkhas, who climbed to close on 19,000 feet (5795 m) to outflank and fire down on the hapless defenders. They also made a surprise night attack on Macdonald's headquarters; but this was beaten off with the usual ratio of casualties – 100 Tibetans killed for every Anglo-Indian wounded.

Soon only one serious obstacle lay between Younghusband and Lhasa: the Brahmaputra. It was now mid-summer, and the river, swollen by monsoon rain, proved a more formidable barrier than the Tibetan army. It ran fast and deep, and the Tibetans had withdrawn all boats to the far bank. Eventually Captain Sheppart of the Royal Engineers rigged up a flying ferry at a spot where the river, hemmed in by high cliffs, narrowed to 200 yards (189 m); and by this means the whole force was ferried across, with the loss of only one man – ironically this one casualty was Major Bretherton, the chief supply and transport officer whose logistical expertise had done so much to bring about the expedition's success.

A few days after crossing the river they sighted Lhasa. 'Here in a lovely valley, covered with trees, rich with cultivation, watered by a river as broad as the Thames at Westminster, and hidden by range after range of snowy mountains, lay the Forbidden City which no living European had before set eyes on.' For the British it was a moment of triumph – 'every obstacle,' wrote Younghusband, 'which nature and man could heap in our way had been overcome.' But for the Tibetans it was a moment of sadness. The veil which for centuries had hidden Lhasa from the outside world had been ripped away. Its

*Top: British troops about to cross the Brahmaputra
River – the boat capsized, drowning the chief supply
and transport officer – and, below, entering Lhasa*

isolation ended, its innocence violated, the Tibetan capital from now on had no option but to join the modern world in its scramble for material progress.

It was the end of an era.

Considering its cost – to the British in effort, and to the Tibetans in lives – the mission achieved surprisingly little. Since the Dalai Lama had fled to Mongolia, Younghusband was obliged to negotiate with his regent Dorjieff, the very man who was suspected of being a Russian agent! The negotiations, carried out with great good humour and politeness, dragged on and on. In the end a convention of nine articles was agreed and signed. Some articles dealt with trade, some with an indemnity, and some with the setting up of political agents. Younghusband reckoned he had used his initiative to drive a good bargain, but some of the articles did not find favour in London, and there was a general feeling that he had 'overstepped the mark'. On his return he was not honoured but reprimanded, and made a scapegoat for Curzon's unpopular jingoism. One cannot help feeling sympathy for Younghusband, although without doubt those baying for his and Curzon's blood were right: the long-term evil that resulted from the mission far outweighed the short-term good.

One short-term advantage was the opening up of Tibet to British explorers, and the moment the convention was signed, an expedition under Captain Rawling set out to survey the upper reaches of the Brahmaputra. 'This expedition,' Younghusband told the Royal Geographical Society, 'with no armed escort, travelled through more than 1000 miles [1600 km] of Tibet, and was everywhere well received. They surveyed 40,000 square miles of country, including the whole course of the Brahmaptura from Shigatse to its source, the Mansorawar and adjoining lakes, and the sources of the Indus and Sutlej. They also proved beyond doubt that no higher mountain than Everest lies at the back of the Himalayas' – a mention which foreshadows half a century of British interest in, some would say obsession with, the mountain. As Younghusband pointed out with justifiable pride, 'the mission was by no means barren in geographical results.'

Politically, it was a different story. For when the Dalai Lama fled from the British, he fled to China; and when, after four years, he returned, it was with Chinese backing.

All the British had done was to upset the age-old balance of power by which Tibet had for centuries preserved her precarious independence. Ever since 1720 the Chinese had claimed to be overlords of Tibet; and now, with the Russians excluded and the British unwilling to garrison a mountain area so remote from their bases, this suzerainty became a *de facto* corollary to Younghusband's mission. In 1906 an Anglo-Chinese treaty recognized this suzerainty, and in 1907 an Anglo-Russian treaty confirmed it – facts which help to explain if not excuse the Chinese invasion of 1950.

◆

One concession Younghusband extracted from Dorjieff was a vague promise that mountaineers would be given permission to climb specific Tibetan peaks – almost certainly he had Everest in mind. This permission, however, was not sought for several years, because there was still a multitude of unconquered mountains of easy access on the borders of Kashmir and Nepal. One of these, Trisul (23,360 ft, 7125 m), was climbed by Tom Longstaff in 1907, a magnificent achievement, for Trisul remained the highest mountain in the world to be climbed for more than 20 years.

It could be argued that an even more magnificent achievement was that of two little-known Norwegians, Rubenson and Aas, who came within a hair's-breadth of climbing Kabru, finally giving up only some 100 feet below the summit at a height of 23,900 feet (7290 m). This climb has never won the recognition it deserves; apart from an article in a Calcutta newspaper and a report in the *Alpine Journal*, no full account of it – at least in English – has appeared in print.

Kabru is the peak some ten miles (16 km) south of Kangchenjunga which Graham erroneously claimed to have climbed in 1883. It is part of the Singalila ridge, and its glaciers and ice-fields can be seen quite clearly from Darjeeling. Rubenson and Aas arrived in Darjeeling during the monsoon of 1907, and in the rare intervals between the rains they studied the mountain's approaches. Neither was an experienced climber, but they planned their assault carefully, and they had one great advantage over many of their predecessors: they won the unswerving loyalty of their 'coolies'.

On 5 October the monsoon clouds lifted, and next day the two Norwegians, together with some 30 porters, set out for the Singalila ridge. They climbed steadily, skirting the Forked Peak and the Dome, and establishing one camp at 18,000 feet (5490 m) and another at 19,500 (5948 m) – the highest point in the history of mountaineering to which porters had, up to this date, carried substantial loads.

Tibetan boat crossing the Brahmaputra,
photographed by Capt. C.G. Rawling, 1903

So far [to quote Rubenson] *the ice and snow had presented no great difficulty; but we now got our first view of the ice-stream which was our only approach to the summit. I must confess it looked hopeless; I didn't think it passable for loaded coolies . . .* [However, they decided to give it a try.] *From this camp it took us five days of hard work cutting steps through a chaos of ice needles and crevasses – a frozen world of the most fantastic and wonderful architecture . . . Halfway up the icefall we established another camp, where we halted two days. The route from here was not so difficult as the first part, but the greatest care had to be taken because of the danger of avalanches. It was from this camp at about 21,500 feet [6558 m] that we decided to make our final attempt on the summit.*

Their first attempt was unsuccessful, but they managed to establish an even higher camp, and from here, on 20 October, they began a second assault.

We passed the night at about 22,000 feet [6710 m]. The cold was intense, the thermometer registering 29° below zero [−34°C]. All the coolies had been sent down to the lower camp, except for two, who passed the night with us huddled up in our small tent. At about 8.30 a.m. the two of us set out on the final attempt to reach the summit. The start was rather late, but the cold, intensified by an icy wind, made it difficult if not impossible to start earlier. We progressed very slowly, cutting steps in the hard snow, and stopping every now and then to attend to our feet, which threatened to freeze solid. Our plan was to climb the saddle between Kabru's two peaks, then attempt to reach the S.W. peak which is marked on the map as the higher (24,015 feet [7325 m]). However, the wind, which grew stronger by the hour, made this impossible. So we bore off to the right to get into the shelter of the N.E. peak. The climb here was exceedingly steep, and provided us with very hard work on rock and ice. Our watch having been lost earlier in the day, we had only a hazy idea of time, but we could tell by the westering sun that evening was approaching. We did our best to hurry. At about 5 o'clock we thought we could see the summit just above us, and knowing that the moon would soon be up, we decided to continue in spite of the lateness of the hour. At about 6 o'clock we reached what we had thought was the top, only to see ahead of us a low snow ridge leading to a summit some 100 feet [30 m] higher. The sun by now had set, and knowing we had a difficult and dangerous descent, we did not dare to go on – although the climbing of the ridge would not have presented any problem. We did not have too much difficulty in breathing, but the cold was almost unbearable. The altitude we reached was about 23,900 feet [7290 m]. We didn't leave anything there, as the place we reached was not marked in any way which could be recognized by future climbers.

On the way down we had a remarkable escape. Descending a very steep slope, I, who was in the rear, slipped off an icy step, fell on my back and shot past my friend like a bullet from a gun. We were roped; and he luckily for both of us was able by a miracle to hold me. The Swiss rope, which was of five strands, almost parted; four strands breaking, so I was held literally by a single thread. I had managed to keep hold of my ice axe, and by ramming this into the ice was able to hold my position, and eventually continue the descent. How Mr Aas was able to check me, I shall never know. But had we both fallen, we could not possibly have survived, for after a slide of some 500 feet [150 m] we would have been flung on to a glacier many thousand feet beneath us.

The moon by now had risen. The wind was icy. But at last we reached our tent, where we found our two boys waiting for us, shivering with cold. We were too tired to eat. Aas complained of pain in his feet, and we found that six of his toes were badly frost-bitten. We applied the only remedy we could: rubbing them with snow. Next day we returned to the lower camps, having spent more than a fortnight on the ice and snow of the upper reaches of the mountain . . . I don't doubt it will prove possible to climb mountains even higher than Kabru. The most important thing is to have good and willing coolies, as we had. Properly fitted out and with kind treatment they will achieve the impossible! We could not persuade them to be roped when loaded; but by making good steps, fixing in pegs and ropes, and helping them over difficult places there seems to be no limit to what they will surmount. Our experience is that the coolies, especially the Nepalese Sherpas, are excellent men when treated properly. What success we achieved was due to the willingness and bravery of these people.

This climb has much to commend it. Rubenson and Aas came within some 100 feet of reaching the highest summit yet attained. They climbed higher than anyone had ever climbed before. They knew when to give up – in the same way that it was a measure of Shackleton's greatness that he turned back when the Pole was within his reach, so it was a sign of the Norwegians' greatness that they did not attempt the final 60 feet, which would almost certainly have cost them their lives during the descent. They persuaded their porters to provision camps at record altitudes. And, best of all, they established with their Sherpas a genuine friendship: a comradeship which, in the fullness of time, was to take Tenzing to the summit of Everest.

◆

A couple of years later, in 1909, there arrived in the Himalaya one of the great figures in the history of world exploration: the Duke of the Abruzzi.

HRH Prince Luigi Amedo of Savoy seems to have been one of those gifted people blessed with every attribute. He was primarily a naval officer – later becoming commander-in-chief of allied fleets in the Adriatic during World War I – but he was also a highly proficient mountaineer, having served his apprenticeship on the Matterhorn which he climbed at the age of 21, and an indefatigable traveller. Few explorers have been so catholic in their choice of terrain. In 1897 he became the first man to reach the summit of Mount Elias in Alaska; in 1899 he wintered on and surveyed Franz Josef Land in the Arctic; in 1906 he climbed and surveyed the Ruwenzori Mountains of equatorial Africa; and now in 1909 he led an expedition to the Karakoram. He would have liked, his biographer tells us, to have attempted Mount Everest; but Nepal and Tibet were now closed to foreigners – so much for Younghusband's concessions! – and he therefore concentrated his attention on the second highest mountain in the world, K2.

He had with him Filippo de Filippi as aide, doctor and naturalist, Federico Negrotto as topographer, Vittorio Sella, a magnificent photographer, seven Italian guides and over 300 local porters. The expedition left Srinagar in April and crossed the Zoji La Pass while it was still deep in snow – 'our lanterns throwing an unearthly light on the features of the coolies resting in long lines, the shapeless loads on their backs transforming them into strange hump-backed dwarfs' – and by mid-May were camped at the foot of the Baltoro Glacier. There followed two months of non-stop research and climbing, recorded in evocative detail in De Filippi's *Karakoram and Western Himalaya*.

If every mountaineering book bar one had to be burned, the one I would save would be De Filippi's. It has everything: everything, that is, except a popular climax in the shape of a summit attained. Here is his description of the Concordia, that vast amphitheatre of peaks, dominated by the pyramid of K2, at the head of the Baltoro Glacier.

> *So vast were the structural lines of the landscape, that we felt ourselves standing in the workshop of nature, in a world of primeval chaos as yet unvisited by the phenomenon of life. In Alpine ascents one knows one has left the green fields, trees and villages only a day or so behind; from the heights, one looks down on a green mantle of verdure; the rocks and ice are limited areas. But here one is conscious of not a single manifestation of life. In this respect, but in no other, it is comparable to the polar regions . . . The scale is so vast that one cannot get an impression of the whole at any one moment; the eye can take in only single portions. And so for a long time we were not fully conscious of the dimensions of the landscape. We had no standard of comparison, and the glaciers, peaks and valleys are so well proportioned that it is hard to judge the size of any one object. This was revealed to us only by detailed observation and by our repeated failures to estimate heights and distances. So it was that our amazement, instead of diminishing, grew greater; and our last day in the Concordia made an even greater impression on us than our first.*

They established a base camp at 16,500 feet (5030 m), close to the southern foot of K2; and from here the Duke reconnoitred all four of the ridges which combine to form the summit of the mountain.

First he attacked the southern rib (the Abruzzi Ridge) with three guides and four porters. For several days they inched their way up a succession of formidable glaciers and ice-walls, eventually reaching a height of 22,000 feet (6710 m). But the climb was too difficult technically for laden porters, and too long to attempt without them. The guides decided – rightly – that the south rib was beyond them, and the Duke decided – wisely – to accept their advice.

He next turned his attention to the west rib, which he approached via the Savoia Glacier. This was dangerous ground: 'We were now in a trough between rock and glacier, exposed to falling stones on one side and falling ice on the other. The surface of the glacier was ragged with seracs: some of them of the strangest shape, with stalactites hanging down from them like long white beards, all hollowed out and eaten away by melt, and often poised over our heads at alarming angles.' From the head of this glacier they examined the southwest and northwest ridges. Both were hopeless. 'Between this west foot of K2 and the summit there is less than a mile of horizontal distance, but more than 10,000 feet [3050 m] of vertical height. We could now see the whole of the west face of the mountain, splotched here and there with snow, but everywhere so steep no glacier could cling to it, and the hopes with which the Duke had begun the ascent were annihilated.'

Thwarted in the south and west, he returned to the Concordia, and from here ascended the upper section of the Godwin-Austen Glacier which wound up towards the mountain's easterly ramparts. From the top of this glacier he reconnoitred the northeast ridge, and ruled it too impracticable. There remained only the southeast ridge. This at first glance appeared to be not only the most spectacular but also the most inviolate of

K2 and the Chogolisa Saddle, photographed by
Vittorio Sella on the de Filippi expedition

K2's defences, and certainly the expedition did not at the time see it as a possible route. However, from a col known as Windy Gap, Sella took a number of superb photographs; several of these featured a great shoulder (of over 25,000 ft, 7625 m) hunched up in the middle of the southeast ridge, and when these were later enlarged and studied in detail it was realized that if only this shoulder could be reached, the way to the summit lay open.

At the time De Filippi wrote: 'The mountain seemed to be equally fortified on all sides against assault. After weeks of examination and hours of contemplation the Duke was finally forced to the conclusion that K2 was not to be climbed.' But he had, although he did not realize it at the time, discovered the route by which the mountain would one day be conquered. In the seeds of his defeat lay the fruits of victory.

'Though our work around K2 was finished,' wrote De Filippi, 'the Duke had no intention of withdrawing. For he still had hopes of climbing some other peak in the region which was higher than any yet attained.' In this he was encouraged by the fact that the climbing season was not yet far advanced, the guides and porters were working well, and the expedition in good health. The peak he selected was Bride Peak (25,110 ft, 7659 m) at the head of the Baltoro Glacier. 'From our camp,' wrote De Filippi, 'we looked with admiration, almost with desire, at the beautiful outline of this unattempted peak. Its great northern wall seemed to afford an easy if tedious route to the summit.' By early July the expedition had established its base camp at the foot of the north face. They then split up: the Duke, three guides and some 40 porters attempting the summit, while the remainder of the party embarked on a programme of glacial research and photogrammetric surveying.

The monsoon by now had broken, and snow was falling endlessly out of a canopy of mist-cum-cloud, although not heavily enough to keep pace with the process of melting. It was the time of avalanches.

In the base camp we could hear the thousand voices of the glacier: a continuous dripping, the murmur of little streams, the deadened rush of distant torrents, the rattle of detritus down icy slopes, the sharp crack of opening fissures. Now and then these smaller sounds would be drowned by the roar of an avalanche. These avalanches fell almost continually from the north face. Often the first ray of sunshine was enough to dislodge the snow, which fell in streams, cascades and cataracts; while in the warm part of the day, so deafening were the collapsing seracs and falling rocks it seemed as though the whole mountain was being torn asunder.

In spite of these difficulties, the glacier party carried out an extensive programme of surveying, a feature of which was their use of the Paganini photogrammetric apparatus. This consisted of a highly sophisticated camera, so calibrated that it was possible to orientate the panoramic picture which it took to a given trigonometrical point. By using this camera it was possible to complete accurately in hours (on glass plates) a survey which would normally have taken days to complete by traditional methods (on maps). The expedition's success in pioneering the use of this apparatus was by no means the least of their achievements.

The Duke, meanwhile, was climbing higher than man had ever climbed before.

Although hampered by bad weather – overcast sky, heavy snowfalls and dense mist – he managed to establish a camp on the Chogolisa saddle (20,778 ft, 6337 m) which connects Bride Peak to the Golden Throne. Much of the credit for this must go to his porters. 'The coolies,' wrote De Filippi, 'performed wonderfully well, coming up over the seracs with full loads, and living in camps on the snow without fires and contrary to all their normal habits. They adapted themselves as well as any Alpine porters.' Three of them, indeed, struggled up beyond the saddle, and succeeded in establishing an even higher camp at 21,670 feet (6609 m) on the mountain's long easterly buttress. From here the Duke and the guides, Enrico and Emilio Brocherel and Giuseppe Petigax, made two determined assaults on the summit.

On their first attempt they managed to reconnoitre what looked like a possible route – albeit between a dangerous cornice and a gaping crevasse. They reached about 23,300 feet (7107 m), then were overtaken by a storm. This continued day after day – 'strong winds and heavy unremitting snow' – and they were forced to retreat to their camp. It was six days before the sky cleared and they were able to try again.

They broke camp at 5.30 a.m. The air was lifeless, the cold numbing, the sun weak, pale and surrounded by a watery aureole of cloud – not a good augury. However, in the first hour they made excellent progress, and by 7.00 a.m. were at 23,000 feet (7015 m). Then the mist closed in. For a while they struggled on, climbing by memory, by recollection of the route they had pioneered the previous week.

They knew they had to keep midway between a cornice to their right, and a great crevasse to their left. The snow was soft and two foot deep. The gradient steep. At each step they could feel no solid ground beneath them; at every ominous creak of the snow they shied away from the crevasse and toward the cornice, until the sight of dark fissures and a chill wind warned them that they were hanging almost literally over the abyss. More than once they heard, terrifyingly close, the crack of snow detaching itself from the slope and slithering into the void. They could see no more than a few yards in any direction, but realized that bottomless gulfs were opening up around them.

By 11 o'clock they reached a rocky prominence toward which they had been climbing blind. They now stood at 24,278 feet (7405 m): higher than anyone had climbed before.

After a short rest they tackled the rockface. And here, due to the increased exertion of having to use their hands as well as their feet, they experienced difficulty in breathing, and progress was slow. However, at the end of a couple of hours, the rocks were conquered. They now hoped to find themselves on the terminal crest. Instead, to their disappointment, another indeterminate snow-slope disappeared ahead of them into the mist. To their right lay the cornice, to their left the mountain 'seemed to fall away precipitously. It would have been madness to go blindly on, up a slope of unknown direction and inclination, flanked by a crevasse and a cornice and covered in deep unstable snow.' They had reached 24,600 ft (7503 m), and the summit lay no more than 500 feet (150 m) above them; in normal conditions they could have reached it in a couple of hours, but in the mist it lay tantalizingly out of reach. They waited for two hours, 'in the hope that some fugitive wind might brush away the mists. But the weather showed no sign of improving, and at 3.30 the Duke gave the order to retreat' – a wise decision, for he had already taken unprecedented risks in climbing as far as he had.

The descent from Bride Peak marked the end of the expedition. 'There had not been a single fine day in the last two weeks, and we saw no reason to hope for better. Below 16,000 feet [4880 m] the glaciers were being visibly consumed by melt, while on the peaks themselves snow piled higher every day.' On 19 July they abandoned the Chogolisa saddle in a blinding snowstorm, and next morning the base camp, too, was dismantled, and they pulled out of the Concordia, 'the crash of avalanches accompanying our retreat, a last threat from mountains victorious but unappeased'.

The Italians failed to climb both K2 and Bride Peak, but in everything else they achieved success. They enjoyed good relations with their porters. By pioneering an important new technique of surveying, they produced excellent and detailed maps. They took photographs of outstanding artistic and technical merit. By reaching a height of 24,600 feet (7503 m), the Duke established an altitude record which was to stand for many years. They discovered the route by which K2 was eventually climbed. And – perhaps most important of all – they proved that large numbers of men, including porters, could live for weeks, and indeed months, at very high altitude. The statistics speak for themselves. For 37 days the entire expedition was camped at over 16,000 feet (4880 m); for 17 days the Duke, guides and porters were camped at over 18,000 feet (5490 m); for nine days the Duke and guides were camped at over 21,000 feet (6405 m), and for five days they were continuously camping and climbing between 21,600 and 24,600 feet (6588–7503 m). And not one of them was any the worse for the experience.

Between them, the British in 1892 and the Italians in 1909 pioneered the technique by which most of the great peaks were eventually conquered: the technique of laying seige to a mountain, and of using Nepalese porters to establish and provision a succession of high-altitude camps, from the highest of which an assault was made on the summit.

It was, however, some time before it was understood that this method of attack called for porters who were both skilful and dedicated.

British Everest expedition, 1922. Top: At breakfast and, above, camped in North Col, below the north-east shoulder

Many expeditions which attempted the major peaks between the wars failed to appreciate the importance of their porters, and this is one of the reasons why they so often failed. A man who might have prevented this was Dr Alexander Mitchell Kellas – if only his reticence and early death had not precluded the lessons he taught being fully understood. He is one of the great if improbable figures in the history of mountaineering.

He was primarily an academic: a research chemist who, in his chosen field – 'the effects of high altitude on the human system' – was the greatest authority in the world; and he conducted his researches with self-effacing enthusiasm, not only in the laboratories of the Middlesex Hospital in London, but at first hand among the peaks of the Himalaya. It is doubtful if anyone – not even the Workmans – spent as much of their lives in the mountains as Kellas did, for between 1907 and 1921 he went on no fewer than seven great journeys among the Sikkim and Kumaun Himalaya. I use the word 'journeys' rather than 'expeditions' because Kellas nearly always travelled alone: alone, that is, except for his devoted Nepalese porters, with whom he established such a bond of friendship that they eagerly met him to go climbing year after year. He was one of the earliest and greatest in a long tradition of mountaineering doctors who gave their time, their knowledge and eventually their lives, to help man reach the highest point on his planet. Every climber and every pilot who has ever used oxygen is in his debt.

One reason why he is not better known is that he was a great deal happier writing technical treatises than popular accounts of his travels. We know of the latter principally from his diary, and this is spare to the point of aridity. Here, for example, is the account which he sent to the Alpine Club of his travels in 1910:

> *April 24.   Started from Lachen, 8 days' march N of Darjeeling.*
> *"   29.   Green Lake Plain (15,400 ft [4697 m]) Snowstorm at night.*
> *May 2.   Ascend to 18,000 ft [5490 m] N. of Green Lake. No easy pass could be found.*
> *"   4.   Ascend Tent Peak icefall.*
> *"   5.   Ascend to close to summit of Nepal Gap (21,000 ft [6405 m]). Small rock-face at summit not ascended.*

It was typical of Kellas that he should get to within reach of the summit, and then not bother to climb it. He was utterly uninterested in conquests or records, and has been nicely described as not so much a mountain climber as a mountain physiologist.

> *May 7.   Tried to cross Lhunak La Pass (19,500 ft [5948 m]). But route too difficult and dangerous for laden coolies.*
> *"   10.   Start for Zemu Gap (19,300 ft [5887 m]).*
> *"   13.   Ascend and camp on summit of Simvu Saddle (17,700 ft [5399 m]). Icefall to the S. would be climbable with some difficulty.*
> *"   15.   Proceed up Tent Peak Glacier and camp on summit of pass.*
> *"   21.   Ascend to summit of Sentinel Peak (21,240 ft [6478 m]).*
> *"   25.   Ascend to Langpo Saddle, but driven back by wind, and camp at 20,700 ft [6314 m].*
> *"   26.   Ascend to near summit of Langpo Peak (22,500 ft [6863 m]) to investigate summit-ridge of Jongsong Peak. Driven back by snowstorm and thick mist.*
> *"   30.   Ascend to summit of Long Ridge Pass (19,520 ft [5954 m]).*
> *"   31.   Attempt on Chabuk La.*
> *June 5.   Cross Lungnak La and arrive at Thango. V. wet and misty, deep snow on pass.*
> *"   13.   Camp at 18,500 ft [5643 m] on Pawhunri.*
> *"   14.   Attempt on Pawhunri. Driven back by high wind at 20,700 ft [6314 m].*
> *"   15.   Move camp up to 20,000 ft [6100 m].*
> *"   16.   Ascend to summit of Pawhunri (23,180 ft [7070 m]).*

There follows a further page-and-a-half of Kellas's itinerary, which include such throw-away lines as: 'July 12. Ascend to summit of Chumiomo (22,430 ft [6841 m]) . . . August 21. Move up camp to 18,500 ft [5643 m] on Kamet, examine W. face, climb snow-peak of 20,200 ft [6161 m] . . . Ascend Doneran Peak (19,000 ft [5795 m]), and examine N. and NW. faces of Kamet.' The final entry reads simply: 'Sept 9. Leave Bombay for London.' The story that emerges from these bare facts is an astonishing one. For four months Kellas rarely camped below 14,000 feet (4270 m); and in a single season he climbed no fewer than nine peaks of over 20,000 feet (6100 m), including one of over 23,000 ft (7015 m) – a feat which would have taxed the stamina of a fully fledged team of professional climbers. Yet Kellas claimed no skill as a mountaineer, and apart from his devoted 'coolies', journeyed alone. One can think of only one other climber who has derived so much pleasure from solitary travel in high places: Eric Shipton.

Throughout the decade before World War I, Kellas continued to lead a double life, alternating between his laboratories in the Middlesex Hospital and the peaks of the Himalaya. And each year when he returned to Darjeeling he found the same local porters queing up to accompany him. One wishes he had not called them 'coolies', but more important than what he called them is what he thought of them. And there is no doubt about that. He came not only to trust and respect them, but genuinely to like them. 'Their behaviour,' he wrote, 'was excellent. By the end of the trip we were all working together most harmoniously. Really they are the most splendid fellows.' He also extolled their virtues on more practical grounds: 'Of the different types of coolie, the writer has found the Nepalese Sherpas superior to all others. They are strong, good natured if fairly treated, and since they are Buddhists there is no difficulty about special food for them – a point strongly in their favour at high altitudes.' Although he was no great mountaineer in the technical sense, Kellas gradually taught his porters the value of European techniques. In particular he overcame their aversion to being roped – an aversion which sprang from their feeling that if they were tied together they could not in an emergency go to one another's aid.

Kellas's relationship with his Sherpas was much talked about by post-war mountaineers, and when, in 1921, a British expedition to Everest at last got under way, he was given the job of recruiting porters. He had, unfortunately, only just recovered from a breakdown in health, brought about by the strain of his work for the Air Ministry during the war when, with Professor Haldane, he had been researching into the use of oxygen for high-altitude flying. Determined to get himself fit, Kellas not only embarked with enthusiasm on recruiting and training a special team of Sherpas, but also made a determined attempt to climb Kabru. He allowed himself only a week's rest between descending from Kabru and joining the team advancing on Everest, and his zeal was his undoing. He had never been strong physically – the few photographs of him depict a slightly built, pale-faced man with glasses and an academic's stoop – and on 5 June, near the Tibetan border, he died suddenly of heart failure.

He died as he had lived: unobtrusively, almost diffidently and without fuss.

Learned societies gave him a valediction. 'His death,' wrote the *Geographical Journal*, 'is a serious loss. For he possessed in a remarkable degree the power of mountain travel, coupled with enthusiasm for the scientific investigation of the physiological effect of high altitude, together with a unique talent for training coolies in mountain work.' 'His scientific studies,' wrote the *Alpine Journal*, 'were connected with problems elucidating the effect of high altitude on the human system; he was the best authority on this subject in the world . . . He often managed to get double work out of his coolies, but was always careful about their comfort and food; they trusted him and liked him . . . He [also] had a unique knowledge of the Sikkim Himalaya, and his death deprived the Mount Everest expedition of one of its most valued members.'

It is, however, doubtful if anyone at the time fully appreciated just how grievous a loss to mountaineering his death was. How often between the wars were expeditions to fail on the last couple of thousand feet, because their high camps were not sufficiently stockpiled with food and oxygen for the climbers to ride out a spell of bad weather. Kellas was the man who pioneered the use of oxygen *and* the use of high-altitude porters. It was by using the techniques which he advocated in the first two decades of the twentieth century that Everest was finally climbed in the 1950s. And although today Mallory is a household name and Kellas virtually unknown, yet it was the latter who made the greater contribution to the technique of mountaineering.

George Leigh Mallory, who died near the summit of Everest, 1924

Oxygen equipment as used in the British expedition of 1922

Memorial cairn on Everest, erected after the British expedition of 1924

Between the wars virtually all the great peaks of the Himalaya and the Karakoram were attempted, but none of over 26,000 feet (7930 m) was climbed. Prior to 1950, only two major summits had been attained: Kamet (25,447 ft, 7761 m) climbed in 1931 by Holdsworth, Lewa, Shipton and Smythe, and Nanda Devi (25,645 ft, 7822 m) climbed in 1936 by Odell and Tilman. Then something happened which opened the floodgates, and led, within the span of ten years, to *all* the giants falling one after another to the assault of mountaineers from a dozen countries:

The French climbed Annapurna.

No nation can claim a monopoly in the climbing of any particular mountain. It would, none the less, be true to say that over the years certain nations have established a special relationship with certain peaks: the French with Annapurna, the Italians with K2, the Germans with Nanga Parbat and the British with Everest. These four great mountains have been described respectively as 'the most beautiful', 'the most formidable', 'the most dangerous' and 'the most unattainable' on earth. With one

Everest, photographed by George Leigh
Mallory, 1922

exception, they were climbed only after some 50 years of blood, sweat and tears.

The exception was Annapurna, which fell at the first attempt to one of the most inspired *tours de force* in the history of mountaineering.

The French did not send many expeditions abroad; yet it was they more than any other nation who helped to bring about the great advance in the technique of climbing which took place between the wars. Names such as Allain, Charlet, de Lépiney, de Ségogne, Lagarde and Vernet may not be well known to the general public, but they are well known to mountaineers. No one doubted French expertise. Nevertheless, when their expedition arrived in India early in 1950, its objective was thought to be impossibly ambitious. The president of the French Himalayan Committee was quite specific about this objective: 'Many expeditions of many nationalities have tried to climb an 8000-metre peak. None has succeeded . . . You will attempt either Dhaulagiri [26,795 ft, 8167 m] or Annapurna [26,493 ft, 8075 m] . . . Up to now Himalayan expeditions have picked objectives in regions already known and explored. We know virtually nothing about our "eight-thousanders". The approaches to them are untrodden by Europeans; the maps of their upper reaches inaccurate. You will therefore have to do a great deal of reconnaissance work before you can launch an assault.'

It sounded, as the leader of the expedition Maurice Herzog admitted, 'a tremendous undertaking'.

The expedition crossed into Nepal early in April 1950 – the country having opened its frontier to Westerners only the previous year – and moved their 4½ tons of equipment and 1½ tons of food northward to Tansing, where they had their earliest glimpse of the Himalaya.

At first glance we could see nothing but filmy mist; then, looking more closely, we could make out in the distance a terrific wall of ice rising above the mist to an unbelievable height, and blocking the entire northern horizon for hundreds of miles. This shining wall was colossal, without break, with seven thousand-metre peaks leading up to the eight-thousanders. We were quite overwhelmed by the magnificence and grandeur of the sight.

A couple of days later the mist and cloud dispersed, and they sighted the mountain that they had decided to make their first objective.

We were woken by a shout from Noyelle: 'Look! Dhaulagiri! Dhaulagiri!'

Everyone was out in a flash, covering his nakedness with whatever came to hand – in Lachenal's case his ski-cap! An immense ice-pyramid, glittering in the sun like crystal, soared up more than 23,000 feet [7015 m] immediately above us. Its southern face, shining blue through the rising mist, was unbelievably lofty: not of this world . . . The sight was magnificent; but from a mountaineering point of view disappointing, for we could see there was not the slightest hope of an ascent via the south face.

Nor, as they were soon to discover, was there a great deal of hope on any other face.

They spent the better part of a month reconnoitring the Dhaulagiri massif, only to be thwarted time and again by stupendous walls of rock-cum-ice every bit as sheer as the north face of the Eiger and twice as high. The climbers' comments say it all: 'We were totally unprepared for the scale; everything is *far* larger than we anticipated . . . Monstrous ice-walls, and the glaciers a jumble of seracs and crevasses; Dhaulagiri isn't just difficult, it's impossible . . . I never want to set foot on the mountain again. I doubt it will *ever* be climbed.' Herzog decided to turn his attention to Annapurna.

Dhaulagiri and Annapurna lie side by side, separated only by the narrow slit of the most spectacular valley in the world, the Kali Gandaki. The two massifs, however, are totally different, for whereas Dhaulagiri is a simple pyramid, Annapurna is a complex ridge: a ridge which is ten miles (16 km) long, five miles (8 km) wide and has many summits – 40 of over 23,000 feet (7015 m), the highest being invisible from the south. So before the French could climb Annapurna they had to find it. And both finding and climbing needed to be done in less than a month, because of the approaching monsoon. It seemed an impossible task.

It was mid-May as the expedition retraced its steps down the Kali Gandaki, then cut eastward into a 'savage and desolate cirque of mountains never before seen by man'. They climbed steadily to 17,000 feet (5185 m), roping the route for their Sherpas. Above 17,000 the ascent became more difficult – 'soon we were holding onto a blade-thin ridge of rock, with our feet dangling free; beneath us the precipice fell near-sheer.' That night, the night of 19 May, they were obliged to pitch their tents on a small, sloping, ice-coated ledge of rock; to stop themselves rolling over the precipice as they slept, they belayed their sleeping-bags to the ice with pitons. Next morning it was snowing hard, but they struggled on, and by 21 May had managed to establish a base camp at the foot of the North Annapurna Glacier. For a couple of days the weather was bad, then they woke one morning to find the sky miraculously clear.

'I can see a route!' Lachenal shouted.

Herzog, scrambling out of his tent, found himself almost blinded by the glare.

For the first time [he wrote] *Annapurna was revealing its secrets. The huge north face, with its great rivers of ice, shone and sparkled in the sunlight. Never had I seen so impressive a mountain. It was a world both dazzling and menacing, and the eye was lost in its immensities. But for once we were not being confronted with vertical walls and hanging glaciers which put an end to all thoughts of climbing. Lachenal was pointing: 'If only we could get to the foot of that sickle-shaped glacier . . .'*

That afternoon they radioed to Paris: 'Following reconnaissance, have decided to attempt the summit via North Annapurna Glacier. Route entirely snow and ice. Weather favourable. Have good hopes.' And within an hour, four climbers – Herzog,

Lachenal, Rébuffat and Terray – were setting out to establish Camp I.

The reconnaissance had become an assault.

What happened next is usually told from the point of view of the climbers, and it tends to be forgotten that the high drama of the assault would have ended in high tragedy if the Base Camp and Camps I, II and III had not been swiftly stockpiled with equipment, food and medical supplies by the almost superhuman efforts of the Sherpas, many of whom, when the assault began, were still some 25 miles (40 km) away and some 10,000 feet (3050 m) lower in the Kali Gandaki. There were, in other words, two simultaneous races against the clock: the climbers racing to gain the summit before they were overtaken by the monsoon, and the Sherpas racing to stockpile the lower camps so that the climbers would have a haven to fall back on. The former could never have survived, let alone succeeded, without the latter.

There was not a breath of wind as the four-man assault party struck out across the North Annapurna Glacier.

With the sun vertically above us, the basin was like a furnace, every ray being reflected back from the surface of the snow. Walking soon became a dull agony. Our faces pasted with anti-sunburn cream, we sweated profusely and felt as though we were being suffocated. Burdened with heavy loads, we had to call on all our resolution not to give way to breathlessness and lassitude.

In the course of the next week they established four camps between 16,750 feet (5109 m), at the foot of the big north glacier, and 23,500 feet (7168 m), on the east flank of the smaller, sickle-shaped glacier pointed out by Lachenal as a possible route; and each time they set up a camp, the Sherpas struggled through, either with them or behind them, to provision it. There were many moments of danger; at one place they had to cross a couloir down which seracs were 'crashing with a hideous din . . . the almost continual rumble of avalanches put us all on edge.' There were moments of difficulty; on one particularly intransigent ice-wall it took them all their strength and all their technical skill to climb a couple of dozen feet in an hour. And there were moments of beauty and elation: 'The air was luminous, the light tinted a most delicate blue. Ridges of bare ice refracted the light like prisms and sparkled with rainbow hues. The weather was fine – not a single cloud, and the air still and dry. I felt in splendid form: at peace with myself and the world. Was this, I wondered, the quintessence of happiness?'

There was, however, little happiness above Camp IV.

On 2 June Herzog and Lachenal emerged on to the great 40° *arête* which leads up via the east peak of Annapurna to the summit. Ahead of them they saw a rib of bare rock which looked like a possible camp-site from which, next day, they could launch their final assault. The following is Herzog's description of Camp V:

We had the feeling that we were climbing across an enormous roof; the slope was uniform, and though it was at an angle of some 40° we were able to crampon up it. Every ten yards we halted, in cold so intense that our feet grew numb. But we couldn't risk delay: 'On to Camp V' became a compulsive refrain. The going was unbelievably exhausting, for the crust of the snow broke beneath our crampons, and we sank up to our knees with every step. With a final spurt of energy we gained the rib of rock.

But what a disappointment! The rocks turned out to be glazed deep in ice; there were no ledges, no holds; we would have to camp on the bare slope . . . With our axes we did our best to make a level space; but about every thirty seconds I had to rest, for I felt as though I was being suffocated, my breathing was out of control and my heart pounding . . . An hour later the shelf was ready, and we tethered the tent to two pitons which Lachenal drove into cracks in the rock . . . We knew it would be a grim night; for the camp site was dangerous and unstable. Driven by wind, snow slid down the arête and piled up against the upper side of the tent. We hoped its weight wouldn't dislodge it. For we knew that our pitons driven into the rock and our ice-axes driven into the snow gave us little more than moral support, and that the tent, and ourselves with it, could all too easily be swept into the abyss.

Our minds worked slowly that night. We couldn't concentrate; conversation lagged; and it was only with the greatest difficulty – and because we urged one another on – that we managed to make some tea and swallow our pills. After dark a fierce wind sprang up, making the nylon-fabric of the tent flap noisily; at each gust we clung in terror to the tent-pole, as drowning men to a straw.

Herzog, on the upper side of the tent, spent the night with the snow as it accumulated above him becoming heavier and heavier, until he felt he was being slowly suffocated. Lachenal, on the lower side, spent the night convinced that any moment he was about to tumble 3000 feet (914 m) down the precipice beneath them. They had virtually no sleep, and at dawn were so exhausted they did not have the energy to prepare themselves a meal or even a hot drink. They simply struggled into their climbing boots, swallowed 'a handful' of Maxiton tablets, and set out, unroped, for the summit. Maxiton has the effect of keeping fatigue at bay for five or six hours. It is an effective short-term stimulant, but if taken in excess it brings about 'a kind of uncaring euphoria' – which may help to explain some of the events of the next 48 hours.

The ascent from Camp V to the summit did not present any technical difficulties; it was more like a very steep walk than a climb. It was, however, 'unbelievably exhausting, every step a struggle of mind over matter'. By midday, after climbing for six hours, Herzog and Lachenal were approaching the little couloir which ran up to the summit, but by now they were in the last stages of exhaustion, their feet were frost-bitten, and they were suffering from hallucinations. 'It was,' wrote Herzog, 'as though I was standing outside myself, and watching our paltry efforts from another world. There was no gravity. The landscape was diaphanous. This wasn't the mountain I knew on which I was standing: it was the mountain of my dreams.'

They struggled on to the summit a little after 2.00 p.m. 'It consisted of a corniced crest of ice, and the precipices on the far [southern] side, which fell away vertically beneath us, were terrifying. Clouds floated half-way down them, concealing the fertile valley which lay 23,000 feet [7015 m] below, almost at our feet.'

They photographed one another and the little French flag, stained with sweat and food, which they had brought with them. Then they began the descent. It was now their troubles started.

'My gloves!

'I saw them sliding down the arête. I stood quite still, stunned, as they glissaded on and on, without stopping. I knew that their loss meant: a race with death. I hurried on, trying to catch up with Lachenal. I felt as though I was running, though I knew that I must in fact be walking slowly, pausing every few paces to pant for breath.' Lachenal ploughed on ahead. His feet were without sensation, and he had a horror – perhaps a premonition – of his frost-bitten toes having to be amputated. It grew colder – and darker. Soon the two men were enveloped in cloud, and lost sight of one another.

Herzog almost fell over Camp V before he saw it, and it was several seconds before he realized that there was now not one tent but two. Rébuffat and Terray had climbed up to join them.

'We made it!' I gasped. 'We're back from the summit.'

Terray, speechless with delight, wrung my hand. But his smile quickly vanished. There was a terrible silence, as he saw that my hands were stained violet and white, and hard as marble.

'Where's Biscante?'

I mumbled that he was somewhere ahead of me; and they looked at one another anxiously.
'Help! Help!'

I was so intoxicated with success, and so remote from reality that I heard nothing. But the others heard, and rushing out saw Biscante Lachenal – minus his ice-axe, gloves, balaclava and one of his crampons – spreadeagled in the snow. He had fallen several hundred feet, and was frost-bitten and concussed. The others helped him back to the tents.

Throughout the night Rébuffat and Terray worked desperately on their friends, massaging their frost-bitten hands and feet in an effort to restore circulation. 'Outside the wind howled and the snow fell; and once again we had to cling to the poles to prevent the tents being carried away . . . That night was absolute hell.' The next morning the storm had deepened to a gale-force blizzard. There could, however, be no thought of sitting it out, for they realized that the one hope of saving Herzog's and Lachenal's lives was to get them to the doctor 5000 feet (1525 m) below in Camp II – and quickly. So the four of them set out, with only two ice-axes between them, and the snow so thick they could not see from one end of their rope to the other. At first they made fair progress, but by midday the wind had dropped and the snow thickened; mist began to close in, and soon they were unable to see where they were going. Sinking up to their waists in the wet snow, and at intervals giving concerted shouts for help, they searched frantically for Camp IV where they knew other members of the expedition would be waiting.

The light faded. The temperature dropped. And the four men's expectation of life ebbed gradually away. Suddenly Lachenal gave a cry of fear, and vanished. He had fallen into a crevasse. This, however, turned out to be no more than 15 feet (4.5 m) deep, a natural cave of ice, a haven. It was the miracle which each of them had prayed for. They half-crawled, half-slid into the ice-cave, and huddled together for warmth, stuffing their feet into their one and only sleeping-bag. They passed another terrible night, each of them withdrawing into a private world of his own. Rébuffat and Terray again worked tirelessly to try and massage life into their companions' frozen-solid hands and feet, oblivious to the fact that their own were badly frost-bitten.

At dawn came the last straw: a mini-avalanche cascaded into the ice-cave, completely burying them. As the others fought their way out and lifted Herzog clear, he whispered, 'I'm dying.' But his companions' condition was very nearly as parlous, for they found, to their horror, that they were snow-blind.

Again the expectation of life – but not the will to live – ebbed out of them. Herzog was convinced that the end was near, 'but it was the end that every mountaineer would wish for. I was conscious of gratitude that the mountains were so beautiful on my last day. "It's all over for me," I said to Terray. "You three go on. You still have a chance." ' But they refused to leave him. The sun was mercifully warm and, the blind and the maimed helping one another as best they could, they unearthed their equipment, struggled into their boots, and started shouting for help. Herzog was now on the point of death. His mind was wandering: 'I had visions of shady slopes, peaceful paths and the scent of pine woods. It was all very pleasant . . . Suddenly I heard a shout. "They're coming!" And there was Schatz, waist-deep in snow, ploughing his way slowly towards us like a boat through heavy seas. The shock was too much.' He came to in Schatz's arms, but he could not feel the warmth of the embrace that enveloped him or the breath that revived him, for he was frozen solid.

The survivors were carried to Camp IV, which in fact was only a few hundred yards from the ice-cave. They were reprieved, but not yet saved, for they had, somehow, to descend another 4000 feet (1220 m) before they got to the doctor and the comparative safety of Camp II.

They started at once: preferring to face the possibility of avalanches (all too likely after a night of heavy snow and a morning of warm sun), to the probability of Herzog and Lachenal dying through lack of medical attention. The descent, for the injured men, was agony. The blind had to be led almost every step: as Herzog lowered himself by ropes over the ice-fall, the skin was torn in great strips from his frost-bitten hands; and a little below Camp III they started an avalanche.

Again a miracle saved them.

Suddenly a crack appeared in the snow under the very feet of the Sherpas. The crack grew wider and longer. A mad idea flashed through my mind: if only I could climb back up the rope to the safety of solid ground! Then an elemental force flung me head over heels. My head crashed into the ice. Snow enveloped me, making it impossible to breathe. I was spun round and round like a puppet. As in a kaleidoscope, I saw flashes of brilliant sunlight through the snow that was pouring past my eyes. The rope joining me to the Sherpas coiled round my neck. Again and again I crashed into solid ice as the avalanche swept me down through the seracs. Suddenly the rope tightened, and I was brought to a stop. In an uncontrollable spasm I passed water, and lost consciousness . . . Opening my eyes, I found I was swinging to and fro, upside down, the rope coiled round my neck and my left leg, in a chimney of blue ice. I managed to stop the pendulum motion, by jamming my elbows into the ice-chimney, and saw, falling away beneath me, the precipices of the couloir. I simply had to get myself out. My hands and feet were useless; but by jerking this way and that, I managed to right myself; then I began to lever myself up, inch by inch, with my elbows . . . I felt something tug at the far end of the rope . . . I looked up, and saw two frightened faces framed against the circle of the sky. The Sherpas were safe, and had come to rescue me . . . At last I was out, and collapsed face-down in the snow . . . The rope had been caught on a ridge of ice, and the Sherpas and I had hung suspended in mid-air from either end of it. It we hadn't been checked, we would have hurtled down another 1500 feet [458 m] to certain death.

The avalanche had catapulted them to within sight of Camp II, and a rescue team struggled up to meet them. By evening everyone was crowded into tents at the side of the North Annapurna Glacier. But what a state they were in, especially Herzog.

The doctor examined me first. My limbs were completely numb well beyond my ankles and wrists. My hands were in a really bad way; there was practically no skin left, and what little there was hung down in long black strips; my fingers were swollen and grotesquely distorted. My feet were not much better; the soles were completely brown and violet, without feeling . . . In my arms and legs my blood pressure was virtually nil.

'What do you think?' I asked him.

'It's pretty serious,' he replied. 'I'm afraid you may lose part of your hands and feet.'

What Doctor Oudot did not tell his patient was that it was not only his hands and feet he feared for; it was his life. He injected the climbers' arteries with zetylcholin in an effort to stimulate the recirculation of blood; he put dressings over their eyes to counter ophthalmia; he and his companions worked late into the night, massaging, anaesthetizing and comforting the injured men. The smell of ether was everywhere. Next day, to stave off gangrene, he began a course of the most agonizing injections: injections which led to convulsions and delirium, and revealed that Herzog's blood was 'thick, clotted and black: black as a black pudding'. The injections were so painful that brave men sobbed in agony and had to be held down by force, but they saved the climbers' lives.

A couple of days later, on 6 June, Camp II was evacuated, and the expedition

A glacial stream in the Himalayan foothills

Flora of the Himalaya, drawn by Joseph Hooker: (top left) Meconopsis Simplicifolia or blue poppy (top right) Rhododendron Thomsoni (above left) Magnolia Campbellii (above right) Rhododendron Nivale – probably the highest-growing shrub in the world

RHODODENDRON DALHOUSIAE, Hook. fil.
(in its native locality.)

Rhododendron Dalhousie in its native locality, from Joseph Hooker's journals

Travellers in Nepal often inscribed prayers on the wayside rocks, thus creating impromptu shrines

began yet another race against time: a race to struggle clear of the mountains before conditions made it impossible to travel. 'Three injured men had to be carried all the way on stretchers, and another two could walk only with assistance. There were miles of glacier to cover, rock precipices to climb down, interminable slopes of scree and moraine to traverse, a major river and a 13,000-foot [3965 m] pass to cross – all in the monsoon.' It was a nightmare journey, with the devoted and self-effacing Sherpas 'weaving yet another leaf into their chaplet of fame'; in the difficult places – and a great many places were difficult – they carried the injured men on their backs.

At last the expedition struggled through to comparative safety in the valley of the Kali Gandaki. But by now Lachenal's feet and Herzog's hands were gangrenous, 'giving off the most nauseating stench, and soaked in puss'. On the last terrible stage of their journey – carried on stretchers through teaming rain and enervating heat – all Lachenal's toes, one by one, had to be amputated. In the same way Herzog lost all his toes and all his fingers. Annapurna had been conquered – but at what cost.

Maurice Herzog subsequently spent the better part of a year in the American Hospital at Neuilly, learning, without bitterness, to live a new and very different life. During his convalescence he dictated – he could not, of course, write – an account of his expedition which he called simply *Annapurna*. *Annapurna*, like De Filippi's *Karakoram and the Western Himalaya*, is a classic: the Italian's book is scholarly, scientific, authoritative and cerebral, the Frenchman's exciting, individualistic, passionate and, at times, uncomfortably honest. Between them these two books say just about all that there is to be said about mountaineering.

Before the conquest of Annapurna, virtually none of the major peaks had been climbed. Within five years of Herzog's success virtually all had been climbed: K2, Makalu, Nanga Parbat, Kangchenjunga, Everest. It was as though the French had broken a psychological barrier.

It was, fittingly, the Italians who were first to the summit of K2.

K2 derives its name from the symbol used by Montgomerie when he first triangulated the peak: Karakoram Peak No. 2. 'Karakoram' is a Turkish word meaning 'black rubble' – a strange misnomer for the world's most beautifully glaciated range. Several alternative names for the mountain have been put forward, the most widely canvassed being Mount Godwin Austen (after the man who first surveyed its environs), and Chogori (from the Balti – the language of Baltistan – *chogo* = big and *ri* = mountain). However, Montgomerie's symbol has now become generally accepted, even by the people of the nearest village who call the mountain – as they have heard successive expeditions call it – 'Ke Tu'. Its height is 28,253 feet (8611 m), which makes it the highest peak in the Karakoram, and the second highest in the world. From the climbers' point of view it has the advantage of being sited in territory which for most of the time has been politically accessible, and the disadvantage of being technically difficult.

The first attempt to climb the peak was made in 1902 by a multi-national expedition of experienced British, Austrian and Swiss alpinists. They had no idea what a task they were taking on, and after struggling with some difficulty up the Godwin Austen Glacier, were forced to withdraw by heavy snow and a mild outbreak of influenza. In retrospect, one can see that they never had a chance in a million of reaching the summit, and it was a pity that the suggestion of attempting the nearby peak of Skyang Kangri (24,750 ft, 7549 m), put forward by the Austrians Pfannl and Wessely, was not taken up.

The second attempt was by the Duke of the Abruzzi. This, as we have seen,

Two celebrated Italian climbers: (left) Professor Ardito Desio and (above) the Duke of Spoleto

achieved just about everything except the actual summit.

In 1929 the Italians were back again, this time led by the Duke of Spoleto, a nephew of Abruzzi's. This was one of those cumbersome expeditions, beloved by planners between the wars, the sheer size of which precluded the success that can sometimes come from mobility. Little new climbing was done, but useful scientific research was carried out by the expedition's geologist, Professor Ardito Desio.

1938 saw an assault by the Americans led by Charles Houston. This was a well organized and eminently sensible expedition which failed, through inexperience, to take advantage of the unusually fine weather which it enjoyed. The Americans reached the foot of the mountain as early as 12 June, and if they had immediately attempted the summit via the Abruzzi Ridge, they might have succeeded. As it was, apparently not trusting the judgement of previous expeditions, they spent more than three weeks reconnoitring other possible routes. By the time they turned their attention to the southeast (Abruzzi) ridge in earnest, they had one eye on the approaching monsoon. The Abruzzi ridge cannot be hurried; it is a steep, dangerous and technically difficult combination of ice and rock, and can only be climbed by porters if they are provided with fixed ropes. It took the Americans a fortnight to climb it, rope it, and establish a succession of adequately stocked camps. By the time Houston and Petzoldt were poised at 25,000 feet (7625 m) to attempt the final summit-pyramid, the monsoon was overdue. The two climbers pushed on for a further thousand feet, then decided that discretion was the better part of valour, and turned back; K2 was evacuated. The monsoon, for once, broke 'not with a bang but a whimper', and the Americans were left with the feeling that perhaps fame had been theirs for the taking, but they had turned their backs on it.

Houston has been accused of being 'over-cautious', but the fate of his successor, Fritz Wiessner, proves, in my opinion, that he made the right decision.

Wiessner was the leader of another American expedition which tackled K2 the following year. His team consisted of six American climbers and nine Sherpa 'Tigers' led by Pasang Kikuli. They were plagued from the start by bad weather and sickness – one climber developing heart trouble, another being unable to acclimatize, and a third being severely frost-bitten. In this diminution of the 'sahibs' lay the seeds of tragedy.

Wiessner followed the well-tried route via the Abruzzi Ridge and the southwest shoulder, and by mid-July had established and provisioned a chain of camps up to 24,700 feet (7534 m). On 19 July he and Pasang made their first attempt on the summit, but were thwarted by a sheer rockface. As they returned that evening to their camp, Pasang fell, and his crampons went crashing 5000 feet (1525 m) on to the Godwin Austen Glacier. A couple of days later they tried again, only to be thwarted a second time by rocks not merely vertical but overhanging. They gave up, expecting to be able to retreat via well-stocked camps occupied by their colleagues. Instead, to their horror, they found some camps evacuated, and others occupied by sick men already short of food. There seems to have been a complete break-down in communication, which led to near-panic, nobody knowing who was in charge and the camps being unnecessarily abandoned. Wiessner himself, frost-bitten and in the last stages of exhaustion, managed to struggle to safety, but the American Dudley Wolfe found himself marooned in Camp VII, and he, and three of the Sherpa 'Tigers' who quixotically tried to rescue him, perished.

At the time Wiessner was severely criticized. 'It is difficult to record in temperate language the folly of this enterprise,' writes Kenneth Mason. 'From 11th July until the end of the month each day added to the errors of judgement. The one redeeming feature was the heroism of the Sherpas.' In recent years, attempts have been made to exonerate Wiessner. He was a brave man and a brilliant mountaineer, but there is no getting away from the fact that he was the leader of an expedition where leadership failed.

In 1953 the Americans tried again. And failed again – this time because of the tragic illness of one of their assault party. They arrived on the mountain in mid-June, rather too late for comfort, and since they had with them inexperienced Hunza porters rather than Sherpas, they took a long time to provision their camps up the Abruzzi Ridge. Nevertheless, by 1 August they had not only established an unusually high camp near the base of the final pyramid, they had also managed to man it with eight skilled climbers and stockpile it with sufficient food for 12 days. Success seemed certain. Then a blizzard set in, and continued unabated day after day. Soon one of the climbers became dangerously ill. On 4 August Arthur Gilkey complained of pain in his leg, and when he tried to put his full weight on it, he fainted. Houston diagnosed thrombo-phlebitis, and realizing that the one hope of saving Gilkey's life was to get him down quickly, they abandoned all thought of the summit. However, when they tried to descend, dragging the injured man behind them, wrapped in the torn remnants of a tent, the blizzard forced them back. For six nightmare days they were confined to their tents, becoming gradually weaker and more dehydrated, while the phlebitis spread to both Gilkey's legs and the blood clots to his lungs. On 10 August the weather was no better but they decided they could not simply lie in their sleeping-bags and watch Gilkey die.

So we wrapped him again in sleeping-bag and tent, and set out in the raging storm. It was a desperate attempt, but there was no alternative. First we dragged him through the deep snow, then we lowered him over a steep ridge and on to the ice-slope. After many hours of exhausting work, we had descended little more than 400 feet (120 m), and realized we would have to spend the night on the small ledge at Camp VII.

We had just lowered Art over a steep cliff, when one of us slipped. We were climbing in pairs, but in some miraculous way our ropes must have crossed and become entangled. Five of us were jerked off the cliff-face. Pete Schoening, who was holding the rope by which we were lowering Art, had the only strong belay, and somehow he held us all. But Bell had fallen more than 200 feet [40 m], and the rest of us little less. Again by some miracle none of us was badly hurt, although Houston was unconscious and Bell had badly frozen hands, having lost his gloves in the fall.

Those of us who were able, made our way to Camp VII and managed to set up a tent on the tiny platform there. We then helped the casualties into the tent. Art meanwhile had been left securely anchored to the snow-slope by two ice-axes. While we were getting the others into the tent we were able to shout back and forth to Art, who was some 200 feet away over a small rise, though we couldn't hear what he was saying above the roar of the wind.

Rescuing the others took about half an hour, and then the three of us who could still move went back to try and do something for Art. We knew we wouldn't be able to move him, but we hoped to cut a level ledge in the slope and make him as comfortable as we could for the night. He wasn't there.

At first we couldn't believe our eyes; it was only gradually, as we stared at the soft and unbroken surface of the snow, that we realized a small avalanche must have swept him away.

The death of Arthur Gilkey was almost certainly an accident. But there is another remote possibility which ought perhaps to be mentioned: could he have pulled out the ice-axes and let himself slide to his death? If he did, then his action – like that of Captain Oates – was that of 'a very gallant gentleman', for by his death he gave the others the chance of life. Another member of the expedition, H. R. A. Steather, in an article in the *Alpine Journal*, made the point very clearly: 'Once over the shock of having lost Art, we realized that his passing was a miraculous deliverance from a situation which might well have meant disaster for all of us. If we had continued the attempt to carry him down over the increasingly difficult climbing below, it is most improbable that we could have avoided further and even more serious accidents.'

As it was, the seven climbers managed somehow to claw their way to safety in the teeth of the blizzard. It took them five days, Bell's feet were so badly frost-bitten that he had at times to be carried; Houston was so concussed that he had most of the time to be helped. But they survived: thanks to 'a magnificent feat of mountaineering which borders on the miraculous'.

The following year – 1954 – 'the Mountain of Mountains' was conquered at last.

The Italian expedition which first climbed K2 had much in common with the British expedition which first climbed Everest. Both were big, heavily subsidized and meticulously equipped; both were combined efforts, with the final climbers being, as it were, 'hoist on to the summit on the shoulders of their team-mates'; and both were led by a man who was not only a first-class mountaineer, but was a brilliant organizer.

The Italian expedition of 1954 reached the Concordia early in June, but instead of the usual relatively fine weather they were greeted by '40 days of almost non-stop storm'; their porters deserted, and one of their finest climbers, Mario Puchoz, died of pneumonia. The omens were not propitious. However, by the end of July the Abruzzi Ridge was again dotted with camps; these were linked one to another by fixed ropes, and a windlass set up between Camps I and V was winching up supplies at the rate of 100 feet (30 m) a minute. 'Life in these tiny camps, spread out like eagles' nests on the spur, was terrible,' wrote their leader Ardito Desio. 'The continuous and violent shaking of the walls of the tents, the difficulty of making even the simplest meal, the prolonged immobility of men confined to a very restricted place, the intense cold: all this was unbelievably wearing both physically and mentally.' By 28 July Camp IX had been established at 25,250 feet (7700 m), on the very spot where the Americans had camped the year before. However, the Italians then proceeded to set up an even higher camp, at the foot of the final pyramid, and it was from here, a couple of days later, that Compagnoni and Lacedelli launched their assault.

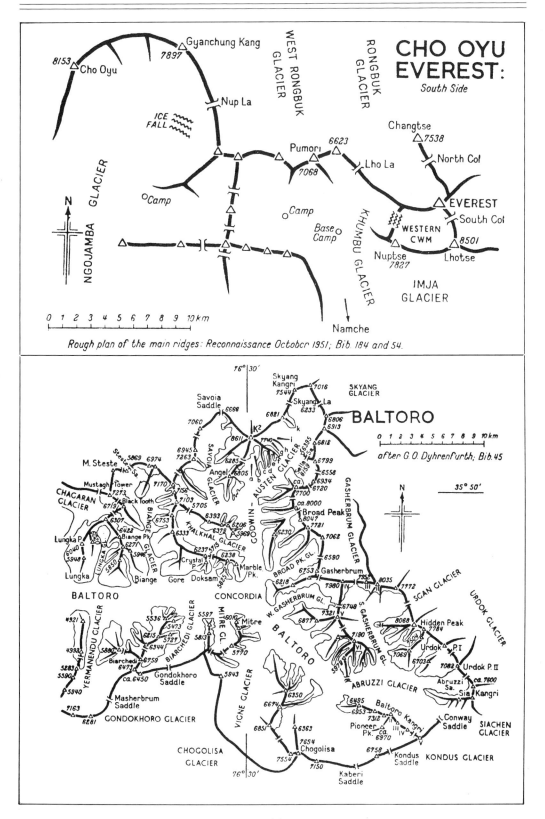

CHO OYU
EVEREST:
South Side

Gyanchung Kang 7897

8153 Cho Oyu

WEST RONGBUK GLACIER

RONGBUK GLACIER

Nup La

ICE FALL

Changtse △7538

North Col

Pumori 6623 △

7068

Lho La

NGOJAMBA GLACIER

N

○ Camp

○ Camp

Base Camp

KHUMBU GLACIER

EVEREST

South Col

8501

WESTERN CWM

Nuptse 7827

Lhotse

IMJA GLACIER

0 1 2 3 4 5 6 7 8 9 10 km

Namche

Rough plan of the main ridges: Reconnaissance October 1951; Bib. 184 and 54.

76° 30′

Skyang Kangri 7544 △ 7016

Skyang La

SKYANG GLACIER

Savoia Saddle 6668

7060

6821

Skyang 6233

6806 6913

BALTORO

K2 8611 7790

0 1 2 3 4 5 6 7 8 9 10 km

after G. O. Dyhrenfurth; Bib. 45

M. Steste 5869 6974

Steste

6945 7263

SAVOIA GLACIER

6285

6818

6135

6799

6558

6934 6720

35° 50′

N

Mustagh Tower 7273

CHAGARAN GLACIER

Black Tooth 6719

6307

Biange Pk 6271

6422

7170

7156

7103

5705

6753

6393

6206 6319

6333

5959

ca 8000

7700

GODWIN-AUSTEN GLACIER

ca. 7800

Broad Peak 8047 7781

7062

GASHERBRUM GLACIER

Angel 6805

Lungka P. 6040

5948

Lungka

BIANGE GLACIER

KHALKHAL GLACIER

5850

6237 5716 6238

Crystal

Gore Doksam

Marble Pk.

6230

5813

6218

6590

BROAD PK. GL.

Gasherbrum 6753

7980 IV

III 8035

7172

SGAN GLACIER

URDOK GLACIER

BALTORO

Biange

CONCORDIA

W. GASHERBRUM GL.

S. GASHERBRUM GL.

6877 7321 V

6748

8068 Hidden Peak 7784

Urdok P.I

7069

6703

7082 Urdok P. II ca. 7600

4921

5536 5597

5473 5731

6060 Mitre

MITRE GL.

5770

BIARCHEDI GLACIER

YERMANENDU GLACIER

4932

5285 5390

5940

6215 5800

Biarchedi 6759 6473

6344

ca. 6450

Gondokhoro Saddle

5943

VIGNE GLACIER

BALTORO

VI 5979

7190

ABRUZZI GLACIER

Urdok Sa. Sia Kangri

7163 6281

Masherbrum Saddle

GONDOKHORO GLACIER

6350

6674

6495 6953 7318

Baltoro Kangri

Pioneer Pk. 6970

Conway Saddle

SIACHEN GLACIER

6851

6363

CHOGOLISA GLACIER

76° 30′

7654 Chogolisa

7554 7150

Kaberi Saddle

6758 Kondus Saddle

KONDUS GLACIER

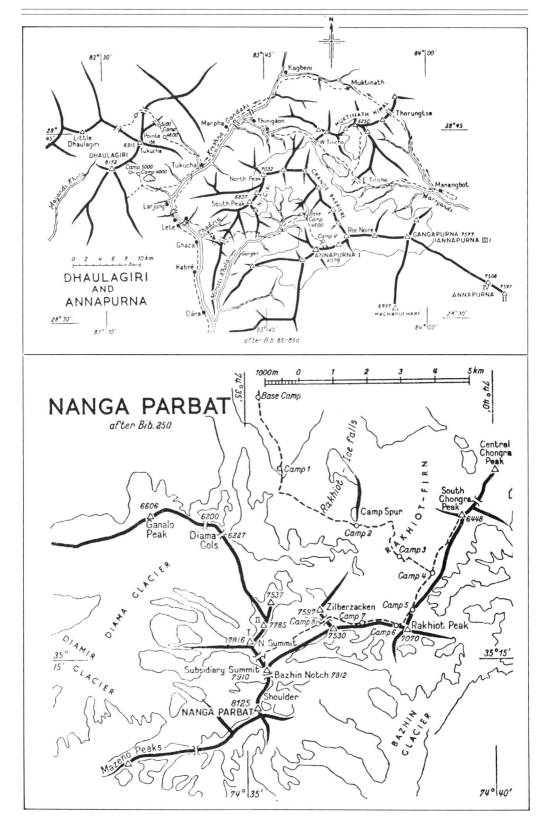

Their first obstacle was the steep couloir which notches the lower rockface of the pyramid. Compagnoni's attempt to climb it ended in near disaster, for he fell the better part of 100 feet – fortunately into soft snow. Eventually Lacedelli managed to claw his way to the top, and the two men emerged on to a steep slope, menaced by great overhanging slabs covered with snow which looked liable to avalanche any moment. Sinking in up to their hips, they traversed first the slope, then the slabs. The latter were so difficult that Lacedelli was forced to remove his gloves, and it took them an hour to climb 50 feet (15 m). Soon fog added to their difficulties, and they were reduced to picking their way near-blind over the ice encrusted rock. *At last*, wrote Desio,

> *a gust of wind swept the fog aside, enabling them to see a series of humps which seemed to lead up to the summit. At this moment both men felt as though they were being suddenly suffocated; a strange warmth enveloped their bodies, and their legs became so weak they could hardly stand. Their oxygen was exhausted. Realizing what had happened, they tore off their masks, and sucked in great gulps of ice-cold air. After some minutes, having assured themselves that their minds were clear and their muscles responsive, they continued climbing – though with great effort. Each moment it seemed the summit was only a few yards ahead; but as soon as they reached the top of one hump, another appeared in front of them. The fog by now had lifted, and a bitter wind lacerated their faces. It was 6 p.m. before they realized the slope was falling away in front of them, and the horizon opening out in every direction.*
>
> *At last, the summit!*
>
> *Filled with joy, they embraced one another, and raised the flags of Italy and Pakistan* [K2 is situated in the Pakistani province of Baltistan.] . . . *They remained on top of the mountain for half an hour, taking photographs. By the time they started down, night was falling.*

As Herzog and Lachenal had discovered on Annapurna, great peaks can be more dangerous to descend than ascend – due partly to the climbers' false euphoria, and partly to cumulative fatigue. The Italians did not so much climb down as tumble down. Within an hour, Compagnoni had fallen 50 feet (15 m), in the process being swept over a gaping crevasse, and next day he fell again, rolling over and over for 600 feet (183 m), only coming to rest in a patch of wet snow on the very edge of the great eastern precipice (5000 ft, 1525 m). Between them they fell on no fewer than six occasions during the descent, and by the time they reached the foot of the Abruzzi Ridge, both were covered in bruises, were badly frost-bitten, and in the last stages of exhaustion. But theirs was the satisfaction of having conquered what many climbers regard as the most formidable of the giants.

The mountaineering phase of the expedition was over, but much of the scientific programme remained, and in the course of the next six weeks the Italians completed an extensive photogrammetrical survey; they also did valuable research in glaciology, morphology and terrestrial magnetism.

Desio sums up their achievements with disarming modesty. 'The basic plan of the expedition, in spite of unfavourable weather, was carried out, with results which I leave the reader to judge. This was due to the enthusiasm, self-sacrifice and discipline of the whole party, and to the efforts of previous mountaineers who had opened up a route along the Abruzzi Ridge.' Some readers, however, may feel that an additional reason for the expedition's success was their leader's flair for meticulous planning.

◆

As the Italians concentrated on K2, the Germans concentrated on Nanga Parbat.

Nanga Parbat is the most westerly buttress of the Himalaya, divided from the

Hindu Kush by the gorge of the Indus. It derives its name from the Sanskrit '*nanga parvata*', meaning 'naked mountain'. It is 26,661 feet (8126 m) in height, and, when viewed from the west, is probably the most spectacular mountain on earth, for it rises near-sheer from the bed of the Indus for 23,000 feet (7015 m): that is, $4\frac{1}{2}$ miles of vertical height in little more than half a mile of horizontal distance, $4\frac{1}{2}$ miles plunging, to all intents and purposes, vertically from the summit ridge, down through fields of ice and snow, down precipices and glaciers, down overhangs and rock-walls, down through scrub and scree and into a gorge which is 100 times more terrifying than the Grand Canyon – a suffocating, rock-bound desert, where nothing grows and nothing lives, and the gneiss disintegrates in an average summer temperature of over 120°F (49°C). This, as Vigne wrote 150 years ago, 'is the most awful and most magnificent sight to be met with in the Himalayas.'

Nanga Parbat was the first of the 8000-m peaks to be attempted. As early as 1895, three experienced British alpinists (Mummery, Hastings and Norman Collie), together with a Gurkha officer (Major Bruce) accompanied by two of his regiment, surveyed the southern face of the mountain and decided it 'not even worth considering'. They then moved round to the north, which struck them as 'more promising'. They carried out some sound reconnaissance on the Diamir Glacier before Collie was taken ill and Bruce's leave expired and he was obliged to return to his regiment. It is obvious from what happened next that Mummery under-estimated the difficulties facing him, for with his depleted party he decided to attempt the summit via the northwest face. He was a fine rock climber, and managed to reach 20,000 feet (6100 m), when one of the Gurkhas who was with him succumbed to altitude sickness. The attempt on the summit was therefore abandoned, and the party split up, Collie and Hastings descending via the route up which they had come, while Mummery and the Gurkhas decided to reconnoitre a col a little to the east. On 24 August the three men set out for the col – and were never seen again.

It is usually assumed that they were the victims of an avalanche; but although their companions searched for them, their bodies were never found. 'The tragic and unexplained disappearance of this famous climber and his brave Gurkhas,' wrote the well known mountaineer G. O. Dyhrenfurth, 'aroused almost as much interest at the time as the disappearance of Mallory or Irvine 30 years later.'

Other and greater tragedies were to follow.

It was 37 years before another major expedition attempted Nanga Parbat. Then in 1932 a German–American team under Willy Merkl made a determined assault which, although it did not succeed, managed to pioneer a possible route to the summit. Merkl's team consisted of climbers who had plenty of alpine but little Himalayan experience; in particular it lacked a transport officer and a liaison officer who could speak the local language. As a result, 'difficulties with the porters runs through the story of the expedition like the red strand through a climbing rope.' The Baltis deserted, refused to eat anything except their specially cooked chapattis, and stole several loads of vital equipment. As a result of these early problems, the expedition did not establish its base camp until the end of June – far too late for comfort, although Merkl consoled himself with the thought that the monsoon in the west arrives later and is less catastrophic than in the east.

They attacked the mountain from the north, via the Rakhoit Glacier. This is the only possible route, and one which presents few problems in the higher reaches, since the summit can be gained via a comparatively gentle snow-ridge. In the lower reaches, however, the glacier is a formidable barrier, heavily crevassed and constantly swept by avalanches. Twice, in their first few days, Merkl and his party came within a hair's-breadth of being swept to oblivion. However, by 18 July they had managed to establish four camps on the glacier, the highest at 20,200 feet (6161 m). All this time the weather had been good; but now it broke, and soon illness was adding to Merkl's problems; Herbert Kunigk developed acute appendicitis and had to be rushed off the mountain, Heron and Simon contracted chills, Aschenbrenner's toes were badly frost-bitten, and the porters without exception reported sick and refused to climb a step higher. For ten days the assault party waited at the top of the glacier for the weather to clear, in the few fine intervals inching painfully higher through the newly fallen snow. With great determination, they struggled to 22,800 feet (6954 m). Then the weather became impossible, and they retreated – only just in time, having to abandon their stores.

As a reconnaissance, this expedition had been a success. As an atempt on the summit, it never came even close to success. To quote Kenneth Mason:

> *The need for careful planning and the scale of the difficulties were under-estimated. Too great a strain fell on the members of the assault party who (due to the failure of the porters) had to make the route and also carry loads in deep fresh snow. Only three out of eight climbers reached 22,800 feet [6954 m], and without porters they could never have gained the summit even in fine weather . . . Merkl took most of these lessons to heart.*

Most, but not all; for when he returned to Nanga Parbat two years later, events were to prove that he still under-estimated the difficulties with which he was faced.

The German–Austrian expedition of 1934 was one of the largest ever to tackle a major peak: nine first-class climbers, three scientists, two transport officers, 35 experienced Sherpas, and no fewer than 500 porters. They left Srinagar early in May, and within a fortnight had established their base camp near the foot of the Rakhoit Glacier. The glacier was in a bad state: unstable, deeply fissured, and covered with heavy snow; 'day and night ice-avalanches roared, and cracking ice detonated beneath the tents.' Nevertheless by early June, four glacier camps had been established and provisioned, and everything seemed set fair for an early attempt on the summit. Then came an unexpected tragedy. Alfred Drexel caught a chill, the chill turned to pneumonia, and although he was helped down to Camp II, his condition rapidly deteriorated. The oxygen which might have saved him arrived too late, and on the evening of 9 June he died of oedema of the lungs.

The events of the next few days are a mystery. The official account of the expedition relates that 'mountaineers and porters were called back from climbing operations to the base camp for Drexel's funeral . . . Everything was then held up because the *tsampa* [the Sherpas' barley-meal] had not arrived on time. Eleven lovely, cloudless days went by – days spent in the base camp.' Few pastimes give rise to such close friendships as mountaineering – when one's life is so often in the hands of one's fellow climber(s) – and one therefore hesitates to criticize the decision to call everyone down to the base camp for Drexel's funeral. But to spend 11 days there is inexplicable. If the *tsampa* really was not to hand, the fault lies with the transport officers – the only two British members of the expedition – but to use the non-arrival of the *tsampa* to explain the delay in climbing simply does not make sense. One of the well-known advantages of employing Sherpas is that they do *not* need a special diet such as *tsampa*; 'they will eat anything.'

It therefore looks as though there must have been yet another misunderstanding between climbers and porters. And in this lay the seeds of tragedy, for the 11 lost days were to lead to one of the most terrible disasters in the history of mountaineering.

On the morning of 6 July, five climbers and 11 Sherpas were poised for the final assault. They had established a camp at 23,130 feet (7055 m) on a step in the snow-slope which leads directly to the summit. Although the monsoon was approaching, it had not yet broken, and the weather was good.

> *There was a strong wind, but not so strong as to be uncomfortable; clouds covered the world like an endless sea, out of which Nanga Parbat alone soared aloft, a solitary island; occasionally the clouds beneath them parted, and through the gaps they could see, 13,000 feet [3965 m] below, the rubble-covered glacier-tongues and the green meadows. After so many weeks in the snow, it was like the glimpse of another world.*

They moved off in good heart, intending to pitch one more camp, Camp VIII, on the saddle immediately beneath the summit. By midday this camp was established, at 25,750 feet (7854 m). The summit was now within their grasp: a mere 900 feet (275 m) above them, and divided from them by no more than a gentle and easily climbable *arête*. Had the fittest of the five climbers attempted Nanga Parbat that afternoon, the first 8000-metre peak would almost certainly have been climbed. But Merkl wanted all five of his team to reach the summit together; so they waited, to give the more exhausted climbers a chance to recuperate, confident that the morrow would bring success for them all.

Instead it brought the monsoon.

What happened next has been gone over in detail by literally hundreds of alpine writers. Professor Dyhrenfurth's account is probably the fairest.

> *In the morning of 7th July a fearful blizzard raged about the tents: so fierce it was impossible to breathe in the open. Snow scud was blown horizontally across the saddle, and all day long it was dark as though it were twilight . . . The surface snow was pressed by the gale into the consistency of hard ice, so it was impossible to dig a hole in which to shelter. During the first night a tent-pole broke. The tents were no longer windproof, and the climbers could only lie huddled in their sleeping-bags under a shroud of snow-dust. They had provisions and fuel for about five days, but in the raging gale it was impossible to get the cookers working, so they couldn't even prepare themselves a warm drink. The second night was worse than the first. Another tent-pole broke, and on the morning of 8th July the weather was as bad as ever. Conditions in the tents had become unbearable. It was therefore decided to withdraw to Camp IV, and wait for better weather. Aschenbrenner and Schneider with three Sherpas were to go ahead and break the track; Merkl, Welzenbach and Wieland, with the remaining eight Sherpas, were to follow close behind them.*

The first party struggled down to safety, descending through Camps VII and VI without stopping, resting briefly at the well-stocked Camp V; then

> *plunging on through chest-deep snow, to arrive, utterly exhausted, at Camp IV late in the afternoon. They expected the second party to join them any moment. When they didn't turn up that evening, Aschenbrenner and Schneider were confident they must have spent the night at Camp V, where the tents were still in position and there were plenty of sleeping-bags and provisions. For the next two days the storm raged with unremitting fury, the wind swirling snow from the ridges in fantastic plumes. At last, on the evening of July 10th, there was a brief clearance; and those in Camp IV, staring up the mountain, saw to their horror and amazement four figures still well above Camp V. They turned out to be four Sherpas, who when at last they struggled down to Camp IV, utterly spent and terribly frost-bitten, brought the unbelievable news that Merkl, Welzenbach, Wieland and the rest of the porters were still marooned in Camp VII.*

In the course of the next week only one man, Ang Tsering, managed to struggle through to safety; and he was so exhausted and so terribly frost-bitten that he was close to death.

The others had died slowly and painfully, huddled together in tents or ice-caves which became their graves.

There have been alpine disasters of greater magnitude – whole expeditions snuffed out by some catastrophic avalanche – but none of such protracted horror: nine days of long, slow, agonizing death from cold, exposure and starvation.

It is easy, in the comfort of an armchair and with the knowledge of hindsight, to blame Merkl: to say if only he had not wasted those 11 days in the base camp, if only he had not insisted that his whole team stand on the summit together. In retrospect, it is obvious there were too many eager men too high, and that the basic mistake had been made on 6 July. On that day, the two fit climbers (Aschenbrenner and Schneider) could have reached the summit, but instead of letting those who *were* fit press on, Merkl let those who were *not* fit struggle up to join them. That Merkl, Welzenbach and Wieland cannot have been fully fit on 6 July may be deduced from the fact that only lack of fitness could have prevented such experienced climbers from following closely behind Aschenbrenner and Schneider in their descent of 8 July. However, after all these years it is kinder and perhaps fairer to remember the expedition not so much for its mistakes as for its heroism: the courageous though unavailing efforts of those in Camp IV to go to their companions' rescue and, above all, the selfless devotion of the Sherpas, more than one of whom gave up his life to stay with the 'sahibs'.

In 1937 the Germans again laid seige to Nanga Parbat. This time there were seven experienced climbers, led by Karl Wien, two scientists, a doctor, a cartographer, a transport officer, 12 experienced porters from Darjeeling and a number of carefully selected Baltis for work in the lower camps. This was a strong expedition, and since the route to the summit had been pioneered and was known to have few technical difficulties, there was every hope of success.

To start with, things went well, and by 24 May, in spite of poor weather, the base camp and Camps I and II on the glacier had been established. However, on 26 May a great avalanche swept the glacier, strewing its debris so close to Camp II that tents were ripped to shreds in the blast, and men flung to the ground.

By 14 June Camps I to V had been set up, and that night Camp IV was occupied by no fewer than seven climbers and nine Sherpas, most of whom intended the following day to stockpile provisions in Camp V. Only one European slept that night below Camp IV, and none above it.

Next morning the lone European in the base camp, Ulrich Luft, kept looking up towards the higher reaches of the glacier, expecting to see climbers and porters on the move. There was no sign of life, and becoming uneasy, he set out for Camp IV. When, a couple of days later, he arrived at what he knew to be the site, he found nothing: 'nothing but silence, a vast expanse of shattered ice, a trail that broke off abruptly, and the debris of a great avalanche, 500 feet [153 m] wide and already covered with powder snow.'

It was several days before a team specially flown out from Germany was able to dig down to the bodies. They were still in their tents. All their watches had stopped at 20 minutes past midnight.

As Nanga Parbat punished Merkl for ambition, so it punished Wien for carelessness. If Camp IV had been sited a couple of hundred feet higher, on the glacier plateau, it would have been safe from any avalanche.

There were two more German attempts on Nanga Parbat between the wars: Bauer's in 1938 and Aufschnaiter's in 1939.

The former failed – as did every venture in the Himalaya that year – because of the weather. 'Week after week of unremitting blizzard,' wrote Shipton on Everest; 'Weather appalling,' wrote Bauer on Nanga Parbat, '19 days of snow without intermission.' Given good conditions, Bauer might well have succeeded, for he was a mountaineer of great ability, experience and caution, unlikely to have repeated the mistakes of his predecessors. As it was, he managed to reach only 23,900 feet (7290 m), before very prudently retreating; and his expedition is chiefly remembered for pioneering the use of aircraft – they had a three-engined Junkers which was used for photography and supply-dropping – and for discovering several bodies from the 1934 disaster – some frozen solid in snow caves, others hanging from fixed ropes on the ice-wall.

Aufschnaiter's expedition was more a reconnaissance than an assault. The previous year Bauer had sent two climbers to the Diamir (northwest) side of the mountain, to look at the rockface which had defeated Mummery. Their report and the aerial photographs taken by the Junkers seemed to warrant further investigation, and in 1939 a strong team of rock-climbers (including Heinrich Harrer who had conquered the north face of the Eiger) tackled this little-known approach to the summit. They found the rockface 'technically every bit as difficult as the Eiger and a great deal higher'; time and again they were brought up short by vertical and unstable walls, swept by avalanches, and with the gneiss brittle and highly dangerous. In the face of great difficulty and constant danger, they managed to reach 19,700 feet (6009 m) – about the same height as Mummery – before 'retreating under an absolute bombardment of loose stones'. Their return to India coincided with the outbreak of World War II, and Aufschnaiter and Harrer were interned. This was bad luck for them, but good luck for many people all over the world; for the two Germans escaped, and managed to make their way across the Himalaya and into Tibet. Here, after almost as many adventures as the mythical Sinbad, Harrer became tutor and confidant to the young Dalai Lama, an experience which he subsequently related in *Seven Years in Tibet*. Few books tell us as much about the Tibetans – or about the likeable character of their author – as this minor classic in the literature of travel.

The next attempt, in 1953, was organized by Dr Karl Herrligkoffer and led by Peter Aschenbrenner.

This was a contentious venture, redeemed only by the one great feat of physical and mental endurance: Buhl's solo attainment of the summit. From its inception the expedition was bedevilled by doubts, opposition, lack of funds and even court proceedings – 'such a ballyhoo,' writes Professor Dyhrenfurth, 'as was never known before and, it is to be hoped, will never be known again'. Its organizer was a doctor who was unqualified to lead the assault on the mountain himself; the leadership was therefore given to Aschenbrenner who, however, made no secret of the fact that he viewed the whole affair with misgivings; he joined the expedition as late as he could and left as early. There were no Sherpas – they had been refused entry permits into Pakistan. The climbers arrived late, and would never have got to the mountain at all if the Pakistan government had not most generously air-lifted them to Gilgit. The weather was poor; it looked as though the monsoon was breaking early, and on 29 June Aschenbrenner gave the order to abandon the few camps which had been set up, and withdrew. It seemed as if the sixth German attempt would go down in history as not so much a failure as a non-event.

There were, however, a handful of men unwilling to give up so easily. And four of them – Buhl, Ertl, Frauenberg and Kempter – refused to obey their leader's instructions to come down. There was, they argued over the radio, still a chance. And as though in answer to their prayers, the last day of June dawned fine. It was the start of a spell of near-perfect weather.

The four men decided to 'go it alone'. They climbed swiftly to Camp V; and by the evening of 2 July, Buhl and Kempter were bedded down a little below the Silver Saddle, ready for an attack on the summit. The summit, however, was still 4000 feet (1220 m) above them, and the two climbers must have known that, no matter how early they started and how easy the climb, they could not get there and back in a single day: that at something like 25,000 feet (7625 m) they would have to spend a night in the open, without tents.

It was the sort of risk that most mountaineers would have thought unacceptable.

Buhl set out next morning at the unlikely hour of 1.00 a.m.! Kempter did his best to follow a couple of hours later, but was soon obliged to give up. It was now a case of one man, against all the odds, taking on Nanga Parbat alone.

Buhl made steady progress by moonlight but the sun, when it rose, was almost unbearably hot and he suffered badly from lassitude. At midday he cached his rucksack, food and spare pullover on the subsidiary summit (25,950 ft, 7915 m). So far the ascent had presented no problems – but the final stage turned out to be not so easy – a steep rockface, followed by a long *arête* with its south face falling sheer for 14,000 feet (4270 m) to the valleys at Buhl's feet. It was 6.00 p.m. before he came to the last gendarme: 'a massive obstruction which had to be traversed with great care. I scrambled up it on all fours – I could climb it no other way – and suddenly realized I was able to go no higher. I was on the summit!'

He did not linger. He unearthed a Tyrolean pennant and a Pakistani flag, tied them to his ice-axe, and took the mandatory photographs. Then he began what he must have known was a race with death, 'for already the sun was disappearing below the horizon, and although the rocks still held a little of the heat of the day, the air at once turned cold.'

The events of the next few minutes could have been fatal.

First, in a state of forgetful euphoria, he left his ice-axe on the summit. Then, halfway down a precipitous ice-slope, his right crampon slipped off his boot, 'leaving me standing like a stork on the smooth, hard ice in one crampoon, supporting myself as best I could with my ski-sticks, and with no idea of how to extricate myself.' Somehow, he managed to inch his way to safety.

Half an hour later it was dark.

Buhl spent the night – incredible as it sounds – standing on a wobbly block of stone in the middle of a steep rockface. There was not enough level ground for him to crouch, let alone to sit; all night he had to hang on to the rockface with one hand and his ski-sticks with the other, and he had nothing – not even a pullover – to keep him warm. All this was at a height of more than 26,000 feet (7930 m).

The following is his description of how he survived:

I woke with a start. Where was I? Terror engulfed me as I realized that I was hanging, like a fly to a wall, to the side a steep rockface, exposed to the cold and the night, a black abyss yawning beneath me. I told myself I must stay awake; but sleep kept on defeating me; I kept dozing off. It was a miracle I didn't lose my balance . . . Next time I prised open my eyes, the plateau below gleamed silver: everything – the Subsidiary Summit, the North Summit, the Saddle – shone in a pale ghostly light etched with shadow . . . My body had not yet, alas, achieved insensibility. As the night progressed, the cold grew more and more unbearable. I felt it on my face; I felt it, in spite of my thick gloves, in my hands; and worst of all I felt it in my feet. I tried to keep my circulation going by stamping up and down; but my little platform was unstable, and I had to be careful. Soon hunger and thirst were asserting their needs, but I had nothing with which to assuage them. Time passed so slowly that I thought the night would never end. But at last, behind a distant fang in the east, a streak of light broadened and rose gradually higher: the new-born day. For me its light was the light of salvation. I tried to prise myself off the rocks. But my feet were like blocks of wood, and my boots frozen solid to the ice. I couldn't move. But at last the sun's rays fell on me with their blessed comfort and warmth, dissolving my rigidity. I began the descent: but with great caution, because everything was now doubly dangerous under a veneer of ice . . . Soon I had the extraordinary feeling that I was not alone: that I had a companion with me, a friend who was taking care of me and belaying me. I knew it must be imagination, but the feeling persisted. At one point I had to take off my gloves, to get the feel of a band of particularly friable rock; and, having taken them off, I couldn't find them.

'Have you seen my gloves?' I whispered.

I heard the answer very clearly: 'You've lost them.'

But there was no one there . . . All the way down the rockface, my companion was with me, his presence particularly strong at points of danger. He comforted me. I knew that if I slipped, his rope would hold me. And at last, after one more terrifying almost vertical pitch, I collapsed face down on the snow-slope.

The long climb was over. The even longer walk was about to begin.

With only one usable crampon, Buhl made slow progress.

I became completely bemused, and raged at my companion for giving me such wretched equipment . . . Soon I was racked by the most terrible thirst. The sun burnt down, viciously and relentlessly; but though the rocks were coated with ice, not a drop could be squeezed out. I began to suffer from hallucinations . . . Opening my eyes, I realized I must have fallen asleep. Where was I, anyhow? Everywhere I looked, I saw tracks and cairns. Of course, I thought, I must be on a ski-ing holiday! It was only gradually that I realized the ski-tracks were nothing but channels made by the wind, and the cairns outcrops of rock. I was still on Nanga Parbat. Still at over 25,000 feet [7625 m]. And still alone. I got to my feet and started to struggle up the snow-slope that led to the Subsidiary Summit. It took me an hour to cover a hundred feet; but at last I got to the top and saw in the far distance the Silver Saddle. But where was the rucksack I had cached? At last I found it, and pulled out a packet of Dextro-energen. When I tried to swallow a tablet it stuck to my furred-up throat. There was only one thing for it. I crushed the tablets, mixed them with snow and swallowed them. For a while the effect was wonderful. But I knew I shouldn't have done it. And sure enough, my thirst was soon even more searing than before, my throat even rawer, my gums even more swollen. I began to foam at the mouth. As I moved down the snow-slope, at a snail's pace, I had to take about twenty breaths with every stride. Every few yards, I kept falling over in the snow. This must, I thought, be my journey's end. Yet the will to live still flickered on, and I stumbled forward . . . It was now evening, and shadows were lengthening. My own shadow pursued me and confused me. I thought I was no longer myself, but my shadow: that was all that was left of me, a shadow . . . It seemed to me, time and again, that I saw my companions coming to meet me; but always at the last moment they vanished, metamorphosed to rocks . . . I remembered my Pervitin, and realized my only chance was that the brief renewal-of-strength it should bring would last long enough to see me over the Saddle. Blood and spittle were now oozing out of my mouth, which was so gummed up that I had to force the tablets down as though they were wooden wedges . . . At half-past-five I was on the upper rim of the Saddle; and, looking down the glacier, could see the chain of camps laid out beneath me, the tents half-buried in the snow. And there, beside the nearest of the tents, were two small dots: that moved. These were no hallucinations. These were real. These were people.

An hour later, just as the sun was disappearing behind the rim of the Saddle, Ertl and Frauenberg were helping him into their tent. 'The joy of our meeting,' wrote Buhl, 'is beyond my power to describe.'

After more than 50 years and 20 deaths, Nanga Parbat had at last been climbed: not, ironically, by a large, well-planned expedition, but by a last-minute solo challenge.

It in no way detracts from Buhl's achievement to say he had been unbelievably lucky. On nine nights out of ten he would never have survived in the open at 26,000 feet (7930 m). As Dyhrenfurth dryly puts it: 'This 40-hours' solo effort by the Tirolean "Wonder-Climber" was a heroic performance; but it should be stressed that his method of attack is not to be recommended on other eight-thousanders!'

As the Italians concentrated on K2 and the Germans on Nanga Parbat, so the British concentrated on Everest.

The story of how the mountain was discovered and climbed is well known. Not so well known, perhaps, is the truth about two key incidents: the fate of Mallory and Irvine, and the discovery of the West Cwm.

Until the middle of the nineteenth century, Chimborazo, a volcano in the Andes, was thought to be the highest mountain in the world. However, for some years the Great Trigonometrical Survey had had on its maps an unobtrusive Peak XV, half-hidden from view by its more southerly neighbours; and in 1852 this was officially triangulated from six co-ordinates and given the height of 29,003 feet (8846 m). It was, to quote the records of the Survey, 'named Mont Everest, to perpetuate the memory of the Surveyor-General, that illustrious master of geographical research'; and in the absence of any widely used native name, this has become generally accepted.

No attempt was made to climb the mountain for almost half a century; for it is one of the most remote and inaccessible peaks in the Himalaya, lying between Nepal and Tibet, two countries inimical to 'Feringies'. However, in the early 1900s discreet reconnaissance was carried out by Kellas and Noel, the latter penetrating to within 30 miles (50 km) of the foot of the mountain – probably the closest a European had so far been. Noel's journey was the spark which triggered off the powder-train of attempts on the summit, for it was while he was describing his exploits to a meeting of the Royal Geographical Society that the idea of climbing the mountain was taken up officially.

In his book *Everest: the Challenge*, Francis Younghusband tells how this came about.

The idea of climbing Everest only took shape after the Great War. The moment came at a meeting of the RGS [on 10 March 1919] *when Captain Noel was giving a lecture about his pre-war reconnaissance. In the discussion which followed, Captain Farrar, President of the Alpine Club, said that his Club would view with the keenest interest any attempt to climb Everest and would be prepared to lend financial aid and to recommend mountaineers. I was sitting beside Farrar as he spoke: and when he had finished I asked the President to let me say a few words. I said that our own Society would be interested in the project, but that this was big business and must be done in a big way, and that the first thing we would have to do would be to enlist the help of our Government . . . It so happened that I was myself about to succeed to the presidency of the RGS, and I determined to make this Everest venture the main feature of my presidency . . . I therefore formed a Mount Everest Committee* [composed] *of representatives of both the Society and the Club.*

This committee, for better or for worse, was to control all official British attempts to climb Everest for the next 35 years.

The first reconnaissance took place in 1921, when a somewhat ill-assorted team under C. K. Howard-Bury achieved considerable success. Their achievements were succinctly summed up by their leader.

The expedition accomplished what it set out to do. All the approaches to Everest from the north, northwest, and east were carefully reconnoitred, and a possible route to the top was found, via the Rongbuk Glacier and the northeast ridge . . . Some 13,000 square miles of new country were surveyed and mapped, a large number of birds and mammals collected, the geology of the region carefully worked out, and a series of photographs taken of a country quite unknown and containing some of the grandest scenery in the world.

The next year a full-scale expedition, led by C. G. Bruce, followed in Howard-Bury's footsteps; and it was now that the formidable nature of the mountain, and in particular its last 2000 feet (610 m), was realized for the first time. The climbers established their base camp at the head of the Rongbuk valley, and managed without too much difficulty to reach the lower slopes of the North Col (21,000 ft, 6405 m). Then the monsoon broke – several weeks earlier than had been anticipated, and Bruce's party found themselves obliged to make a quick attempt on the summmit before they were properly acclimatized. The wonder is not that they failed, but that they got as high as they did. For nearly three weeks a succession of climbers – Mallory, Norton and Somervell, and Finch, Bruce and the Gurkha, Telgbir Bure – clawed their way across the upper slopes of the mountain. They suffered from altitude sickness, shortage of food, frost-bite, winds of frenetic violence and, above all, from complete and utter physical exhaustion. But they climbed higher than men had ever climbed before: Mallory and Norton to 26,800 feet (8174 m), Finch, Bruce and Telgbir Bure to 27,300 feet (8327 m), before a succession of avalanches drove them off the mountain.

Having studied Bruce's report, the Committee came to the conclusion that

the difficulties and hardships endured by this expedition were understated, and their published accounts give little idea of how formidable the mountain really is. The last 1700 feet [519 m] are technically very difficult, and an ascent seems impossible unless there are four consecutive fine days . . . The idea that the ante-monsoon season might provide the necessary fine weather was too sanguine. The truth seems to be that the weather about Everest is nearly always wild, and the greatest obstacle to a mountain already difficult enough . . . The work of the porters was beyond praise, and the Tibetan authorities and the chief lamas of the monasteries were most friendly and helpful.

It may have been partly because Bruce went out of his way to respect Tibetan beliefs and customs – no animal was killed within 20 miles of the Rongbuk monastery – that permission was given for another attempt on the summit in 1924.

It has been said that this third expedition was 'over-organized'. Certainly it was the largest so far to approach the mountain, no fewer than 350 porters being needed to carry its supplies and equipment through Tibet. It was led by Colonel Norton, who came within a hair's-breadth of success. Indeed, some people claim he met with complete success, arguing that Mallory and Irvine are quite likely to have reached the summit before they fell to their deaths. Whatever the truth about Mallory and Irvine, the 1924 expedition and its tragic climax have become part of mountaineering legend: a legend never more evocatively told than in Norton's *Despatches to the Royal Geographical Society*, published only a couple of weeks after they were dictated by their snow-blind leader at the foot of the Rongbuk Glacier.

We reached Base Camp on April 29th; exactly according to plan, and the way seemed clear for a possible assault on the summit somewhere about May 17th . . . On May 7th we arrived at Camp II, but that evening it became clear all was far from well. For who were these weary crippled men, staggering and straggling down through the seracs of the glacier from Camp III? They are porters who have encountered such low temperatures and bitter winds that they have been driven clean out of their camp by exposure and exhaustion . . . That night there began a blizzard lasting continuously for 48 hours. We woke next morning to find the tents full of fine powder snow, and the temperature

Everest: the East Rongbuk Glacier

−22°F [−30°C] (10° lower than anything recorded in 1922) . . . There was nothing for it but to retreat . . . and tomorrow we hope to get the whole expedition, and especially the sick, blessed by the Head Lama at Rongbuk.

A week later the assault was renewed. But again snow, high winds and a temperature of −24°F (−31°C) made climbing to all intents and purposes impossible. By the end of May both Europeans and Sherpas were close to the limit of their endurance but it was decided to make two last-minute attempts on the summit. Somervell described the first.

[On 4th June] *we got up as dawn was breaking. There was an early delay because the Thermos had shed its cork during the night, and we had to waste nearly an hour melting snow to make more liquid. But we got going about 6.45, and trudged slowly up a rocky shoulder in the direction of the summit. Our side of the shoulder was in shadow and very cold; but at length, panting, puffing and sometimes slipping back on the scree and compelled to stop and regain our breath, we attained the sunlight and began to get warm. We crossed a patch of snow, with Norton chipping steps, and reached the band of yellow rock which is such a conspicuous feature in distant views of the mountain. This rock has weathered into horizontal ledges some ten or more feet wide, and provides a safe and easy route towards the summit ridge. So up these ledges we went, pulling ourselves with heavy breathing from one to another, and occasionally walking along them for respite, but always heading up and to the right to avoid loose-looking rock on the northeast ridge.*

But the altitude was beginning to tell. At about 27,500 feet [8388 m] there was a change. Lower down we had been able to walk almost comfortably, taking three or four breaths for each step; but now eight or even ten complete respirations were needed for every step forward. And even at this slow rate of progress we had to rest every 20 or 30 yards. We were coming to the limit of our endurance. At about 28,000 feet [8540 m] I told Norton I could only hinder him and his chances of reaching the summit. I suggested he should go on alone, and settled down on a sunny ledge to watch him. But Norton too was not far from the end of his tether. I watched him move slowly, but oh how slowly, upward. After an hour I doubt if he had risen more than eight feet above my head . . . and after a while he returned. We agreed reluctantly that the game was up . . . So with heavy hearts, beating over 180 to the minute, we retraced our steps. The view was beyond words for its magnificence. Gyachang Kang and Chouyo (among the highest mountains of the world) were over

1000 feet [305 m] beneath us. Around them lay a perfect sea of peaks, all giants among mountains, but all as dwarfs below us.

They struggled back to Camp IV, Norton snow-blind and unable to see, Somervell with a constricted throat and unable to speak.

We are both rather done in, wrote the latter,

but we have no complaints, no excuses . . . We were beaten by the height of the mountain and our own shortness of breath. But the fight was worth it. We now await news of Mallory and Irvine, who to-day are making another attempt with oxygen. May the Genie of the Steel Bottle aid them! All of us are hoping he may, for nobody deserves the summit more than Mallory.

The weather on 8 June was good, with a light wind drifting layers of mist-cum-cloud across the upper slopes of Everest. Mallory and Irvine had been expected to set out from Camp VI at dawn; and later that morning, in the hope of spotting them as they neared

Andrew Irvine, who died near the summit of Everest, 1924

the summit, Odell struggled up towards the camp where the two climbers had spent the night. And spot them he did. A little after 12.30, the clouds for a moment lifted, and Odell saw two figures, almost certainly on the lower of the 'steps' which led to the summit ridge; he reckoned they were at a height of about 27,950 feet (8525 m). Then the clouds closed in. Mallory and Irvine vanished. And were never seen again.

What happened to them?

Probably the mystery will never be solved, and it will never be known if they fell to their death (soon after Odell sighted them) during the *ascent*, or if they went on to reach the summit and fell subsequently during the *descent*. For years, the former view was the more widely held, but recent discoveries make one wonder . . . The evidence we have to go on is (a) Odell's testimony, (b) an ice-axe, which must have belonged to one of them, found in 1933 on a snow-slope immediately below the second or lower 'step', (c) persistent reports that the Chinese expedition of 1975 found a body some thousand feet below the ice-axe.

Odell at 90 is as clear-minded today as he was 60 years ago when he caught that brief glimpse of Mallory and Irvine; but he was not certain then and he certainly is not certain now which of the two 'steps' the climbers were on, nor whether they were going up or coming down. This is not surprising. Heights and distances at extreme altitude are notoriously difficult to judge, visibility that afternoon was poor and Odell had just climbed 2000 feet (610 m) without oxygen. However, his general impression, he says, was of surprise that the climbers were not higher – it therefore seems probable that they were still on the lower step. He also thinks that they were going up rather than coming down – although this may have been wishful thinking. If Odell is right, then Mallory and Irvine, when he saw them, had climbed no higher than Somervell and Norton; and it used to be argued that if by midday they had reached only 27,950 feet (8525 m), they would never have even attempted the summit, through fear of being overtaken by darkness in the open. But one wonders. Other climbers – Buhl, Herzog and Lachenal, for example – were subsequently to attempt (and achieve) more, for a lesser prize. And suppose in the early part of their climb Mallory and Irvine had not used oxygen, either because Mallory wanted to see how far they could get without it, or because the extreme cold had frozen up the valves in their oxygen cylinders: suppose that round about midday they had boosted their performance by taking oxygen – perhaps by now the heat of the sun had unfrozen their valves – might not they have thought that climbing the 1100 feet (336 m) to the summit in about five hours was worth a try? It has been rightly pointed out that most of the early Everesters climbed at an average rate of less than 250 feet (76 m) an hour; but there were exceptions. On the previous expedition Finch (at 26,000 ft, 7930 m) averaged 800 feet (244 m) an hour; that very afternoon Odell (at 25,000 ft, 7625 m) had averaged 700 feet (214m) an hour, *without oxygen*. And in recent years men such as Hackett and Kopczynski have climbed Everest after averaging, on the final slopes, 340 feet (104 m) per hour and 600 feet (183 m) per hour respectively. For Mallory and Irvine to have reached the summit that evening they would have needed to average 220 feet (67 m) an hour. Difficult, yes. Unlikely, perhaps. But impossible, certainly not.

There is therefore nothing in Odell's testimony which precludes Mallory and Irvine's success.

The ice-axe tells us little. When discovered, it was an emotive find, a link with the past. But its position proves only that Mallory and Irvine were on or near the lower step when they fell. There seems to be no way of telling if they were climbing up or down.

One might have thought that this vital point would remain unresolved even if their bodies were found. This, however, is not so.

It is now more than 12 years since Tom Holzel published his possible reconstruction of Mallory and Irvine's ascent of Everest in the magazine *Mountain*. His article brought down on him the wrath of the mountaineering hierarchy, who were quick to point out that 'Mr Holzel has never done any serious mountaineering or had any practical experience of the problems of high-altitude climbing.' Many people wrote him off as a crank. Holzel, however, stuck to his guns, and begged every expedition intending to set foot on Everest to search the snow-slopes, below where the ice-axe had been found, for a body. A body, he insisted, would prove he was right.

The point he was making was a simple one, which many people seem to have overlooked. Both Mallory and Irvine had cameras with them: cameras loaded with Eastman Kodak film. And Eastman Kodak had assured Holzel that even after 60 years in the ice, their films should develop into recognizable prints, prints which would surely, if Mallory and Irvine had succeeded, contain photographs taken from the summit.

In 1975 a body was found.

The discovery seems to have been deliberately hushed up at the time, and it is only recently that reports of what took place have filtered through to the outside world. One of these reports is of a conversation which took place between two climbers, the Chinese Wang Hong Bao and the Japanese Ryoten Hasegawa. The former, one of China's best and most experienced climbers, was killed by an avalanche in 1979, and it seems that the day before he died he told Hasegawa that during his 1975 ascent of Everest he found 'two deads'. The first (at about 21,500 ft, 6558 m) was undoubtedly Maurice Wilson, the Yorkshireman who had tried to climb Mount Everest alone, and whose body had already been found and buried by Shipton in 1935. The second (at about 26,600 ft, 8113 m) was found in the snow-slopes directly beneath the second 'step'. Wang apparently told his colleague: 'When I touched the clothes of this dead at 8100 metres, the cloth fell to pieces and blew away in the wind.' Hasegawa asked if the body could have been that of a Russian, and Wang said, 'No, the Russians never climbed that high;' and he several times repeated 'English! English!'; he then etched in characters in the snow the word 'Englishman 8100' (metres).

For years the Chinese denied that any body had been found. They then suggested the body was that of Wu Tsung-yueh, who fell to his death from only a little below the summit during the Chinese expedition of 1975. However, this makes nonsense of Wang's testimony; for how could he have confused the body of a recently deceased Asiatic in modern kit, with the body of a Westerner, in old-fashioned and disintegrating kit which had been lying on the mountain for 40 years?

Our only other evidence is that of a well-known and highly respected British mountaineer – he insists on remaining anonymous – who was recently present when a Chinese climber was questioned about the body found by Wang. Apparently the Chinese climber said in public, 'There is no truth in the story that any other body [apart from Maurice Wilson's] was found on Everest in 1975.' However, he told the Britisher *sotto voce* that a body *had* been discovered, and he believed there had been a camera with it. He is also reported to have said that if the camera had contained photographs taken from the summit, the Chinese Mountaineering Association would have been unwilling to admit their existence, since this would negate the Chinese claim to have made (in 1975) the first ascent of Everest from the north.

One wonders why, if there was not a camera on the body and the camera did not contain such photographs, the Chinese should have been so secretive about its discovery?

The more closely one looks into the story of Mallory and Irvine, the more likely it now seems that they did indeed reach the summit.

◆

It was Tilman and Shipton who, between them, pioneered the route by which Everest was climbed by Hunt's expedition of 1953.

Throughout the 1930s the British had launched numerous attempts on the summit. All were unsuccessful. Teams led by Ruttledge in 1933, Shipton in 1935, Ruttledge again in 1936 and Tilman in 1938 were thwarted either by bad weather, by lack of supplies, by lack of oxygen or by the sheer technical difficulties of the final 1800 feet (549 m). It began to look as though the mountain was inviolate. However, soon after the war, two things happened which led to a veritable spate of successful climbs. In 1949 Nepal opened its frontiers to foreigners, and in 1950 the French climbed Annapurna. Not only could the great peaks now be approached from the south, but the psychological 8000-metre barrier had been breached.

First to reconnoitre Everest from the south, along what has since become the classic route not only of expeditions but of countless trekkers, were Bill Tilman (then 53 years old), Oscar and Dr Charles Houston (the former 67), Mrs Betsy Cowles (an experienced American climber) and Anderson Bakewell (a novitiate in the Jesuit college in Darjeeling). Tilman, who liked to pretend he was a misogynist, wrote: 'Hitherto I had not regarded a woman as an indispensable part of the equipage of a Himalayan journey, but one lives and learns. Anyway, with a doctor to heal us, a woman to feed us, and a priest to pray for us, I felt I could face the future with confidence!' This unlikely entourage developed into what was not only a wonderfully happy team, but a wonderfully successful one, and their progress that autumn up the valley of the Dudh Kosi to the foot of Everest took on the magic of an idyll. Houston wrote:

Betsy was a charming and understanding woman; she quite won Tilman's heart, and after the first few days they became inseparable. We had perfect Fall weather, and the ten-days' walk – little more than a picnic – was an unforgettable experience: virgin territory, incredibly beautiful scenery, and a small bandobasta [Hindustani for an informal party]*; our evenings about the fire were never to be forgotten . . . Bill and I were first up the ridge to Thyangboche, the first Westerners ever to see that beautiful place. We were royally welcomed: Tibetan tea, devil dances, ceremonies, exchanges of presents – the whole lot. Even Bill was deeply moved. We were lodged in a small stone house, liberally ventilated, although this did little to dissipate the smoke from the fire built for us each morning by the monks. They aroused us at dawn with liberal doses of* rakshi [Nepalese rum] *served in a huge old-fashioned glass-stoppered pickle-jar, still bearing the label 'Heinz, 57 varieties'. While Bill and I went on up the valley, the rest of the party basked in the sun at Thyangboche, enjoying the freshness of Eden.*

Tilman describes their progress beyond the monastery, through open woods of twisted juniper and silver birch. 'We strolled past a little white-washed hamlet, when suddenly a bend in the path brought into view the foaming river and beyond it a massive rock-shoulder, like the grey roof of a church, from which sprang the preposterous snow-spire of some un-named, unmeasured peak . . . Few stretches of the track were without *mani* walls, and every convenient boulder was inscribed with a religious text.' In the evenings their Sherpas built enormous log fires, 'big as a holocaust'. At nights, 'frost stilled the murmur of the stream, and only the faint note of a bell on some restless yak broke the silence.'

It was like a walk through Eden before the fall.

Soon they came to the moraine of the Khumbu Glacier, a mighty river of ice above which lay a cirque of some of the most beautiful mountains on earth: Pumori, Nuptse, Lhotse, Makalu and Everest. Houston takes up the story:

Next day we went up the glacier, going quite slowly, because we were not adequately acclimatized. We climbed high on Pumori to look into [Everest's] West Cwm, but our strength was not enough to let us see round the corner. We could see that the West Cwm would be dangerous, but cautiously suggested to each other that here was a route which would go. After many photographs, we turned back to Thyangboche – having to carry one of our porters who went down with malaria . . . This was in the Fall of 1950, when the Chinese had just [invaded Tibet] and the whole sub-continent seemed about to burst into flame. I remember vividly walking with Bill through the autumn gold, reflecting on what we had seen, and what damage we and others like us might have set in train for this innocent, backward, beautiful country. We were all sad, knowing we were witnessing the end of something unique and wild, and the beginning of a period of great danger and immense change.

One can understand how they felt. It was not, however, they or their compatriots who were about to desecrate Tibet's 2700 monasteries, and make nearly a million people homeless. This, as a recent American climber of Everest has pointed out, was the work of the Red Guards, who mobilized discontented Tibetan teenagers and assigned them the task of destroying 'the monuments of an obsolete lifestyle'.

It would be wrong to suggest that Tilman and the Houstons pioneered a route up Everest via the West Cwm. They did, however, pioneer the approaches to such a route, and were the first people ever to look into the cwm. The cwm itself and the icefall that guarded its approaches were pioneered the following year by Eric Shipton.

Shipton in 1951 probably had a greater knowledge of the mountains of central Asia than any man alive; for as well as taking part in many expeditions in the 1930s – on Everest, Kamet, Nanda Devi and in the Shaksgam – he had been British consul in both Kashgar and Kunming; he therefore knew the north face of the mountains as well as, if not better than, the south. In 1951 the Himalayan Committee invited him to lead a reconnaissance party to look into the possibility of climbing Everest from the south. Shipton accepted, and on the spur of the moment agreed to include in his team two unknown New Zealanders. As he himself put it, 'my momentary caprice was to have far reaching results', for the New Zealanders' names were Riddiford and Hillary.

Prior to 1950 mountaineers had, of necessity, concentrated their attention on the north face of Everest, their eyes on the deceptively gentle-looking northeast ridge which seemed to offer a not-impossible route to the summit. This northern approach, however, had many disadvantages: above 23,000 feet (7015 m) it was exposed to the full force of the northwest gales which lash the summit for four days out of five; the northerly tilt of the rock strata meant there were few footholds and almost no level ledges on which to pitch a tent; the lack of morning sun precluded climbers making an early start; and the most difficult climbing was in the last 1700 feet (519 m), at an altitude at which mountaineers were least able to cope with difficulties. A southern approach appeared, at first glance, to present even more problems, for the south face of Everest consists of stupendous cliffs and sheer, beautifully fluted walls of ice. However, in the southwest, a broad and relatively gentle ridge rises to the summit from the col between Everest and its neighbour Lhotse, and if only this ridge could be reached, the final 1700 feet promised to be a good deal easier from the south than from the north.

It was Shipton's task to see if a route to this ridge could be pioneered: possibly by the mysterious West Cwm.

Hillary described the key moment of their reconnaissance.

The next fortnight was one of the most exciting I have ever spent . . . Shipton and I descended into a paradise of blazing colour. In our ten days up the Khumbu [glacier] every leaf, branch and twig had assumed its autumn coat. To my eye, accustomed to the evergreen forests of New Zealand, it was unbelievable. It was like being in a new world: a world of crimson and gold, and above it the white purity of soaring ice and the deep dark blue of the sky. For ten days we climbed and explored in country that men had never seen. We crossed difficult passes and visited great glaciers. But at the end of it, it wasn't so much our achievements I remembered, exciting as they had been, but the character of Eric Shipton: his ability to be calm and comfortable in any circumstances; his insatiable curiosity to know what lay over the next hill or round the next corner; and, above all, his remarkable power to transform the discomfort, pain and misery of high-altitude life into a great adventure . . . On the morning of September 30th it was fine and clear, and Shipton was anxious to climb to a position where we could get a look into the Western Cwm . . . We scrambled onto the bottom of a ridge which came down off Pumori. We were both fairly fit and climbed steadily. But eventually the height

The 1951 Everest Reconnaissance team. Left to right: (back row) Eric Shipton, Bill Murray, Tom Bourdillon, Earle Riddiford (seated) Michael Ward and Edmund Hillary

started taking its toll. In the rarified air our lungs were working overtime and rapid movement was impossible. [They were now well beyond 'the corner' which Tilman and Houston had not been able to negotiate.] *At 19,000 feet [5795 m] we stopped for a short rest and admired the wonderful views that were opening up around us. Then we pushed on up the last pitches. We scrambled up a steep bluff, chipped a few steps over some firm snow, and collapsed with relief on a little ledge at about 20,000 feet [6100 m].*

Almost casually I looked towards the Western Cwm, although I didn't expect to see much of it from here. To my astonishment the whole valley lay revealed to our eyes. A long, narrow snowy trough swept from the top of the ice-fall and climbed steeply up the face of Lhotse to the head of the Cwm. And even as the same thought was simmering in my own mind, Shipton said, 'There's a route there!' And I could hear the note of disbelief in his voice. For from the floor of the Cwm it looked possible to climb the Lhotse glacier – steep and crevassed though it appeared – and from there a long steep traverse led to a saddle at 26,000 feet [7930 m] – the South Col. Certainly it looked a difficult route, but a route it was. In excited voices we discussed our find. We had neither the equipment nor the men to take advantage of our discovery, but at least we could try and find a route, and then return next year and attack the mountain in force.

The key to their proposed route was the ice-fall which guarded the approaches to the cwm: a steep, frozen, 2000-foot (610 m) cataract of unstable seracs and crevasses. They made two attempts to climb it. On the first, ice conditions were bad, and Hillary, Pasang, Riddiford and Shipton were very nearly swept to their deaths in a crevasse. On the second, although menaced by avalanches and frustrated by crevasses, Bourdillon and Shipton managed to reach the top of the ice-fall, and, looking up the mountain, could confirm that the rest of the route to the summit would be 'relatively easy'.

◆

A couple of years later Hunt climbed where Shipton had reconnoitred.

One reason for the success of the 1953 expedition is that it tackled the summit via a practicable route which had already been partially pioneered; another is the leadership of John Hunt. When appointed by the Himalayan Committee, Hunt was not a 'big name' in mountaineering circles, but he was good with people and better with logistics.

He welded his disparate climbers into a particularly happy team with a real *esprit de corps*, and he organized their assault on the summit with quiet but unerring efficiency; to quote Hillary, 'he hit the nail on the head every time.' His campaign was based on the use of oxygen and the use of high-altitude porters – which Kellas, 45 years previously, had argued were the prerequisites of success. To quote the then President of the Royal Geographical Society, James Wordie:

> *This expedition differed in one vital respect from those of former years. The intention of the earlier expeditions was to try and reach the summit without the use of oxygen, and to turn to oxygen only when absolutely necessary. As a result no climbers above about 26,000 feet [7930 m] were in prime physical condition. The Himalayan Committee took the view that oxygen was needed on a much larger scale than formerly, that it was in fact the secret of success. This involved a very heavy lift for porters right up to the South Col; and the amount of oxygen to be carried decided the size of the expedition. A small party was out of the question; a large party was essential.*

The Committee's plan was adhered to, and half a dozen fit climbers, with plentiful supplies of food and oxygen, were established only a couple of thousand feet below the summit. All that could stop them now was the weather, and the weather held. At almost exactly 11.30 a.m. on 29 May 1953, Hillary and Tenzing were levering themselves on to the top of the world – 'A few more whacks of the ice-axe, a few more weary steps, and we were on the summit of Everest.' It was a great moment in the history of mountaineering.

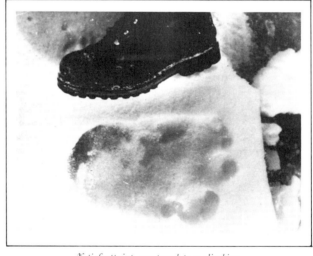

Yeti footprint, compared to a climbing boot, photographed by Eric Shipton, 1951

Within a few years, all the major peaks in the mountains of central Asia had been climbed: Everest in 1953, K2 in 1954, Makalu and Kangchenjunga in 1955, Lhotse, Mustagh Ata and Tomur in 1956, Dhaulagiri in 1960. Mountaineers, however, continued to be drawn to the great peaks as moths to a candle. They took to climbing mountains of lesser height but greater technical difficulty or, like Chris Bonington, to attempting major summits 'the hard way'. There were a number of brilliant solo efforts – such as Pelissier's ascent of Kanjut Sar – and a number of mass assaults – like the Chinese 214-strong expedition to Everest, when three climbers, one in his stockinged feet, reached the summit. These will continue, politics permitting, for as long as people find

Everest, 1953: second base camp on the
Khumbu Glacier

mountains a challenge.

Why, it is often asked, *do* they find mountains a challenge?

One remembers the bodies frozen solid on to the ice-walls of Nanga Parbat, the suppurating stumps of Herzog's fingers and toes, the long agony of Gilkey's thrombosis, the quick stab at Kellas's heart. What, one wonders, would these men, in the last analysis, have to say about their love affair with the mountains? When asked why he was so anxious to climb Everest, Mallory replied, 'Because it is there' – a fatuous answer, made in a moment of exasperation, to get rid of a persistent journalist. How on earth, one wonders, did such a remark achieve near-immortality? The reason, I suggest, is that Mallory's answer enables everyone to put his or her own interpretation on it, thus solving to their satisfaction a problem to which there is, in fact, no solution. Certainly men more intellectually gifted than Mallory have delved deeply into the springs of their motivation, and failed to come up with a satisfying answer.

If, however, at some final court, mountaineers had to choose two advocates to defend their calling, the men I would suggest would be Winthrop Young and Eric Shipton. The former defined mountaineering as 'a journey into adventure, into beauty, and, best of all, into the unknown'. The latter said of it: 'The springs of enchantment lie within ourselves; they arise from our sense of wonder, that most precious of gifts, the birthright of every child.'

Whatever the motives that inspired them, there is no doubting the mountaineers' importance. During the last 100 years, the ice-axe has superseded the theodolite as the most potent instrument in laying bare the secrets of Central Asia.

This process seems likely to be reversed soon, for as the number of unconquered peaks diminishes, so expeditions are becoming less interested in climbing *per se*, and more interested in gathering scientific facts. History may prove that, as the attainment of Lhasa marked the culmination of a century of exploration, so the attainment of Everest marked the culmination of a century of mountaineering. Once the Forbidden City and the invincible peak had fallen, men's energies were diverted into other channels. And if the nineteenth century belonged to the explorers, and the twentieth to the mountaineers, it seems likely the twenty-first will belong to the scientists.

CHAPTER SIX

THE SCIENTISTS

As long ago as the thirteenth century, *The King's Mirror*, a Norwegian encyclopaedic scientific treatise, attempted to analyse the motives which make us want to explore our planet: 'If you wish to know why men journey to far places, often at great danger to their lives, it is the threefold nature of man that draws him thither. One part of him is the desire of fame, another part is the desire of wealth, and the third part is the desire of knowledge.' Few explorers or climbers deliberately sought fame in the mountains of Asia; fewer still sought wealth. Most of them, however, directly or indirectly, did seek knowledge; they were all, in a manner of speaking, scientists. Alexander, while crossing the Hindu Kush and campaigning in Sogdia, found time to collect and classify Asian flora. British and Russian surveyors triangulating the roof of the world found time to write appendices on the Pamirs' birds and fish. Bill Tilman, often accused of climbing purely for pleasure – as though there was something wrong with that! – had until recently the honour of finding the highest living plant ever classified. Almost every individual and every expedition have contributed something to science.

It is therefore impossible to make a list or even a précis of the scientifically important expeditions which penetrated the mountains; if you list one, you might as well list all. Instead I have selected two journeys which seem to me to typify all that was best in the old invididual approach to science, and all that is best in the new collective approach: Hooker's travels in Sikkim in 1848–50, and the Royal Geographical Society's expedition to the Karakoram in 1980.

Few men have led such interesting and academically distinguished lives as Joseph Dalton Hooker. He was born in Suffolk in England, but brought up in Glasgow in Scotland, where his father was the university's professor of botany. He knew at an early age what he wanted from life: the opportunity to travel and do botanical research. 'When still a child,' he said, 'my father used to take me on excursions to the Highlands, where I fished a good deal and botanized. I well remember on one occasion, after returning home, that I built a heap of stones into a representation of one of the mountains we had ascended, and stuck upon it specimens of the mosses I had gathered, at heights relative to those at which I had found them. This was the dawn of my love for geographical botany.'

An occasional visitor to the Hooker house in those days was James Clark Ross, the polar explorer, and when in 1839 Ross set out for the Antarctic, he took young Hooker with him as his naturalist. It was during their long, hazardous and highly successful voyage that Hooker, then only 22 years old, acquired that love of the lonely reaches of the world which was soon to take him to unprecedented heights in the Himalaya.

On his return from the far south, Hooker published his first major work, *Flora Antarctica*, which established him as one of the leading botanists of his generation. He was given a post with the Geological Survey, and for several years was engaged in research which was of particular interest to Britain's coal industry. It was not long, however, before his love of travel overcame his love of palaeobotany, and in 1847 he set out on what was to be the greatest of all his journeys: to India. He chose India, he tells us, because 'it was a country of equal interest to the traveller and the naturalist': a remark which pinpoints a fundamental difference between Hooker and the scientists of today. He was not a specialist. He was a man who turned an orderly and enquiring mind to a whole range of disciplines – botany, zoology, meteorology, geology and ethnology – which is one reason why his *Himalayan Journals* make such interesting reading.

He arrived in India in January 1848, and went almost at once to 'Dorjiling' in the foothills of Sikkim. Here he remained for two years, exploring an area of great natural beauty where few Europeans had yet set foot.

What makes Hooker's travels of particular interest is that, as he climbed from *terai* to snowline, he was able to study, in a comparatively short distance, virtually the whole spectrum of the world's flora, starting with the gargantuan, rain-soaked sals of the rain forest, and ending with the minute, acid-secreting lichen of the Tibetan desert.

He began botanizing in the *terai*, 'that low malarious belt, about 20 miles broad, which skirts the base of the Himalaya from the Sutlej to the Brahmaputra'. He described the area as 'covered with a loose forest of trees common to the hotter parts of India, especially the sal (*Shorea robusta*), together with a rich undergrowth of shrubs, coarse grasses and plants of the Ganetic plain . . . There is much swamp, and many small streams, their banks richly clothed with brushwood and climbing convolvulus, vines, *Hirea*, *Leea*, *Menispermea*, *Cucurbitacea* and *Bignoniacea*.' The two features of this zone which seem to have impressed him most were the vapours and the leeches. He pointed out that, although the former were often fatal to Europeans – malaria, in those days, was thought to be caused by 'noxious vapours' – they had no ill effect on the local inhabitants, 'a sallow-skinned but robust people who live by burning the *terai* and cultivating the areas they have cleared'. The leeches were a constant tribulation.

Much of the time we were wading through deep mud. Leeches swarmed in incredible profusion in the streams and damp grass and among the bushes. They got into my hair, hung onto my eyelids, and crawled up my legs and down my back; the sores they produced were not healed five months afterwards, and I retain the scars to this day. Snuff and tobacco leaves were an antidote; but when marching in the rain it is impossible to apply these remedies. Another pest is the midge or sand-fly, which is the most insufferable torment; the minutest rent in one's clothes is detected by this insatiable bloodsucker, which is so small as to be barely visible without a microscope. We often arrived at our camp-site streaming blood and mottled with bites.

In this small area Hooker classified no fewer than 850 different species of trees and plants, noting that most of the former were 'Malayan in character'.

It must have been a relief to leave the swamps and climb some thousand feet to the forest.

Hooker was one of the first botanists to set foot in a tropical rain forest and to note its three principal characteristics: a diversity of flora, a paucity of mammals, and a super-abundance of insects.

Up to about 5500 feet [1678 m] the hills are clothed in dense, deep-green, dripping forest. The trees are huge, and festooned with climbing Leguminosea, Bauhinias and Robinas *which sheath their trunks and join tree to tree with enormous cables. Their trunks are coated also with parasitical* Orchids, *and, still more beautifully, with* Pothas, Peppers, *vines and convolvulus. Of the smaller trees the wild banana is particularly abundant, and bamboo abounds, often well over 100 feet [30 m] high and thick as a man's thigh at its base. In one small area I counted no fewer than thirty species of luxuriant and handsome ferns . . . Elephants, tigers, wild boar, leopards and occasionally the rhinoceros inhabit these forests, but none is numerous . . . Ants, on the other hand, are exceedingly numerous, as are earthworms and cicadas; while my tent at nights, when the candle was burning, was a veritable Noah's Ark of moths, cockroaches, may-flies, glow-worms, flying beatles and earwigs; a large species of daddy-longlegs sweeps itself constantly across my face as I write.*

In the rain forest Hooker classified 1150 species: the most common trees being Sal, *Magnoliaceae* and *Anonaceae*, and the most common plants, orchids (over 400 varieties) and ferns (280 varieties).

Above 5500 feet, as the tropical zone gave way to the temperate, the rain forest was superseded by open and mainly deciduous woodland.

In the lower slopes of this woodland the principal trees were oaks, chestnuts, laurels, magnolias and rhododendrons. The latter were Hooker's favourites. He discovered 22 new species, and helped to introduce these beautiful trees first to the Botanical Gardens at Kew in London, and then to almost every country in Europe.

During this part of his travels he was usually accompanied by a small retinue of Bhotias, Gurkhas and Lepchas, who carried his food, equipment and specimens, did his cooking and acted as guards. The last of these duties had its dangers, for although Hooker had been given permission to enter both Sikkim and Nepal, he was frequently threatened and more than once imprisoned. His *Journals* evoke the dual nature of his travels: the juxtaposition of luxury and hardship, idyll and odyssey.

My tent was a blanket thrown over the limb of a tree; to this others were attached, and the whole supported on a frame like a house. One half was occupied by my bed, the other half by my books and writing material. My barometer hung in one corner, my thermometers under a special canopy in the other. In the evenings a small candle burned in a glass shade, and I had the comfort of seeing my knife, fork and spoon laid out on a white napkin. After dinner, which usually consisted of meat, rice and tea, my occupations were to ticket and store the plants collected during the day, write up my Journal, plot my map and take observations. As soon as I went to bed, one of the Nepal soldiers was accustomed to enter, spread his blanket on the ground, and sleep beside me as my guard. In the morning, collectors were sent to change the plant papers, while I botanised, took observations and breakfasted. By 10 a.m. we would be ready to move off.

As he climbed higher, he found that the number of species diminished: over 1100 had been classified in the rain forest, under 600 in the deciduous woodland; and he was to meet still fewer in the coniferous woodland.

At about 8000 feet (2440 m) he now entered one of the most beautiful regions of the Himalaya, and almost every page of his *Journals* has vivid descriptions not only of the flora, but of the scenery, the people and the faith by which they lived. Of the flora he wrote:

The monarch and most common of the conifers is the Silver Fir Abies webbiana which is also the most gregarious; others are Yew, Spruce, Larch (the only deciduous conifer in the Himalaya) and Juniper, which in stunted form ascends also into the alpine zone. The absence of Pine or Cypress is notable. Of shrubs the most conspicuous are the Rhododendrons (25 species) some of them forming impenetrable thickets; and, in the lower slopes, the Magnolias, starring the hillsides in spring, while still leafless, with their magnificent flowers. Dwarf bamboos (six species) abound, but there are only two palms. Other shrubs include species of Clematis, Berberideae, Ilex, Rosa, Rubus, Cotoneaster, Spiraea, Hydrangea, Buddleia, Elder, Viburnum, Ivy, etc. Beautiful herbaceous plants are plentiful – Anemones, Aconites, Violets, and many species of balsam, potentilla, etc.

*Top: Members of the Pamir Boundary
Commission and, above, fish and reptiles from the
Yassin River recorded in their Proceedings, 1896*

Of the scenery:

It is truly grand: rivers roaring in sheets of foam, sombre woods, crags of gneiss, and tier upon tier of lofty mountains crested with groves of black fir and terminating in snow-sprinkled peaks.

Of the people:

Almost every day we passed parties of ten or a dozen Tibetans, laden with salt. The men are middle-sized, square-built and muscular; they have no beard, moustache or whiskers, the few hairs on their faces being removed with tweezers. The women have their hair parted in two tails, and their necks adorned with strings of coral, amber and agate. They are a good-humoured, amiable people, Mongolian in countenance, with broad mouths, high cheek-bones, flat noses and low foreheads. White is their natural colour, but all are so begrimed with filth and smoke and so weatherworn from exposure to the most rigorous climate in the world, that their natural hue can hardly be recognised . . . It was here that I first saw a praying machine turned by water; it was enclosed in a little wooden house, and consisted of an upright cylinder containing prayers, with the words Om mani padme om *painted on the circumference; it was placed over a stream, and made to rotate on its axis by a spindle going into the water and terminated by a wheel.*

These are among the earliest descriptions of the Tibetans and their way of life to be read by the general public in Europe.

In this upper part of the temperate zone Hooker classified some 400 species, before ascending to the alpine zone. This extends from roughly 12,000 feet (3660 m) to the highest level at which plants survive – a little over 20,000 feet (6100 m). Hooker subdivided it into two regions: 'a lower south-facing humid region', and 'an upper north-facing dry region'. In the former he botanized with care. In the latter, as he was the first to admit, he barely scratched the surface.

He loved the alpine zone. In its softer moods it reminded him of the Scottish Highlands, in its bleaker, of Antarctica. He had always taken a particular interest in mosses and lichens; he now had the chance of studying some of the finest in the world, and his *Journals* are full of breath-taking (if somewhat long-winded!) descriptions.

Between the moraines, near my tent, the soil was level, and consisted of little lake-beds strewn with huge boulders, and covered with hard turf of grass and sedge and little bushes of dwarf rhododendron and prostrate juniper, as trim as if they had been clipped. Here too were the remains of so many kinds of primrose, gentian, anemone, potentilla, orchis, saxifrage, parnasica, campanula and pedicularis that in summer they must be the most perfect gardens of wild flowers. Around each plot was a girdle of stupendous rocks, many 100 feet [30 m] high and crested with junipers, while at their base were more mosses, lichens, etc. than I had dreamed of.

He was to spend six months in the alpine zone, climbing to 18,000 feet (5490 m) and venturing several times to the top of passes leading into Tibet. To have climbed so high at a time when few peaks of over 14,000 feet (4270 m) had been even attempted elsewhere in the world was no mean achievement. Not surprisingly he suffered from headaches, altitude sickness and snow-blindness; also from cold, although in this respect his unfortunate Lepchas from the Ganetic plain suffered a great deal more, and on several occasions Hooker was to lend his own clothing to men 'almost beside themselves with misery'. The following is his description of their climb to the top of the Wallanchoon Pass.

We left the valley and struck north up a narrow gorge, with an immense moraine at its mouth. The path, which we followed for 7 or 8 miles [11–13 km], kept to the southeast slope of the gorge, this being the sunniest and freest from snow. The morning was splendid, the atmosphere vibrating from the power of the sun, while vast masses of blue glacier and snowfield choked every gully. At 15,000 feet [4575 m] the snow closed in from all sides, the path being cut some three feet [1 m] deep through it. For several miles we proceeded over snow much honeycombed, and treacherous from the icy stream it covered, into which we every now and then stumbled. There was scarcely a trace of vegetation . . . Towards the summit of the pass the snow became very deep, the walls being breast-high on either side of us . . . Just below the summit was a complete bay of snow, girdled with peaks of red schist and gneiss, thrown up at all angles with no prevalent dip or strike, and permeated with veins of granite. The top itself, the boundary between Nepal and Tibet, is a low saddle between two rugged ridges of rock; a cairn is built on it, adorned with prayer flags and inscriptions. The view into Tibet was entirely of mountains, piled ridge upon endless ridge . . . The ascent had been most laborious, and the three of us who gained the summit were utterly knocked up. My barometer gave a height of 16,764 feet [5113 m] . . . The plants gathered near the top were Compositae, Arenaria, and most curious of all Saussurea gossypina, *which forms clubs of the softest white wool, six inches to a foot high [15–30 cm], its flowers and leaves seemingly clothed with the warmest fur that nature can devise. Generally speaking, the alpine plants of the Himalaya are unprovided with protection of this kind; it is the conspicuous nature of the exceptions that induce the careless observer to generalise falsely from solitary instances. For the prevailing alpine genera – Arenarias, primroses, saxifrages, fumitories, Ranunculi, gentians, sedges, etc. – have uniformly naked foliage.*

A little below the top of the pass, he came across an unexpected friend: a rhododendron nearly three feet (about 91 cm) across but no more than two inches (5 cm) high. He took a specimen for dissection, sketching and classification, and eventually wrote the following description:

R. nivale. *Distribution and range: Sikkim Himalaya, in the dry valleys of the interior, at elevations of 16,000 to 18,000 feet [4880–5490 m].*

The hard woody branches of this curious little species, as thick as a goosequill, straggle along the ground for a foot or two, presenting brown tufts of vegetation where few other plants can exist. The branches are densely interwoven, and wholly depressed, being raised barely 2 inches [5 cm] above the soil. The surface of the branchlets and foliage is covered by small scales of bright ferruginous-brown. Leaves one-sixth to one-eighth of an inch [4–3 mm] long, pale green. Corolla one-third of an inch [8 mm] across the lobes, of a purple colour. The whole plant is very odoriferous. It appears indifferent to all changes of climate, remaining buried under many feet of snow for 8 months of the year, while at other times the soil around it is heated to 150° [66°C]. Snow-storms, even in summer, are frequent; they do not, however, injure its blossoms, which remain open until fertilization has taken place. This species attains, I believe, a loftier elevation than any other shrub in the world. Its nearest allies are R. setosum *and* R. lapponicum, *from which latter it differs in its smaller stature and solitary sessile flowers.*

This is one of the briefest of Hooker's botanical classifications. In his monumental seven-volume *Flora of British India* (the introduction alone is over 260 pages), he describes in detail some 4000 Sikkimese trees, shrubs and plants, almost every one of which he individually collected, dissected, studied and classified. The mind boggles at the magnitude of such a task, especially when one remembers the finicky nature of some of the dissecting.

I do not know [he wrote] *which is the more difficult task – to remove and dissect a flower, to classify its species, or to describe its variable organs for which there is often no technical terminology. Many single flowers take two or even three hours to lay out the parts for drawing and description; and after all is done I sometimes doubt if what I see, draw and describe will fit the living flower! For I defy even the acutest botanist to tell from dried specimens whether there are two or four lateral sepals, whether the anthers are acute or didymous, or the true form of a floral envelope. To get at these you must remove and moisten the flowers and spread out every organ flat under water. This done, I secure them all on slips of gummed paper as evidence of the fidelity of my sketches.*

When one reads the *Himalayan Journals*, with their graceful evocation of the wonders of Sikkim, it is easy to forget the long hours of research which formed the basis of Hooker's descriptions. When one looks at his portrait, with its frail aesthetic features, it is easy to be unaware of the inner steel which drove him, streaming with blood, through the *terai*, or led him, reeling with nausea and snow-blindness, to work at heights to which few men before had even climbed. As well as being a dedicated and academically brilliant botanist, he was incredibly tough.

Hooker never had the chance to study the flora of the Tibetan plateau. This was a pity, for the lichen and mosses which cling to life on the roof of the world would have excited not only his interest but his admiration. He shared with them a rare resilience and tenacity.

Few parts of our planet, except Antarctica, are more hostile to life than the northern desert of Tibet: minimal rainfall, virtually no soil, violent extremes of heat and cold, and a lacerating near-perpetual wind. Yet for a few weeks each summer this desert is metamorphosed to a mosaic of almost unbelievable beauty, as life – which for nine months has been sealed-up under a canopy of snow and ice – reawakens, and lichens, mosses and dwarf alpine shrubs burst into brief but glorious bloom.

What revives them is not only warmth but humidity. Because the air at 12,000 to 15,000 feet (3600–4575 m) is so clear and thin, the effect of solar radiation in summer is intense, the surface of the Tibetan plateau fairly shimmers with heat, and the ice melts. In many parts of the world, the resulting meltwater would soak away through the soil and be lost; but beneath the Tibetan plateau, only a couple of feet under the surface, is a solid layer of permafrost; the meltwater is trapped, and conditions in the moist subsurface soil become ideal for the growth of roots. This explains the principal characteristic of Tibetan flora: that the size of the plants is greatly exceeded by the size of their roots. A sedge only one inch (2.5 cm) in height may have roots three feet (1 m) in length. Therefore, once a plant roots, it establishes a life-support system impervious to the rigours of the surface climate.

The pioneers in the process of rooting are lichen – one of the most basic forms of plant life – whose spores stain the damper rocks dull-green. These lichen secrete acid, which dissolves and fragments the rock into the most primitive form of soil. As the lichens expand, they extract nutrients, and at the same time create the basic conditions for other plants. Mosses begin to grow on and among the dead lichen; they perform photosynthesis more quickly than their primitive hosts, and produce a fine soil into which they can root. Once rooted, Tibetan flora becomes very nearly as enduring as Tibetan rock.

Over the millennia, species proliferated and became more sophisticated: sedge and stonecrop, gentian and edelweiss, delphinium and rhubarb, shrubs such as rhododendron and jasmine, dwarf trees like juniper and willow. All have the same prostrate growth – a bush of jasmine may be 12 feet (3.65 m) in diameter and only six inches (15 cm) in height. All are long-lived – a juniper may be only two feet (0.60 m) high but 200 years old. All have the same brief season – *Pegoephyter scapiforus* emerges from its roots, sprouts, flowers, bears fruit and recedes to ground level all within a month.

These plants briefly transform the Tibetan plateau into a wonderland not only beautiful but useful, for they provide the basis of the Tibetans' pharmacopoeia. Chinese poppies are a source of opium, and fritillaria, a source of cough syrup; gentians alleviate

*Top: Glacier of Panmah, Baltistan by Godwin Austen, 1872, and,
above, Thomas Holdich's painting of the Wardak Pass near Kabul*

*The magnificent peaks of Pasu overlooking the
Karakoram Highway and Hunza River at Gulmit*

*Top: Holy masks – white for good spirits, black for evil –
worn by Lamas celebrating Buddha's birthday. Above:
Horsemen playing 'Boz-Kashi' on the steppes of Turkestan*

Members of the dance troupe who fled Tibet with the Dalai Lama, wearing traditional dress at Dahram-sala, India

fever, delphiniums dysentry.

Hooker no more than scratched the surface of this highest echelon of alpine flora. But at every other level he was the greatest of a distinguished line of botanists – men like Thomson, Jacquemont, Heber, Semyonov, Przhevalski, Kingdon-Ward and Polunin – who have helped to classify the mountains' 4500 species of trees, plants and shrubs.

Hooker worked alone. He did have the researches of Wallich and Griffith of the Botanic Gardens in Calcutta on which to base his studies, and he did have a certain amount of practical help from his 'guard' of Bhotias, Gurkhas and Lepchas. However, his classification of Indian flora was basically a great solo effort: years of single-handed research in the field, followed by years of single-handed dissection and drawing at Kew. Like nearly all the great scientists of his day – Darwin, Bates, Wallace – he was a loner.

British and Pakistani surveyors working together in the Karakoram, 1980

This individual approach is now out of fashion. Today is the day of the team, with experts in a number of highly specialized disciplines working together with highly complex equipment. The Royal Geographical Society's International Karakoram Project was such a venture, with more than 60 scientists making an intensive study of a selected area: the Hunza valley and its environs.

Such an expedition poses political and financial problems. It took the Society three years of painstaking planning and negotiation to ensure the support of Pakistan and the co-operation of Chinese scientists; and the price for this was the unfortunate alienation of the Russians and the Indians who claimed the project was a CIA-inspired reconnaissance to site missile bases! This was particularly to be regretted since one of the Society's objectives in launching their expedition was to demonstrate the *international* nature of scientific research, and the benefits that can stem from it to *all* nations. As the expedition leader, Keith Miller, very mildly says: 'It is to be hoped that the two volumes of scientific

*Top: Members of the Frontier Works Organisation who see that the Karakoram
Highway is kept open to traffic, despite frequent landslides and mudslips, and,
above, Land Rover belonging to the International Karakoram Project, 1980*

papers that will result from our studies will correct this mistake.' As for finance, at one stage the expedition's balance sheet read: 'expenditure £75,000; income £16,000'! And it was only with the help of the British and Pakistan governments, the Society itself and over 200 generous commercial sponsors that expenses were covered.

The expedition began to assemble at its headquarters in the Hunza valley in the summer of 1980.

The Hunza valley can be reached by either the most sensational air flight in the world – past the sheer 23,000-foot (7015 m) face of Nanga Parbat to land on the airstrip at Gilgit – or by the most sensational road in the world – the Karakoram Highway (the KKH), which runs for 4500 miles (7240 km) from the Indian Ocean to the heart of China, cutting *en route* through the highest and most unstable mountains on earth. Many who have seen this superb piece of engineering rate it as the greatest man-made structure of the modern world, but the price of building it, in more ways than one, has been high. A plaque invites those who drive along it 'to say a prayer for those silent brave men of the Pakistan army, who gave their lives to realize a dream' – and almost every day this death toll rises. The road is being continually strewn with the debris of landslide and avalanche, submerged by flood and shattered by earthquake; every hour of every day some part of it is temporarily blocked. It needs a huge corps of dedicated engineers to keep it open, while its tunnels, hairpin bends and sheer drops of up to 1000 feet (305 m) to the river below, lead to frequent accidents – UN observers who use the road regularly have the doors removed from their Jeeps so they can quickly jump clear in emergency! Keith Miller summed up the expedition's feelings about the road. 'On the one hand, without the KKH, and the rapid means of deployment it presented to our scientific groups, we should never have achieved our long list of successes . . . on the other hand we were convinced that if any accident was to occur, it would be here.'

From the Hunza valley, the scientists fanned out on research work. The surveyors were the mountaineers of the expedition. Their task was to re-triangulate the peaks surrounding the Indus valley to the south of Gilgit and the Hunza valley to the north. This area was described by Curzon as 'that great workshop of primaeval forces . . . where avalanches of snow and mud come plunging down the slopes, and distort the face of nature.' Put in more scientific terms, the area spans one of the most active belts of tectonic activity in the world; for this is where the subcontinent of India is boring into the underbelly of Eurasia. It was the hope of the surveyors that, by comparing peak positions as shown in Mason's very accurate survey of 1913 with peak positions today, they could measure the rate at which movement was taking place. To quote one of the survey team, Nigel Atkinson: 'Sixteen stations [on prominent peaks] were occupied. This involved us in some 600,000 feet [183,000 m] of ascent! The stations ranged from 12,000 to 17,000 feet [3660–5185 m] in altitude, and each required a mini-expedition of at least three days for occupation. On one occasion three parties were marooned on separate stations during persistent bad weather, with food and water running perilously short.' Triangulation was carried out with extreme precision, using the most sophisticated theodolites, tellurometers and laser geodimeters. Full details have not yet been published, but in general terms some peaks were found to have moved by as much as five metres (16 ft 5 in) in 67 years, which indicates that India is boring into Eurasia at a 'speed' of roughly 80 millimetres (3.15 in) a year.

The geomorphologists and glaciologists concentrated on the Hispar, Batura and Ghulkin glaciers. These great rivers of ice at the head of the Hunza valley are not only among the largest in the world outside the Arctic and Antarctic – some are 50 miles (80 km) long and 1000 feet (305 m) deep – they are also subject to the largest fluctuations in the world, in extreme cases receding or advancing as much as ten miles (16 km) in a single year. This movement is of interest not only to academics, but to the people of the Hunza, whose fields and laboriously constructed irrigation channels can run dry or be devastated by flood according to the position of the glaciers. And today another edifice is at risk: the Karakoram Highway. Twice within the last few years a change in the position of the glacier snouts and their meltwater streams has devastated the KKH, sweeping away bridges and submerging whole sections under 50 feet (15 m) of water. Here, obviously was a case where research work could be of benefit to the everyday lives of the local people.

Glacial meltwaters washing away part of the
Karakoram Highway

The glaciologists concentrated mainly on the Hispar: a 30-mile (48 km) long river of ice descending from 17,000 feet (5185 m) to 11,500 feet (3508 m): a fascinating but almost inaccessible and dangerous field for research. According to Keith Miller:

> *Our intention was to sound the depth of the ice* [by using] *electromagnetic radiation (radio waves) which travels through ice and is reflected back from the glacier bedrock to a receiver. Using the fact that the speed of radio waves in ice is 169 metres (554 ft) per microsecond (a millionth of a second), it is possible to measure the thickness of the ice from the time interval between transmission and reception of signals. By moving the equipment over the ice, manually or in an aircraft, and plugging the receiver into a synchonised cine-camera, it is possible to record the depth and profile of the ice automatically, and so determine the three-dimensional shape of a glacier – something that had never been done before in the Karakoram or Himalaya.*

In spite of many difficulties and not a few dangers, this programme was successfully concluded.

The geomorphologists, meanwhile, were concentrating on their analysis of scree, moraine and lake sediment. The terrain in which they were working was the most spectacular on earth and it was being disintegrated in front of their eyes, for everything in and around the Hunza valley is conducive to destruction on the grand scale: slopes of extreme steepness, an arid climate, a paucity of vegetation, salt-impregnated and friable rock, and rivers that quadruple their discharge inside an hour. It has been estimated that the Hunza river discharges more debris than any other of comparable size on earth, while the landscape around it is being worn and swept away at the rate of 5000 tonnes per square kilometre per annum; for comparison, the Thames basin in England is being worn away at a rate of 50 tonnes per square kilometre per annum. It is a land where disaster cannot be prevented. It can, however, sometimes be predicted, thus saving lives. In the past, whole villages and entire army corps have been obliterated by the bursting of dammed-up floods. Much of the geomorphologists' work was devoted to finding the cause of and predicting such disasters, and their findings should help to provide a measure of safety to a people whose lives are, to say the least, precarious.

The ethnologists of the expedition were also intent on helping the Hunzakut people. Their team consisted of doctors, social anthropologists, architects, disaster analysts and civil engineers. The doctors found that there was quite a high degree of mental stress among the villagers, although this seemed to stem not from their hazardous environment, but from changes in their social pattern brought about by sudden contact with the outside world. One of the team's more interesting studies was that of the local houses which, it had been reported, were unusually resistant to earth tremors. Careful analysis, however, disproved the use of any secret technique. The buildings were strong because once erected they were deliberately rocked by the owners; if they fell down, the remedy was obvious!

The seismologists' programme was of particular importance. Of all the disciplines associated with geography, seismology is the most elemental – its devotees would say the most fundamental – for earthquakes and earth tremors have not only shaped our planet in the past but continue to shape it today. Each year, as a result of quakes and eruptions, millions of tonnes of the upper crust of the earth are redistributed, thousands of people are killed and hundreds of thousands made homeless. To give just a few examples from the last 100 years: in the Kwanto earthquake of 1923, Tokyo was virtually destroyed and a minimum of 143,000 people were killed; in the Krakatoa eruption of 1883 in what is now Indonesia, rocks were flung 34 miles (55 km) into the air, dust fell for ten days over a radius of 3300 miles (5310 km), and the death toll has been estimated at between 180,000 and 200,000; in the mountains of central Asia the earthquake of 1976 is reported to have killed nearly 400,000 in the Chinese industrial city of Tang Shan; while in the Quetta

*Operating a seismograph to record earthquake
activity in the Karakoram*

Views from the Karakoram
Highway

[Baluchistan] earthquake of 1935, 30,000 people died in 30 seconds. All of which proves that the primordial forces which shaped our planet are not dead but lightly slumbering.

The Karakoram in general and the Hunza valley in particular are the scene of some of the most intense and continuous volcanic activity in the world. To be caught in such activity is, to put it mildly, terrifying. The following is Keith Miller's account of what happened to a group of people visiting the 600-year-old Baltit fort overlooking the upper reaches of the Hunza.

A deep subterranean rumble caused them to run out onto the castle roof. Little comfort, however, could be found on the roof, since the fort is perched on a knoll surrounded by high precipices. There followed three hard shock waves a minute apart, with continuous shock waves between. The old castle swayed and creaked, but it seemed so flexible as to be almost earthquake-proof. However, as the earthquake stopped, a new and spectacular scene developed as tremendous avalanches thundered down every gorge in the vicinity, and for a further five minutes a continuous rumble was heard and felt. Suddenly a great snow cloud spilled out of the mouth of a gully to the east. This avalanche was timed at 62 mph [100 kmph]: a wild, tumbling mass of cold air in which powdered snow was suspended. When the 2000-feet [610 m] high avalanche cloud struck the castle, it shivered again, and everyone had to lie flat to avoid being blown off the roof . . .

The duration, strength and aftermath of such earthquakes bring home the fact that man is not the master of his environment, but a [mere] transient on the surface of a world in constant upheaval. Even a small earthquake is an unforgettable experience. An initial sense of wonder turns to helplessness and panic. You can no longer trust your eyesight since your brain cannot register a true horizontal; it is impossible to stand upright. A primitive response is to fall to the ground in order to make a more secure contact with what should be solid earth. But the earth vibrates up and down and sways from side to side. A feeling of physical sickness is not uncommon, since co-ordination between sight and touch is disrupted, and new smells and fearful sounds add to the sense of inevitable destruction. These sensations are magnified in villages and towns where buildings collapse and fires start. There is no time to crawl away from potential death traps, and it is not unusual for entire populations to die from fear, thirst, suffocation, fire or by being crushed.

In human terms, seismologists deal with matters of life and death, and much of their research today is devoted to earthquake prediction and possible prevention. In academic terms, their work is equally important, for it provides the basis of the theory of plate tectonics.

As long ago as 1756 the German theologian Theodor Liliethal pointed out that the facing coastlines of many continents were like a jig-saw puzzle, and could be slotted one into another: for example, the bite out of the west coast of Africa coincides with the bulge in the east coast of South America; hence the idea that these land masses must, over countless millennia, have been prised apart. From this sprang the theory of continental drift, which visualized the continents drifting hither and thither over a sort of viscous jelly – an idea which was plausible but not very accurate scientifically. Plate tectonics is a refinement of the theory of continental drift. It sees the earth as consisting of a number of plates, which may be land mass or ocean bed. The land mass plates are known to be thick (approximately 22 miles, 35 km) and heavy: the ocean plates are known to be thin (approximately 4 miles, 6.4 km) and light. The former are solid, but the latter are being constantly renewed by material welling up from the core of the earth; the disruption caused by this welling-up makes the plates move and, in places, grind together and ride one-over-the-other. Where this takes place mountains are formed – such as the Andes, the Himalaya and the Karakoram.

This theory accounts for the arcs of volcanoes which proliferate where seismic activity is greatest at the confluence of land-mass and ocean-bed plates – the Aleutians and the islands of Japan are an obvious example. Millions of years ago a similar volcanic arc is believed to have existed along the confluence of the old Sea of Tethys and the coastline of Eurasia. As the Sea of Tethys was replaced by the advancing land mass of India, these volcanoes were pushed north and tilted sideways, until they arrived at their present position along the fault-line which runs through the Karakoram. It was among these ancient volcanoes, of which Rakaposhi is the highest, that the team carried out their research work.

The Chinese surveyor Chen Jian Ming working with the International Karakoram Project, 1980

It is spectacular terrain – spectacular to the layman because of its vast distances, steep slopes and almost lunar-like aridity (except for the Indus and Hunza valleys, the area is almost devoid of vegetation), and spectacular to the specialist because as one travels south through the faulted-zone between Pasu and Patan, one passes volcanoes of the old arc which have not only been squeezed upward but tilted sideways by the colliding continents. So as one drives horizontally along the surface, one finds oneself at the same time making a seismic journey downwards towards the centre of the earth, seeing progressively unveiled the rock strata of something like 30 million years. What a field for the seismologists!

Their team consisted of five British, four Pakistanis and one Chinese. In order to plot the exact location and strength of the earth tremors which were taking place almost continuously below the surface, they needed to establish a wide network of recorders. They set up 17 recording stations in all, 'travelling in Land Rovers and Jeeps for several thousand kilometres across high deserts and steep precipices under loose cliffs and glacier snouts, through rivers and avalanching boulders on tracks likely to subside if not collapse any instant.' They had many narrow escapes, but thanks to a combination of skill and good fortune, no fatal accidents – although in one village they were nearly murdered, 'because it is not the wish of Allah that earthquakes should be predicted'. In spite of these difficulties the programme was successfully completed.

Their hard work, tenacity and courage sum up the spirit of the expedition.

In the beginning, the *Mahabharata* tells us, the Himalaya and the Karakoram were fashioned out of the bones of Mother Earth. And as it was in the beginning, so it is today: the Himalaya and Karakoram are *still* being raised out of the earth, are *still* thrusting ever higher in an upheaval which has been going on for a couple of million years and seems likely to go on for many more.

These great ranges which have been prised up by the colliding continents form the most significant and spectacular physical feature of our planet; they encompass the lushest rain forest, the highest peak, the deepest gorge, the most arid desert. They are worth preserving.

We will not, however, preserve them by ignoring them: by telling ourselves they are in another country, and the concern of another people. In the past we ignored the rain forests, and as a result over half of them today have been totally destroyed, never to return, and one species of forest flora or fauna is becoming extinct every eight hours of every day of every week of every month of every year. What happened to the forests could happen to the mountains; for if trees continue to be felled on the slopes of the Himalaya, the area *could* become another dust bowl; if the Amu-Daria continues to be siphoned off for irrigation, vast reaches of Turkmenistan and Uzbekistan *could* be metamorphosed to desert.

Today the veil of mystery which for so long enveloped the mountain complex is being lifted. First the explorers, then the climbers and finally the scientists have laid bare its secrets, and our knowledge of this last great wilderness area is increasing every year. This augurs well for the future; for out of knowledge may, in time, come wisdom.

Out of knowledge, too, will surely come an even greater sense of appreciation. . . If you stand on the hairpin bends of the Karakoram Highway, a little above Gilgit, you can hardly fail to experience a sense of awe and wonder at what is probably the most spectacular view on earth: behind you the near-sheer face of Rakaposhi rising to 25,000 feet (7625 m), in front of you the even-sheerer face of Nanga Parbat rising to 26,000 feet (7930 m). And your wonder will be heightened if you know what you are looking at: if you identify Rakaposhi as the mightiest of the great volcanoes which a million years ago girdled the Sea of Tethys, and Nanga Parbat as the outrider of the Indian subcontinent bearing down on Eurasia like the bow of the leading ship in a vast armada.

As Hooker wrote nearly 140 years ago: 'Nowhere else on earth are the wonders of the Natural World displayed with such majesty and in such variety and profusion.'

This is our heritage.

APPENDIX I

PRINCIPAL EVENTS IN THE HISTORY OF THE MOUNTAINS

Cretaceous era *c.* **70 million** B.C.
Gondwanaland subdivides into the land masses of Africa, India, Australia, South America and Antarctica.

Pliocene era *c.* **3 million** B.C.
India, drifting northward, crashes into Asia: mountains are squeezed up between the converging continental plates.

Pleistocene era *c.* **500,000** B.C.
Homo erectus migrates into the mountains.

c. **200,000** B.C.
Mongoloids settle to the north of the mountains, Negroids to the south, Primitives (Naga) to the southeast.

c. **1000** B.C.
Hindu pilgrims trace the great rivers of India to their sources on the Tibetan plateau.

330–325 B.C.
Alexander the Great crosses the Hindu Kush and explores the approaches to the Pamirs.

A.D. **602–5**
Hsuan Tsang's pilgrimage from China to India, via the Takla Makan, Tien Shan and Hindu Kush.

1219–22
Genghis Khan and the Golden Horde (200,000 cavalry) pillage the north-facing slopes of the mountains; many great cities, already affected by the worsening climate, never recover.

1271–5
Travels of Marco Polo.

1398–9
Tamerlane's invasion of India: sack of Delhi; spoliation of the Indo-Ganetic plain leaves five million dead.

1603–7
Father Bento de Goes' journey from India to China.

1624–8
Father Antonio de Andrade attempts to found the first Jesuit mission in the Himalaya.

1661–2
Fathers Grueber and D'Orville travel from Peking to India via Lhasa and the Nepal Himalaya.

1774–5
Bogle's mission to Tibet: first detailed reports on the eastern Himalaya to reach Europe.

1811–2
Manning's journey to Lhasa.

1819–25
Moorcroft's travels in Ladakh, Baltistan and Turkmenistan: first detailed reports on the western Himalaya to reach Europe.

1830–43
George Everest, Surveyor-General of India: work begins on the Great Trigonometrical Survey.

1831–2
Jacquemont's travels in Kashmir and Baltistan.

1834–9
Vigne's travels in Kashmir and Baltistan: first attempt to penetrate the Karakoram.

1838
John Wood's journey to the source of the Oxus (Amu-Daria).

1843–5
Wolff's mission of mercy to the snake pit in Bukhara.

1845–8
Sikh Wars: British annexation of the Punjab.

1848–9
Joseph Hooker's botanical studies in Nepal and Sikkim.

1849
Triangulation begins in the Lower Himalayas (Siwaliks).

1850–7
The artist Thomas Atkinson and his wife travel extensively in central Asia.

1852
Mount Everest triangulated and found to be the highest mountain the world.

1856/7
Peter Semyonov's exploration of the Tien Shan: discovery of Khan Tengri ('Lord of the Spirits').

1857–65
Johnson and his Khalasi surveyors traingulate and climb many peaks of over 20,000 feet (6100 m) in the Karakoram.

1865/7
Olga and Alexis Fedchenko's travels in the Pamir.

1865–85
Pundit explorers under the direction of Montgomerie carry out route surveys in Tibet and Sinkiang.

1870–88
Przhevalski's four great expeditions through the Takla Makan, Ala Shan, Kun Lun and the north Tibetan plateau not only explore but study scientifically the unknown heart of Asia.

1872
Kostenko leads military expedition to Lake Karakol; Russians annex Pamirs and Trans-Alai.

1872–90
Ney Elias' journeys in the Gobi desert, the Karakoram and the Pamirs.

1883
Graham, 'the first man to climb in the Himalaya purely for pleasure', reaches the summit of Forked Peak (20,340 ft, 6204 m).

1892
Conway's expedition to the Karakoram.

1894
Sven Hedin, the famous Swedish traveller, makes four attempts to climb Mustagh Ata, one of them mounted on a yak. Reaches 20,600 feet (6283 m).

1895
Mummery and two Gurkhas killed on Nanga Parbat. Pamir Boundary Commission delineates the Afghan/Russian frontier.

1898–1913
Fanny and William Workman's expeditions to the Himalaya and Karakoram; first major peaks to be climbed by a woman.

1903–4
Younghusband's 'diplomatic mission' to Lhasa.

1906
Great Britain and Russia acknowledge Chinese suzerainty over Tibet.

1907–13
Kellas climbs and trains Sherpas in the Sikkim Himalaya; first scientific studies of the effect of high altitude on the human system.

1909
Abruzzi's expedition to K2: pioneer work in the technique of photogrammetric surveying.

1913
Final links between British and Russian triangulation surveys completed.

1921
Howard-Bury leads first British reconnaissance to north face of Everest.

1922
Bruce leads first British attempt on Everest: seven porters killed by avalanche.

1924
Second British attempt on Everest: Norton reaches 28,126 feet (8578 m): deaths of Mallory and Irvine.

1928
Allwein, Schneider and Wein climb Mount Lenin (23,383 ft, 7132 m).

1929
Bauer's first reconnaissance of Kangchenjunga.

1931
Holdsworth, Shipton, Smythe and Lewa climb Kamet (25,447 ft, 7761 m): first ascent of a peak of over 25,000 feet (7625 m); first ascent of any major peak by a Sherpa.

1932
Merkl's first Nanga Parbat expedition.

1933
E. M. Abalakov leads joint British/Russian expedition to the summit of Peak Communism (24,548 ft, 7487 m).

1934
Merkl's second Nanga Parbat expedition: deaths of four Germans and six porters.

1937
Third German attempt on Nanga Parbat: deaths of seven Germans and nine porters.

1944–50
Peter Aufschnaiter and Heinrich Harrer escape from POW camp in India, and in two years walk over 1000 miles (1600 km) to Lhasa, where they are accepted into Tibetan society, Aufschnaiter working in engineering and Harrer as tutor to the Dalai Lama.

1947
Independence and partition of India.

1950
Chinese Communist armies invade Tibet. Herzog and Lachenal reach the summit of Annapurna: the first 8000-metre peak to be climbed. Tilman–Houston reconnaissance of the southern approaches to Everest.

1951
Shipton's reconnaissance of the south face of Everest: a route found to the summit.

1953
John Hunt leads British expedition to Everest: the first proven ascent of the world's highest mountain by Hillary and Tenzing Norkay.
Herman Buhl's amazing 40-hour solo climb to the summit of Nanga Parbat.

1954
Ardito Desio leads Italian ascent of the world's second-highest peak, K2; Compagnoni and Lacedelli reach the summit.

1955
Kangchenjunga (world's third highest peak) climbed by British expedition led by Charles Evans. The climbers stop a few feet short of the summit in deference to the wishes of the people of Sikkim who regard the mountain as sacred.
Makalu climbed by French expedition led by J. Franco. Three groups of three climbers reach the summit on three successive days.

1956
Vitaly Abalakov leads a joint Sino-Soviet expedition to Mustagh Ata, the highest of the Tien Shan. 19 Soviets and 12 Chinese reach the summit after a highly successful – and highly political – massed assault.

1959
Gasherbrum I (Hidden Peak) climbed by the Americans P. Schoening and A. Kauffman.
Mammoth Chinese expedition to Mustagh Ata; 25 men and 8 women, including many Tibetans, reach the summit.

1960
Large Chinese expedition of 214 climbers makes the first (proven) ascent of the north face of Everest. Three climbers, Wang Fu-Chou, Konbu and Cho Yin Hua (the latter in stockinged feet) reach the summit just before dark after a gruelling 19-hour climb. Cho Yin Hua subsequently loses all ten toes from frost-bite. For years this claim was regarded with unjustified scepticism by the West, but is now recognized.

1963
American team led by Norman Dyhrenfurth reach the summit of Everest and achieve the first traverse of the mountain.

1964
Last 'eight-thousander', Gosaintham, is climbed by a Chinese expedition.

1970
Chris Bonington leads British expedition up the south face of Annapurna: the start of rock-wall climbing in the Himalaya.
Tony Waltham leads expedition to explore the limestone caves of the Harpan River.

1975
Japanese Ladies' Expedition attains the summit of Everest.
Large Chinese expedition carries out extensive geological and medical research on the Rongbuk Glaciers.

1978
Reinhold Messner climbs Everest and Nanga Parbat without oxygen.

1980
Reinhold Messner climbs Everest solo.
Royal Geographical Society's International Expedition to the Karakoram carries out extensive programme of geological, geomorphological, seismic and ethnic research.

APPENDIX II

THE PEOPLE OF THE MOUNTAINS

S TARTING in the extreme west of the mountain complex, and working clockwise round the ranges, the following ethnic communities are to be found:

THE TURKOMEN

Population: 1.5 million; *language:* Turkic; *religion*: orthodox Sunni Muslim.

The Turkomen live in the barren plateau centred on the junction of Iran, Afghanistan and the Soviet Republic of Turkmenistan. They are a Caucasoid people, some being almost Nordic in appearance, with aquiline features, blue eyes and pale skin.

Until recently they were nomads, living in small dome-shaped tents, and forever driving their sheep, goats, horses and camels from one seasonal grazing area to the next; when on the move they banded together into communities small enough to avoid overgrazing but large enough to defend themselves. In recent years, Soviet influence and the introduction of collective farms have brought about a more static way of life, and many Turkomen today spend half the year on a state-owned wheat, barley or cotton farm, and the other half tending their herds.

Their society is religious, conservative and male-dominated. The majority still pray the obligatory five times a day, and observe Ramadan – when food, drink and sex are prohibited for much of the time. The winds of change are anathema to them. Women are second-class citizens: 'When a husband's guests are present, a wife must cover her mouth with her head-cloth and not speak. She must sit quietly in a section of the tent reserved for people of low status, and quickly obey any orders given her by the men.'

They are an independent but not an influential people who, until recently, have been left to their own devices because the land in which they live is almost devoid of wealth.

THE UZBEK

Population: 7 million; *language*: Uzbek; *religion*: unorthodox Sunni Muslim.

The Uzbek live in the Soviet republics of Turkmenistan and Uzbekistan: an area of desert-cum-plateaux bisected by one of the great rivers of the world, the Oxus/Amu-Daria. This river is the essence of Uzbek life, 'the lifeline thrown down by Allah to the desert people when they were dying of thirst'; it supports 20,000 desert wells and a complex system of irrigation. 'If the Amu dies today,' runs a proverb, 'everyone dies tomorrow.'

The Uzbek are a mixture of Caucasoid and Mongoloid. The original cultivators of the oases were Caucasoids: a tall, rather dark-skinned people with Nordic features and much facial hair. They were over-run during the Middle Ages by successive waves of Mongoloids: a thick-set, sallow-skinned people with flat features and little body hair. The two races intermingled, with the result that the Uzbek today are as heterogeneous as almost any people on earth: a diversity reflected in their sophisticated clothing, cosmopolitan cuisine and religious tolerance.

Until recently most Uzbek were either steppe-nomads (on the plateaux) or bazaar-artisans and traders (in the valley of the Amu). The last 50 years, however, have seen increasing industrialization, and Uzbekistan today is one of the most prosperous republics in the Soviet Union. Its collective farms give high yields, its factories steady outputs; there are chemical plants, oil wells, coal, tin, copper and gold mines. One might

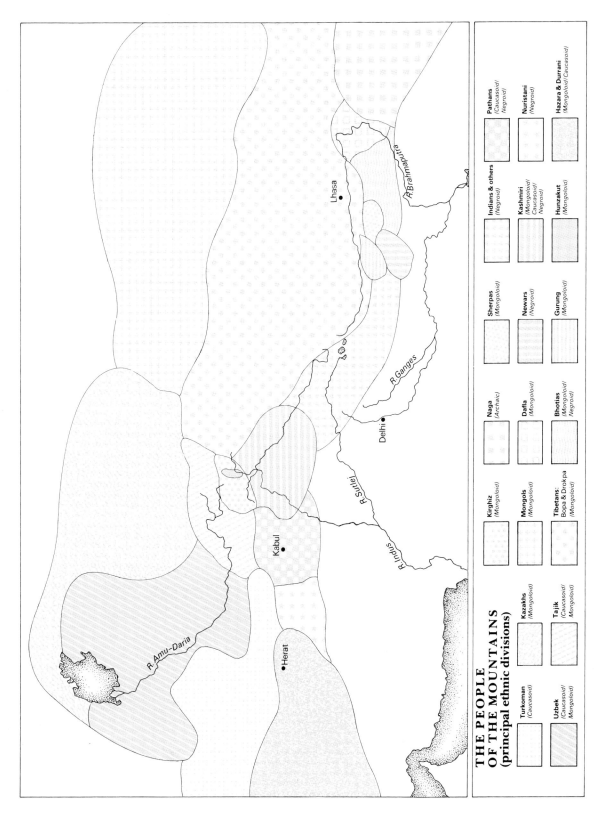

THE PEOPLE
OF THE MOUNTAINS
(principal ethnic divisions)

Turkoman
(Caucasoid)

Uzbek
(Caucasoid/
Mongoloid)

Kirghiz
(Mongoloid)

Mongols
(Mongoloid)

Tibetans:
Bopa & Drokpa
(Mongoloid)

Kazakhs
(Mongoloid)

Tajik
(Caucasoid/
Mongoloid)

Naga
(Archaic)

Dafla
(Mongoloid)

Bhotias
(Mongoloid/
Negroid)

Sherpas
(Mongoloid)

Newars
(Negroid)

Gurung
(Mongoloid)

Indians & others
(Mongoloid/
Negroid)

Kashmiri
(Mongoloid/
Caucasoid/
Negroid)

Hunzakut
(Mongoloid)

Pathans
(Caucasoid/
Negroid)

Nuristani
(Negroid)

Hazara & Durrani
(Mongoloid/Caucasoid)

R.Amu-Daria

Herat

Kabul

R.Indus

R.Sutlej

R.Ganges

Delhi

Lhasa

R.Brahmaputra

225

*Left: Turkoman woman and, below,
Tajik men*

have thought so much 'Russification' would have led to a loss of independence, but this is not so. The Uzbeks still retain their language, culture and freedom; they are an independent resilient people, one of the world's minorities who make themselves felt.

THE KAZAKHS

Population: 4 million; *language*: Turkic; *religion*: Muslim.

The Kazakhs live in the heart of the steppe country, in the plateaux of Kazakhstan, the foothills of the Tien Shan and the periphery of the Kyzylkum desert.

Ethnically they, too, are a heterogeneous people, although with more Mongoloid and fewer Caucasoid characteristics than their neighbours to the southwest.

They are a widely scattered, disunited race, ever merging yet never uniting with their neighbours; some are so rich they own 2000 horses, others so poor they cannot afford a single goat. They are ever shifting, ever migrating from one grazing area to the next, ever at odds with authority, ever hospitable to the few strangers who come their way. They build no cities; like their neighbours, the Mongols, 'their kingdom is the back of a horse'.

Since World War II, some of them have deserted their wholly nomadic life to work part-time in the collective wheat, barley and maize farms which have sprung up in the few fertile valleys of Kazakhstan. However, they are wanderers at heart, and return when they can to the life of wagon and *yurt*: a life which has proved as enduring as the steppe over which the wagon-fleets roll today, very much as they rolled 2000 years ago.

THE TAJIK

Population: 5 million; *language*: Tajiki (Persian); *religion*: Sunni Muslim.

The Tajik live in the scattered oases and steep-sided valleys of the upper reaches of the Amu-Daria: a remote and spectacular region of plateaux and peaks astride the Soviet–Afghan border.

Like their neighbours, they are a mixture of Caucasoid and Mongoloid, the former strain predominating in the west, the latter in the east. But whereas with the Uzbek and Kazakhs the two strains have mingled, with the Tajik they have frequently developed in isolation; for so remote are some of the oases and valleys that their inhabitants have lived for millennia virtually cut off from the rest of the world, have married among themselves and have thus preserved the ethnic purity of the original settlers. More than one traveller has noted that in this part of the world 'the inhabitants of one village will be dark-haired, dark-eyed and with much facial hair, [whereas] in the next village they are blond, blue-eyed and with complexions fair and smooth as a Flemming's.'

Until recently most Tajik were subsistence farmers, growing wheat, barley, millet, onions, turnips and nuts in the scattered oases and south-facing slopes of their valleys. This traditional way of life is now threatened by Soviet plans to harness the Amu-Daria for irrigation; for the Tajik fear that if water is syphoned-off to irrigate the state-owned cotton and fruit farms, the 20,000 wells – the very warp and weft of desert life – will dry up. To quote Nikifor Petrovich, one of the river-pilots:

The Amu is not the river she was when I first knew her. Man has raped her. She gets feebler each season, as her water is diverted here for irrigation, there for a canal. She's not a cow. You can't milk her like that. Today the engineers may have their cotton fields and orchards, but tomorrow the desert wells will run dry.

One can only hope that the lifeline thrown down by the mercy of Allah is not lost by the foolishness of man.

The people of Turkmenistan, from a
photograph c. 1885

THE KIRGHIZ

Population: 1.5 million; *language*: Turkic; *religion*: Sunni Muslim.

The Kirghiz live in the highest inhabited plateau in the world: the Pamirs, a 14,000-foot (4270 m) tableland of barren peaks and featureless valleys astride the Kirghizia/Tadzhikstan borders – a world of vast distances and lunar solitude.

They are a Mongoloid people who came originally from Siberia. Migrating into the Pamirs during the ninth century, they have remained there ever since, virtually cut off from the rest of the world.

The Pamirs provide grazing that is poor in quality but almost limitless in quantity, and the Kirghiz evolved into nomads *par excellence*: little groups of four or five families banding together, and driving their herds of horses, yak, cattle, sheep, donkeys and camels from one pasture to the next, continually on the move, locked in combat with weather and terrain, dwarfed by an immensity of steppe and sky.

They are a proud, independent race, with a long tradition of military prowess. Of all the peoples of the Soviet Union they showed the fiercest resistance to collectivization. Witness their battle-song:

> *Like a mountain torrent we ran down against them,*
> > *We ravaged their campsites.*
> *We destroyed their lines of communication,*
> > *And laid our excrement on their food dumps.*
> *At nights we attacked them from all directions.*
> > *We severed their heads,*
> *And laid our brand on their horses.*
> > *The red flag flew;*
> *The dust rose over their graves.*

They have an equally short way with animal predators. This is Sven Hedin's description of how they deal with wolves: 'When possible, they would capture one alive, tie a heavy pole to his neck and a piece of wood between his jaws, and wind ropes about him. Then they would torture him with whips, blind him with glowing coals and stuff his mouth with dry snuff.' Yet these same people, to their friends, are kind, gentle and unfailingly hospitable. When Tilman and the Shiptons tried to climb Mustagh Ata, Mr Shipton had no qualms about leaving his wife near the base camp to stay with a Kirghiz family in their *yurt*, 'for these nomads have a well-deserved reputation for hospitality'.

Like the Bedouin of the desert, a Kirghiz is an enemy to fear, a friend to cherish.

228

A Tibetan princess, from a photograph c. 1900

THE MONGOLS

Population: 1.5 million; *language*: Altaic: *religion*: Shamanism with occasional communities of Christians and Lamist Buddhists.

The Mongols live in and around the Takla Makan depression, an arid wilderness of gravel, sand and rock, lashed by bitter winds and encircled by a horseshoe of gauntly beautiful mountains: the Kun Lun, Tien Shan and Alai – a tremendous but merciless landscape.

As their name implies, they are pure Mongoloid: round-headed, thickset and with little body hair. Genghis Khan welded them into one of the most lethal armies the world has ever known, and for a brief period their empire was more extensive than Alexander's.

Today they have fallen on hard times. With their huge indefensible territory and a life style centred on their horses, it could not be otherwise; and for the last 100 years Russia and China have been systematically moving into the Takla Makan, reducing the herdsmen-archers, with their unchanging society and out-dated weapons, to sub-servience. Today the descendants of the Golden Horde no longer ride herd over the steppe, but live in semi-permanent settlements of *yurts* on the outskirts of industrial cities. Here they exist in a sort of limbo, tied to the past but not yet attuned to the future: an anti-climax for a people whose empire once extended over half the known world.

THE TIBETANS

Population: 2.2 million; *language*: Tibetan; *religion*: Lamist Buddhist.

The Tibetans live in the high, bleak and extensive plateau which lies between the Himalaya to the south and the Kun Lun to the north: an area, far larger than France and the Iberian Peninsula combined, which is virtually cut off from the rest of the world.

Ethnically, they consist of two Mongoloid races who migrated on to the plateau about 1000 years ago: the sedentary and house-dwelling Bopa, who are mainly farmers-cum-artisans; and the nomadic and tent-dwelling Drokpa, who are mainly farmers-cum-traders. Their outward characteristics have been summed up by the historian Swami Pranavananda: 'both men and women are strong, sturdy and hard-working; they have great powers of resistance to cold and hardship; they are primitive, cheerful, pleasure-loving, peaceful, religious-minded, hospitable and contented; but dirty in their habits and customs.' Their inward characteristics are not so easy to pin down.

Tibetan life has always been overloaded with dualities: extreme alternations of heat and cold; an exterior of glittering splendour, an interior of darkness and poverty. And the same is true of Tibetan character: extreme generosity goes hand in hand with mindless cruelty, spontaneous laughter with contemplative ritual. Until recently, this duality was given an overall cohesion by religion: a third of the population were monks, nuns or hermits; *mantra* (sacred texts) were everywhere, painted on walls, rocks and houses; *korlo* (prayer wheels) were endlessly turning. Religion was the be-all and end-all of Tibetan life.

The destruction of this idiosyncratic system came not with the Chinese invasion of 1950, but with the Chinese suppression of the subsequent rebellion of 1959. This resulted in the total military, political and spiritual subjugation of Tibet; some 100,000 people were killed, some three-quarters of a million were made homeless, and some 2600 monasteries razed to the ground. It was the destruction of an entire culture unparalleled in modern history.

Since then a lot of nonsense has been written about life in Tibet. *Reader's Digest* claim the country has sunk into 'a quagmire of barbarism'; Marxists claim it has been liberated – 'to give an example, the butter which used to be wasted in making candles (the Jokhang monastery alone burned 4000 lb a day!) has been redistributed among the people.'

The truth seems to be that temporally the Tibetans are marginally better off under the Chinese, but spiritually they are a great deal worse off, denied their old gods and unresponsive to their new. The sewers in Lhasa may be improved, but the prayer wheels no longer turn; *mantra* are used to floor public lavatories, and the heartbeat of the nation's life, religion, has been stilled.

THE NAGA

Population: 500,000; *language*: Tibeto-Burmese or English; *religion*: Shamanism or Christianity.

The Naga live in Assam, in the densely forested mountains where China, Tibet, India and Burma converge, one of the least accessible regions on earth.

They are a pale-skinned, handsome people with straight hair and regular features, quite unlike either the Mongoloids to the north or the Negroids to the south. Indeed they are unlike any people within 1000 miles of Assam – their next-of-kin live in Taiwan, the Philippines and Borneo – for they are one of the last surviving remnants of an archaic civilization which, in prehistoric times, extended over most of southeast Asia, but which now exists only in the last redoubts of the rain forest. They are Primitives.

Nothing shows their origin more clearly than the buildings in which they live; for whereas Mongoloids live in tents and Negroids in small individual dwellings of mud or stone, the Naga live communally in massive wooden longhouses, some of them more than 300 feet (92 m) long. Each longhouse is a close-knit, self-sufficient community, around which all activities are centred. Not so long ago the walls were decorated with trophies: the heads of buffalo and elephant and the skulls of rival warriors killed in battle – the latter being fed with rice-beer to keep their souls happy and so bring good fortune to the longhouse.

But the days of headhunting are over. In the last 50 years, an amazing change has come over the Nagas' lives. Today, thanks to missionaries and agricultural advisers, two-thirds of the people are Christians, English is the universal language, and the old and wasteful 'slash and burn' method of agriculture has been replaced by the planting of cash and subsistence crops. 'Thus [to quote *The Family of Man*] a population previously divided into warring units and separated by the threat of headhunting, is being transformed into a people with an ethnic identity.'

THE DAFLA

Population: 25,000; *language*: Tibeto-Burmese; *religion*: sun and spirit worship.

The Dafla live in the remote and inaccessible Arunachal Pradesh, astride the India–Tibet border, a little to the west of the Naga.

They are Mongoloids, totally different in physique and physiognomy from their neighbours: a turbulent, disorganized people, whose lives are unbelievably chaotic. Their agriculture is chaotic, for they roam haphazardly through the mountains, felling, burning, sowing and cultivating one patch of jungle, then moving on to the next. Their home life is chaotic, for they live in small, single-room longhouses with up to a dozen families eating and sleeping on top of one another without privacy. Their social life is chaotic, for they have no laws, no organization and are constantly feuding. Even their religion is chaotic, for they worship one benevolent sun-god, but are forever propitiating evil spirits with sacrifices. Yet in one respect they are in tune with modern life. Dafla women enjoy a privileged status and complete independence; before marriage they engage in farming and trade, sometimes amassing considerable wealth; after marriage they take charge of all their husband's earnings and valuables.

Until recently their poverty and isolation were ameliorated by trade. However, the closing of the India–Tibet border sealed off the traditional trade routes, and this has denied the Dafla that touch of wealth, colour and variety which made their lot endurable. They are now one of the world's threatened people who have not a great deal in their favour.

THE BHOTIAS

Population: 2 million; *language*: Tibeto-Burmese; *religion*: Lamist Buddhist.

The Bhotias live in the northern part of Bhutan, Sikkim and Nepal, on the south-facing slopes of the Himalayas: a world of high valleys, high rainfall and relatively high population.

They are a Mongoloid people, who, over the centuries, have been gradually forced off the Tibetan plateau by its worsening climate, and have intermingled with the Negroids of the South.

Until recently their economy was based on crop growing, animal husbandry and trade. Because their valleys are covered in snow for much of the year, their crops need to be tough and quick-maturing – barley, buckwheat, radishes and potatoes. For the same reason their animals also need to be tough – sheep, goats and yak, the latter being especially prized since they are both beasts of burden and a source of milk, fat, meat and hide. Up to 1950 the Bhotias acted as middlemen in the trade between the plains of India and plateaux of Tibet. The closing of the border has knocked away one of the props of their economy, and it is therefore vital that they now take advantage of improved techniques in agriculture.

Because of the altitude of the land they farm – between 8000 and 13,000 feet (2440–3965 m) – most Bhotias are seasonal nomads, alternating between a winter house in the lower reaches of the valley and a summer tent in the upper. This means that husbands and wives are frequently parted, the former spending the summer with their animals in the high pastures while the latter, some 5000 feet (1525 m) below, look after the family houses. Since both sexes have their own work to do and their own lives to lead, they regard one another as equals, and a degree of sexual permissiveness is condoned.

Realizing that the mountains surrounding them are not only aesthetically beautiful but economically invaluable (as the source of the water on which their lives depend) the Bhotias are forever singing their praises. They are a deeply religious people, most of them Lamist Buddhists who believe in reincarnation, and their homes are nearly always adorned with brightly coloured religious frescoes. Even the smallest village has its temple, even the least frequented track is gay with prayer flags, *mantra* and shrines.

THE SHERPAS

Population: 30,000; *languate*: Tibetan; *religion*: Buddhist.

The Sherpas live in the glacial valleys at the southern approaches to Everest. Their territory is flanked by Gosainthan in the west and Kangchenjunga in the east, which means they control the Nangpa La and Arun passes, two of the most important trade routes over the Himalaya.

Their name tells of their origin – *Sha* = east, and *pa* = people – and it was roughly 600 years ago that these 'people of the east' migrated from the Tibetan plateau to their present home. They are Mongoloids: a tough, resilient race, with a reputation for courage and physical strength – a Sherpa can carry a load for hours which a European can hardly lift.

This load-carrying ability stems from their expertise as traders; for they not only established themselves as middlemen in the trade between India and Tibet, they also took over as organizers, guards, guides and porters to the merchants' caravans, guaranteeing them safe conduct through the Himalayan passes: their price, a toll on the southbound salt, wool, jewellery, Chinese silk and porcelain, and on the northbound butter, meat, rice, sugar, paper, dye and kerosene. Therefore, long before the first climbers set foot in the Himalaya, the Sherpas could boast a high standard of living and the reputation of being porters and guides *par excellence*.

Like their neighbours, they are a deeply religious people, the cornerstone of their faith being a belief in reincarnation. They believe that in this life each person acquires a degree of *sonam* – religious merit – good deeds increasing one's *sonam* and bad deeds diminishing it. When a person dies, they believe this *sonam* is weighed in the balance, and the person's next life is decreed accordingly. Being a practical people, they have evolved rules by which *sonam* can be augmented: plus marks for good deeds, good relations with one's neighbours and kindness to animals; minus marks for strife, theft, fraud and the taking of any form of life. To quote Toni Hagan's excellent book *Nepal*: 'The consequence of these doctrines on the daily life of the Sherpas is their deep respect for the dignity and independence of their fellow-creatures, and their active charity.'

The drying up of trade between India and Tibet struck at the very root of their prosperity, but they have recently found an alternative source of wealth. In the old days, with their tradition as porters and guides, they were ideally suited to help the big expeditions. Today, big expeditions are being replaced by a steady influx of tourists and, in particular, trekkers. These trekkers need guides; and Sherpas are becoming increasingly involved in the opening up of their homeland to the outside world – and who better to forge bonds of friendship between the nations than these robust but gentle people?

THE NEWARS

Population: 90,000; *language*: Tibeto-Burmese; *religion*: originally Buddhist, but now with a sizeable Hindu minority.

The Newars live in the foothills of the Himalaya, in the fertile and beautiful valleys around Kathmandu. They are unique among the people of the Himalaya in having remained in the same area for several millennia, and their mythology is rich and their level of culture high.

Originally they were a Paleo-Mongolian race, with sallow complexion and slit eyes, but over the centuries they have absorbed many Indian/Negroid characteristics, and are now slightly built and graceful, and have as much in common with the people of the plains as with the people of the mountains.

Their economy, like their culture, is a unique blend of the primitive and the sophisticated. The plough is unknown, and they till their fields with Stone Age mattocks; yet their irrigation system is complex, efficient and run on the lines of a trade union. They are one of the few people who harvest twice a year, and their fields grow a wider and a better range of fruit and vegetables than anywhere else in the Himalaya except Kashmir. Their homes are attractive – brickwork within decorated wooden frames, with big windows and pagoda-style roofs – while their villages are the prettiest imaginable, and bear comparison with the most beautiful German or Swiss alpine towns. The care and artistry which they lavish on their homes they also lavish on their metal, stone, and woodwork, and on their books and paintings. They are a delightfully idiosyncratic people, whose lives have altered little in the last millennium.

THE GURUNG

Population: 200,000; *language*: Tibeto-Burmese; *religion*: originally Buddhist, now predominantly Hindu.

The Gurung live in the shadow of the Annapurna massif, another beautiful and fertile part of the world, controlling the approaches to the Kali Gandaki gorge, the most spectacular of the trade routes through the Himalaya.

They are of Mongoloid stock: a strong, hardy and fearless people with a long tradition of military prowess. As early as the sixteenth century, they were much sought after as mercenaries in the wars between the Indian princes, and in the nineteenth century, large numbers enlisted in the British army in India. It was then the name 'Gurkha' originated. Contrary to popular belief, there is no such race as the Gurkhas: the Gurkhas are Gurung who came originally from the fortress town of Goraknath; the name is therefore geographical, not ethnic. Even today, their lives are centred on military service. Almost all the young men enlist for a minimum of three years, and most of them remain in the army a great deal longer; the result is that in a typical village at least half of the males between 19 and 45 are likely to be in British or Indian regiments. It is this extended service in India which has led many to desert the Buddhist faith in favour of the Hindu.

Since so many Gurung leave their homes, one might suppose their standard of living was low or their social life unsatisfactory. On the contrary: their villages are among the most attractive in the world, and their life the happiest. Their circular houses, usually laid on great slabs of rock, are grouped together on terraced hillsides; they are built of stone and roofed with thatch, their south-facing verandahs often surrounded by exotic flowering trees and shrubs. Their family life is hierarchical but not tyrannical. Many visitors have been struck by the contrast between the villages of the plains, and the Sherpa and Gurung villages of the hills: the former quiet as the grave, the latter full of dogs barking, cocks crowing, and people forever singing, chattering and laughing.

'Happiness,' a retired Gurkha once told me, 'is a cluster of thatched-roofed houses, watched over by the Bringer of Life.'

In west Nepal and the northwest tip of India, the different races are as interwoven as the threads of a cat's cradle. This is the 'ethnic turn-table of Asia', where some dozen races – Thakurs, Brahmans, Bhotias, Garhwals, Rais, Kumaons, Indians and Mangars, some Mongoloid, some Negroid, most a mixture of the two – live cheek by jowl in a mosaic too intricate to unravel. Not until we come to Kashmir do we find a people that it is possible to treat as an entity.

THE KASHMIRI

Population: 4.5 million; *language*: various; *religion*: Buddhist, Hindu and Muslim.

The Kashmiri live in the west Himalaya, where the ranges abut the Karakoram to the north and the Hindu Kush to the west. Politically, Kashmir embraces the provinces of Jammu, Kashmir, Ladakh, Baltistan and Gilgit, an area of nearly 100,000 square miles. Ethnically, it embraces pure Mongoloids in the north, pure Negroids in the south and a sizeable Caucasoid minority in the west. Its people worship different gods, speak different languages, have diverse cultures. What, one wonders, holds them together?

A romantic might say 'beauty'. Kashmir has long enjoyed the reputation of a latterday Eden: 'that paradise on earth of which priests have prophesied and singers sung'. Poets have eulogized it in execrable verse:

> *Who has not heard of the Vale of Cashmere*
> *With its roses the brightest that earth ever gave,*
> *Its temples and grottoes and fountains as clear*
> *As the love-lighted eyes that hang over their wave?*

while modern textbooks enthuse over its 'snow-capped peaks and sparkling streams, its high pastures carpeted with alpine flowers, its fertile valleys rich with fruit and grain, and its magnificent chains of lakes.' As for its women! From time immemorial travellers have noted that their beauty surpasses even that of the land in which they live; poets in a dozen languages have extolled their slim build, pale skin and delicate features; in Arab slave markets it was the Kashmiri *nautch* girls who traditionally commanded the highest prices.

A more prosaic reason for Kashmir's cohesion is that its various peoples are so many in number and so similar in size and strength that no one group can hope to gain dominance over the rest. Hindus and Muslims, Sikhs and Jats are therefore obliged to live side by side in uneasy peace. Uneasy because, as well as being internally divided, Kashmir lies astride the traditional route of invaders. The country's mountains failed in the past to keep out successive waves of conquerors, and the Kashmiri today, as they look to the north and east, are conscious that what happened before could happen again. Their life is like their shawls: beautiful and colourful, but of such gossamerlike fragility one wonders how long it will last.

THE HUNZAKUT

Population: 80,000; *language*: Burushaski; *religion*: Muslim.

The Hunzakut live in the valley of the Hunza, a river which slices through the Karakoram from north to south. Here is some of the most spectacular scenery on earth: great peaks rising near-sheer to over 20,000 feet (6100 m) on either side of a gorge so precipitous that in places the sun's rays never plumb its depths. For most of its course the Hunza flows through a world of almost lunar desolation, but a few days' trek up-river from Gilgit, one comes, unexpectedly, to an isolated pocket, intensely cultivated and densely populated: a community cut off from the world, the inspiration of James Hilton's Shangri-la.

The Hunzakut consist of two quite separate races: the Wakhi and the Burusho. The Wakhi were originally nomadic Mongoloids from Turkmenistan, who settled in the upper reaches of the Hunza about 1000 years ago. They now own all the usable land above about 8000 feet (2440 m); since this is too high for crop growing, they are animal husbanders.

The Burusho are an enigma. Nobody knows where they come from, although some ethnologists claim they are descendants of the troops of Alexander the Great. In support of this theory, they point out that the Burusho language is completely unrelated to any neighbouring tongue, and their irrigation channels are made in exactly the same way as those in Macedonia and Thrace. Whatever their origin, there is no doubt about the skill with which they have converted the stony reaches of the Hunza into a garden of Eden: an oasis of lush green strips of fields lined with poplar and willow, of aquaducts and runnels, and of orchards of apple, peach, mulberry and pear.

Both races are Muslims: strict, law-abiding and resistant to change. Their basic unit is the family, and the prosperity of a man is judged not by his acres but his sons. They have a reputation for sagacity and longevity – more shades of Shangri-la – and both races consider the most serious crime to be not adultery or murder, but the theft of (irrigated) water: evidence that for the Hunzakut the harnessing of their river is the very essence of life.

THE PATHANS

Population: 15 million; *language*: Pashtol (Iranian); *religion*: Sunni Muslim.

The Pathans live in north Pakistan and Afghanistan: a bleakly beautiful terrain of barren plateaux and deep-cut valleys, epitomized by the Khyber Pass.

They are a Caucasoid race, who emigrated from the Middle East during the first millennium B.C., popular tradition identifying them as the lost tribe of Israel who disappeared into the desert. Physically, they are taller and stronger than the Negroid races to the south, and slimmer and more hirsute than the Mongoloids to the north: a tough, proud and fiercely independent people who call no man master.

They occupy a vast territory, follow a wide variety of callings, and are subdivided into numerous small and semi-independent groups, rather like the old Scottish clans; the constant fueding between these groups has led them to be dubbed 'the largest and most chaotic tribal society in the world'. What binds them together is a common language – Pashtol – and a common code of behaviour – *Paktunwali*: the way of life for a Pathan. The latter in particular gives them a sense of cultural unity which over-rides their many divisions. *Paktunwali* promulgates three basic laws: the law of vengeance, which insists on retribution for every wrong no matter how slight; the law of hospitality, which must be extended to all strangers; and the law of sanctuary which must be given to all who ask for it. Although the Pathans' adherence to this code in the long-term binds them together, in the short-term it can have just the opposite effect. For every little dispute is blown up into a vendetta, and the repercussions of even the most petty crime are felt long after the crime itself was committed. To quote *The Family of Man*: 'The persistence of personal and family feuds means that Pathans rarely combine for united action on any long-term basis. Their code encourages a fascinating combination of generosity, justice, democracy, independence and violence.'

THE NURISTANI

Population: 75,000; *language*: Dardic (Indo-Iranian); *religion*: originally Hindu, now being forcibly converted to Muhammadanism.

The Nuristani live in south Afghanistan, on the slopes of the Hindu Kush. This is a world of extreme isolation; caravan routes pass to the east and west, but in the whole country there is only one road, a dirt track leading halfway up a single valley.

They are a Negroid-Hindu people, who for 1000 years have been struggling to stem the tide of Caucasoid-Muslim invaders from the northwest – the original Muslim name for Nuristan was Kafiristan, 'land of the infidels'. According to *Peoples of the Earth*:

> *They are a proud race, and although they are hospitable and friendly, they are also aggressive and quick to avenge any injury. They enjoyed centuries of independence, and raised their sons to be warriors and hunters, first with spear and bow and later with rifles. For eight or nine centuries they held out against the tide of Islam, raiding Muslim settlements and caravans . . . and a successful warrior was accorded rank in proportion to the number of Muslims he killed.*

At the end of the last century they came under the suzerainty of Afghanistan, a loss of independence summed up by one of their older warriors: 'In *my* day we drank wine and were strong. Then came the Muslims with their "civilization". Today we drink tea and are weak.'

One wonders how these proud and individualistic people have reacted to Soviet occupation? It would seem that, to outward appearances, their lives are little changed. They still live in villages of 100 to 200 wooden houses, clinging precariously to the steep-sided valleys; the women still till their fields by hand, while the men look after their irrigation channels – vital in a land where the rainfall is under five inches (13 cm) a year. Each village would still seem to be a world of its own, cut off economically and socially from its neighbours; but one cannot help wondering if, sometimes at night, these men of a warrior race might not be stalking commissars with the same enthusiasm as their grandfathers used to stalk mullahs.

THE HAZARA

Population: 1 million; *language*: Hazaraji (Persian); *religion*: Shi-ite Muslim.

The Hazara live in the desolate heights of central Afghanistan: an impoverished area, covered in snow for six months of the year. A 'hazare' was the old Mongol army unit of 1000 cavalry, and they are descendants of the waves of Turko-Mongols who flooded into Afghanistan between the thirteenth and fifteenth centuries. The *yurts* in which they live in summer are almost identical to those of the Kazakhs and Mongols.

They are the have-nots in a land where there is not, for anyone, a great deal to have: a poor but seemingly contented people, who have forsaken the warlike ways of their ancestors in favour of a nomadic and wholly pastoral life. In winter they live in communities of 30 or 40 small, mud-and-stone, single-room houses: no windows, just a fireplace and a smoke-hole; which in time of extreme cold can be blocked up. Each house has its adjoining stable, also with a fireplace and smoke-hole; and a Hazara will go without a fire himself rather than deny his animals comfort and warmth. In summer the community splits up, a minority staying at home to tend their fruit and crops, while the majority set off with their flocks for the high grasslands. Here, for five months, they move their animals from one meagre pasture to the next, menaced by dust storms and predators – principally wolves and eagles. It is a hard, cramped and often unhygienic life. Illness is endemic: eye-diseases (brought about by dust storms and smoke) are common; there is a high incidence of tuberculosis, and leprosy is not uncommon; girls of 20 look 40, and a man of 40 could be mistaken for a septuagenarian. But in spite of their afflictions the Hazara are good-tempered and easy-going. They are Shi-ite Muslims yet have none of the fanatical bigotry of some of their neighbours. In sexual matters they are permissive; their attitude to women is enlightened – it would be impossible to imagine them stoning a woman to death for adultery.

THE DURRANI

Population: 2 million; *language*: Pashtol (Indo-European); *religion*: Sunni Muslim.

The Durrani live in central and western Afghanistan. This is much the same area as the Hazara, but whereas the latter occupy the least attractive territory, the Durrani occupy the fertile valleys and the cities. For they are the élite of Afghan society: a Mongoloid people who migrated into the area about 1000 years ago, integrated with the original Caucasoid inhabitants, and established themselves as the ruling class. Today they monopolize the higher ranks in both government and armed forces.

Their life style is basically the same as the Hazara, though their winter mud-brick houses tend to be more comfortable, and their summer flocks and herds more numerous. They, too, are seasonal nomads, setting out each May for the mountain pastures – great caravans of up to 100 people and 3000 animals, trekking 250 miles (400 km) over 12,000-foot (3660 m) passes, to the choice grazing lands of the Hindu Kush – and returning at the end of August to harvest their millet, maize, apricots, grapes and melons.

They are Sunnite Muslims, stricter and more orthodox than their easy-going neighbours. Each village has its mosque, each campsite its square roped off for prayer. This is a man's world, in which women – like the Hazara – are second-class citizens.

APPENDIX III

◆

NATIONAL PARKS AND PROTECTED AREAS

THE mountains of Central Asia, with their wide range of flora and fauna and their unsurpassed natural beauty, are ideal territory for the creation of national parks and protected areas. On their south-facing slopes, several million hectares are now protected – Bhutan and Nepal being particularly committed to the cause of conservation. On their north-facing slopes, the situation is not easy to determine. The USSR has designated large areas of Turkmenistan, Uzbekistan, Kirghizia and Tadzhikistan as nature reserves, forest management areas or peoples' parks; these appear to be well-sited and well-run, although details are not readily available outside the Soviet Union.

In China the situation is obscure. We are told that 'because of destruction by successive reactionary governments and their failure to protect wild animals and plants, China's biological resources have been seriously depleted . . . However, major reserves are now being established, 13 in the province of Sichuan alone.' The truth seems to be that the heartland of China is reasonably well provided with nature reserves, but in the outlying provinces, conservation has a low priority – in the whole of Tibet, for example, there appears to be only one national park (a wildfowl sanctuary on Lake Koko-Nor).

The following list, compiled mainly from information produced by the Protected Areas Data Unit is, of necessity, incomplete, and in some cases even the exact location of a park is difficult to determine; however, it is hoped that all the major protected areas are listed.

AFGHANISTAN

Dashte Nawar (33°40′N, 67°45′E): 70,000 hectares; established 1977. A salt lake in the Hazarajat.

Pamir-i-Buzurg (37°N, 73°E approx.): 50,000 hectares; established 1978. Plateau in the foothills of the Pamirs: yak, Persian gazelle and Marco Polo sheep.

Ajar Valley (35°N, 67°30′E): 80,000 hectares; established 1980. Plateau and valley in the Koh Bata.

BHUTAN

Bhutan has done more for conservation than any other country in the world. Hunting is banned, timber felling is prohibited, a special elephant 'corridor' enables the animals to migrate. More than 20 per cent of Bhutan is now designated a 'protected' area, by far the largest reserve being:

Jigme Dorji Wildlife Sanctuary (27°N, 90°E): 781,000 hectares; established 1979. A cross-section of the Himalaya between 8000 and 24,000 feet (2440–7320 m). Many rare species, including snow leopard, clouded leopard, blood pheasant, red panda and musk deer.

Smaller reserves are sited at Doga, Pochu, Mochu, Coley, Manes and Khalnij.

BURMA

Piduang Game Sanctuary (25°30′N, 97°20′E): 70,000 hectares; established 1978. Tropical rain forest in the valley of the Irrawaddy; leopard and tiger.

Tamanthi Wildlife Sanctuary (25°20′N, 95°30′E): 215,000 hectares; established

A Sikkimese coolie woman,
photographed by
Chandra Das, c. 1879

1974. Rain forest on the slopes of the Temein: the only place in the world known to contain the very rare Sumatran rhinoceros – only 14 are believed to exist.

CHINA

Out of 51 nature reserves in China, only four are in the vicinity of the central mountains:
Baishuaijing Nature Reserve (32°36′N, 104°45′E): 180,000 hectares; established 1963. The foothills of the Kara Shan: coniferous forest; snow leopard, and many species of deer and goat.
Fanjing Mountains Nature Reserve (in West Yunnan Province, exact location unknown): 37,000 hectares; established 1978. Virgin sub-tropical forest with 'over 1000 varieties of trees, including the rare dove tree, and many medicinal herbs . . . leopard, deer and 17 protected species of fauna.'
Qinghaihu Bird Sanctuary (37°05′N, 100°30′E): 8000 hectares; established 1975. Ibisbill, bar-headed geese and many species of waterfowl.
Tianguan Labahe Nature Reserve (30°10′N, 102°47′E): 12,000 hectare; established 1974. Coniferous forest and sub-alpine flora.

INDIA

Corbett National Park (29°40′N, 78°50′E): 52,000 hectares; established 1955. Based on the Ramganga River in the Uttar Pradesh, an area of marshland and sal forest; tiger, rhinoceros and several endangered species of gharial crocodile.
Dachigam National Park (approx. 33°50′N, 75°30′E): 14,000 hectares; established 1978. Foothills of Ladakh Range; leopard, brown bear and many species of deer.

NEPAL

Nepal is second only to Bhutan in its commitment to conservation. The country used to be a hunter's paradise; in a single day's shoot in the 1850s, one of the Indian princes, it is said, 'killed 21 elephants, 31 tigers, seven stags, one rhinoceros, one crocodile, four bears, 20 deer and three leopards'. A hundred years later, due to indiscriminate slaughter for sport and the conversion of much of the animals' habitats to farming land, many once numerous species were threatened with extinction. The government initiated a comprehensive programme of conservation, and since then, no fewer than 15 national parks and reserves have been established, the larger and more important being:
Koshi Tappu Wildlife Reserve (26°40′N, 87°E): 6500 hectares; established 1979. *Terai* swamp and savannah grassland in the flood plain of the River Koshi; many birds and the remnants of the last herd of Asiatic wild buffalo (about 60 survivors).
Langtang National Park (28°15′N, 85°40′E): 170,900 hectares; established 1976. Scenery typical of the Himalayan foothills; deciduous and coniferous forest. Wild boar, black bear, leopard and snow leopard, musk deer.
Royal Chitwan National Park (27°30′N, 84°20′E): 93,000 hectares; established 1973. *Terai* swamp and sub-tropical lowland bordering the Rapti and Reu Rivers. Ideal habitat for the rare Indian one-horned rhinoceros (which exist only in this park) and the Royal Bengal tiger; other rare species include leopard, gaur, black bear, deer, red jungle fowl, Gangetic dolphin, gharial and mugger. Tiger Tops Jungle Lodge provides first-class facilities for visitors.
Sagarmatha National Park (27°50′N, 86°45′E): 124,000 hectares; established 1976. The upper catchment of the Dudh Kosi River, including Mount Everest. This is the home of the Sherpas and contains some of the most beautiful scenery on earth. Most of the park lies above 10,000 feet (3050 m); birch, rhododendron, pine, fir and juniper

forest. Rare animals include musk deer, tahr, red panda and snow leopard. Facilities for visitors at Namche, Thyangboche and Shyangboche. The development of the park owes a great deal to Sir Edmund and Lady Hillary.

PAKISTAN

Khunjerab National Park (approx. 31°N, 77°E): 23,000 hectares; established 1975. A remote and desolate tract of the Karakoram, close to the Chinese border, which contains not a single human inhabitant. Rare animals include Marco Polo sheep, mountain deer and goats and possibly snow leopard.

Kirthan National Park (approx. 26° 40′S, 66° 40′E): 309,000 hectares; established 1974. An arid semi-desert environment, rich in fossils.

SIKKIM

Khangchendozonga National Park (27°40′N, 88°40′E): 525,000 hectares; established 1977. Slopes of the Himalaya between 6000 and 20,000 feet (1830–6100 m), north of Darjeeling. Mixed coniferous and alpine flora; rare animals include musk deer, snow leopard, Tibetan sheep, red panda and blood pheasant.

USSR

The USSR takes conservation more seriously than China. Its protected areas are well-sited and managed, although information about them is often hard to come by.

Alma-Atinsky (43°N, 78°E): 90,000 hectares; established 1931. The bleak north-facing slopes of the Tien Shan, including Mount Telgar. Typical coniferous forest.

Altaisky (52°N, 88°E): 863,000 hectares; established 1932. One of the largest national parks in the world on the north slopes of the Altai Mountains around Lake Teletsky; coniferous forest and steppe.

Badkhysky Nature Reserve (43°N, 37°E): 88,000 hectares; established 1941. Desert and semi-desert, on the edge of the windswept Karakum – the name 'Badkhysky' means 'the wind is rising'. A brief rainy season in March/April is followed by a long hot summer and a short sharp winter. Animals include gazelles, Kulan (wild ass), Khorozan agamas, lizards and possibly the very rare gepard (Asiatic cheetah). Interesting plants include ferulas, which lie dormant for seven or eight years before bursting into spectacular flower, and pistachio nut trees, some 1000 years old with 35-yard (32 m) roots.

Chatkal Forestry Reserve (42°40′N, 57°50′E): 36,000 hectares; established 1947. The headwaters of the Syr-Daria: an area of great natural beauty, sheltered from the blizzards of Siberia by the Tien Shan, and from the dust storms of Afghanistan by the Alai: contains 1500 varieties of trees and shrubs, and over 250 species of birds.

Kaplankyrsky Nature Reserve (42°N, 54°E): 570,000 hectares; established 1979. A huge reserve on the border of Turkmenistan and Uzbekistan 'reserved for the study of desert ecosystems'.

Repetek Nature Reserve (38°10′N, 63°20′E): 34,000 hectares; established 1978. A small desert research station near the centre of the Karakum: desert grasses and scrub, numerous desert reptiles and insects.

Sarychelek Forestry Reserve (42°40′N, 71°50′E): 23,000 hectares; established 1978. A remote woodland area in the foothills of the Chatkal Mountains. Its botanical research station is experimenting with grafting southern varieties of fruits and nuts on to indigenous fir and birch. A special feature are the magnificent stands of junipers, many more than 1000 years old, their huge roots clinging to the crags like the tentacles of some great sea monster; the roots grow to such an enormous size to withstand earth tremors.

BIBLIOGRAPHY

THE literature of the mountains is vast – on the Himalaya alone there are more than 3000 articles and books. I have listed only those I have used.

Basic sources are the *Journals* of both the Royal Geographical Society and the Geographical Society of the USSR, the *Alpine Journal*, the *Himalayan Journal*, the *Journal of the Asiatic Society of Bengal* and *Asiatic Researches*.

No book dealing with the whole mountain complex has been written. However, two volumes in the Time-Life series *The World's Wild Places* give a good general description of the area: *The Himalayas* by Nigel Nicolson and *Soviet Deserts and Mountains* by George St George.

In the following booklists, the place of publication, unless otherwise stated, is London.

CHAPTER ONE

The primary source is A. Gansser, *Geology of the Himalayas*, 1964. Other sources include:
Burrard, S. G. and Hayden, H. H., *A Sketch of the Geography of the Himalayan Mountains and Tibet*, Dehra Dun, rev. ed. 1933.
Desio, A. and Zanettin, *Le spedizione geografica Italiana al Karakoram*, Milan, 1936.
Hagen, T., *Nepal*, 1960.
Hagen, T., Dyhrenfurth, G. O., and Schneider, E., *Mount Everest: formation, population and exploration*, 1963.
Hedin, S., *Southern Tibet* (9 vols.), Stockholm, 1917.
Mushketov, D., *Modern Conception of the Tectonics of Central Asia*, Moscow, 1936.
Petrov, M. P., *Deserts of Central Asia* (2 vols.), Moscow, 1966.
Wadia, D. N., *Geology of India*, rev. ed. 1957.

CHAPTER TWO (AND APPENDIX II)

Primary sources are *The Family of Man* (Marshall Cavendish Encyclopaedia, 98 vols.), and *Peoples of the Earth* (20 vols.), ed. E. Evans-Pritchard, 1973.
Basic information about the early migrations can be found in Time-Life Books, *The Emergence of Man*. Other sources consulted include:
Bacon, E. E., *Central Asia Under Russian Rule*, New York, 1966.
Coon, C. S., *History of Man*, 1967.
Dor, R., *The Kirghiz*, Paris, 1974.
Dupree, L., *Afghanistan*, Princeton, N. J., 1973.
Furer-Haimendorf, C. von, *The Naked Nagas*, Calcutta, 1962.
    Cast and Kin in Nepal, India and Ceylon, 1963.
    The Sherpas of Nepal, 1964.
Gorer, G., *Himalayan Village*, 1938.
Robertson, G. S., *The Kafirs of the Hindu Kush*, 1896.
Shor, J. and F., *A World's End in Hunza*, 1952.

CHAPTER THREE

The main sources for the travels of the early pilgrims are *The Vedas* and *The Mahabharata*; for the campaigns of Alexander, Robin Lane Fox, *Alexander the Great*, 1973; for the pilgrimage of Hsuan Tsang, Hui-Li (compiler), *The Life of Husan Tsang*; for the campaigns of Genghis Khan, H. A. Lamb, *Genghis Khan*, 1928: for the travels of Marco Polo, H. Yule, (ed.), *The Book of Ser Marco Polo*, 1903; for the campaigns of Tamerlane, Ibn-Arabshab, *Tamerlane*, 1936; for the journeys of the Jesuits, C. J. Wessels, *Early Jesuit Travellers in Central Asia*, The Hague, 1924.
Other works consulted include:
Andrade, A. de, *Novo Descrobimento do Gran Cathayo ou Reinos de Tibet*, Lisbon, 1651.
Arrian, *Campaigns of Alexander the Great*, 1962.

Blunt, Wilfrid, *The Golden Road to Samarkand*, 1973.

Carpine, J. P., *Histoire des Mongols*, Paris, 1961.

Gonzales-de-Clavijo, Roy, *Embassy to the Court of Tamerlane*, 1859.

Huc, E., *Christianity in China, Tartary and Tibet*, Peking, 1857.

Legg, Stuart, *The Heartland*, 1953.

Mandel, Gabriele, *The Life and Times of Genghis Khan*, 1970.

Olschiki, H., *Marco Polo's Asia*, Berkeley, Calif. 1960.

Philipps, E. D., *The Mongols*, 1969.

Poloutsoff, Aleksander, *The Land of Timur*, 1932.

Schuyler, E., *Turkistan*, 1876.

Skrine, F. and Ross, E. D., *The Heart of Asia*, 1899.

Vernalsky, G., *The Mongols of Russia*, New Haven, Conn., 1953.

Waleg, A., *The Secret History of the Mongols*, 1863.

CHAPTER FOUR

Two splendid books on the west Himalaya and adjacent ranges are: John Keay, *When Men and Mountains Meet*, 1977 and *The Gilgit Game*, 1979. I am particularly indebted to John Keay for permission to quote and to paraphrase extensively from *When Men and Mountains Meet* with regard to the explorers William Moorcroft, Victor Jacquemont and Godfrey Thomas Vigne. Other useful general works are:

Kenneth Mason, *Abode of Snow*, 1953 and John MacGregor, *Tibet: a Chronicle of Exploration*, 1970. More specialized books include:

Alder, G. J., *British India's Northern Frontier (1865–95)*, 1967.

Atkinson, T.W., *Oriental and Western Siberia*, 1858.
    Travels in the Regions of the Upper and Lower Amoor, 1861.

Atkinson, Mrs, *Recollections of the Tartar Steppes*, 1863.

Bell, Sir Charles, *Tibet Past and Present*, 1924.
    The People of Tibet, 1928.
    Portrait of the Dalai Lama, 1946.

Burnes, Sir Alexander, *Travels into Bokhara*, 1834.

Curzon, G. N., *The Pamirs and the Source of the Oxus*, 1896.
    Russia in Central Asia, 1899.

Das, Sarat Chandra, *Journey to Lhasa and Central Tibet*, 1902.

Davis, H. W. C., *The Great Game in Asia*, 1926.

Fedchenko, Alexis and Olga, *Topographical stretch of the Zarafshan Valley*, Moscow, 1870.

Gerard, M. G., *Report on the Proceedings of the Pamir Boundary Commission*, 1897.

Holdich, T. H., *Indian Borderland*, 1901.
    Gates of India, 1910.

Jacquemont, V. V., *Voyage dans l'Inde 1828–32*, Paris, *c.* 1840.

Kipling, Rudyard, *Kim*, 1901.

Lunt, J., *Bokhara Burnes*, 1969.

Maes, Pierre, *Victor Jacquemont*, Paris, 1934.

Moorcroft, William, *A Journey to Manasarovara*, Calcutta, 1816.

Moorcroft, William and Trebeck, George, *Travels in the Himalayan Provinces of Hindustan and the Panjab*, 1840.

Morgan, G., *Ney Elias, Explorer and Envoy Extraordinary in High Asia*, 1971.

Phillimore, R. H., *The Historical Records of the Survey of India*, Dehra Dun, 1945 onwards.

Prezhevalski, N., *Mongolia, the Tangut Country and the Solitudes of Northern Tibet* (2 vols.), 1876.
    From Kulja across the Tien Shan to Lob Nor, 1879.

Semenov, A., *Semenov – Tyan Shansky*, Moscow 1965.

Semyonov, Peter, *First Ascent of the Tian Shan or Celestial Mountains*, Moscow, 1859;
    Djungaria and the Celestial Mountains, Moscow 1863.

Vigne, G. T., *A Personal Narrative of a Visit to Ghazni, Kabul and Afghanistan*, 1840.

Travels in Kashmir, Ladakh, Iskardo etc., 1842.

Wolff, Joseph, *Researches and Missionary Labours among the Jews, Mohammedans and Other Sects*, 1835.

Travels and Adventures, 1860.

Wood, J., *A Journey to the Source of the River Oxus*, 1872.

Woodcock, George, *Into Tibet*, 1971.

CHAPTER FIVE

A good general guide to climbing in Central Asia is Francis Keenlyside, *Peaks and Pioneers*, 1976. Other works consulted include:

Anderson, J. R. L., *High Mountains and Cold Seas*, 1980.

Bairnsfather, Col. P. R., *Sport and Nature in the Himalaya*, 1914.

Bruce, C. G., *Twenty Years in the Himalaya*, 1934.

Buhl, Hermann, *Drüber und Drunter*, Munich, 1956.

Conway, W. M., *Climbing and Exploration in the Karakoram Himalayas*, 1894.

Desio, A., *Ascent of K2*, 1955.

Dyhrenfurth, G. O., *To the Third Pole*, 1952.

Filippi, Filippo de, *Karakoram and Western Himalaya*, 1912.

Fleming, Peter, *Bayonets to Lhasa*, 1961.

Harrer, Heinrich, *Seven Years in Tibet*, 1953.

Herzog, Maurice, *Annapurna*, 1952.

Hillary, Edmund, *High Adventure*, 1955.

Houston, Charles S., *The American Karakoram Expedition to K2*, 1938.

Howard-Bury, C. K., *Mount Everest: the Reconnaissance*, 1922.

Hunt, John, *The Ascent of Everest*, 1953.

Kinloch, A. A. A., *Large Game Shooting in Thibet and the Himalaya etc.*, 1885.

Merkl, W., *Der Angriff auf den Nanga Parbat*, Berlin, 1933.

Merzbacher, C., *The Central Tyan Shan Mountains*, 1905.

Mingtao, Zhang, *The Roof of the World*, 1983.

Rowell, Galen, *Mountains of the Middle Kingdom*, 1983.

Shih, Chan-Chun, *Conquest of Minya Konka*, Peking 1959.

Shipton, Eric, *The Mount Everest Reconnaissance Expedition*, 1952.

    That Untravelled World, 1969.

Stone, S. J., *In and Beyond the Himalaya*, 1896.

Tilman, H. W., *Nepal Himalaya*, 1952.

Workman, W. H. and Mrs Fanny Bullock, *In the Ice-World of the Himalaya*, 1900.

    Ice-bound Heights of the Mustagh, 1908.

    Peaks and Glaciers of the Nun Kun, 1909.

    The Call of the Snowy Hispar, 1910.

    Two Summers in the Ice-Fields of the Eastern Karakoram, 1917.

Yang, Ke-Hsien, *The Ascent of Mustaghata*, Peking, 1959.

Younghusband, Francis, *Everest: the Challenge*, rev. ed. 1936.

    The Heart of a Continent, 1896.

CHAPTER SIX

Hooker, J., *Flora of British India* (7 vols.), 1872–97.

    Himalayan Journals (2 vols.), 1854.

    A Sketch of the Flora of British India, 1906.

Miller, Keith, *Continents in Collision*, 1982.

ACKNOWLEDGEMENTS

Mountains of the Gods has been written with the encouragement and co-operation of the Royal Geographical Society.

My best thanks are due to the Society for letting me use their library, map room and archives; without access to these the book would have been a labour rather than a pleasure to write. I should also like to record a personal 'thank you' to the Director, John Hemming; to the Keeper of the Map Room, George Hardy; and to the Librarian, David Wileman, and his assistants. Their kindness and help have been deeply appreciated.

In the text quotations from the Society's publications are made by permission of the Royal Geographical Society. Quotations from *The Alpine Journal* are made by permission of the Alpine Club, Norman Dyhrenfurth and Colonel H. R. A. Streather. I acknowledge with thanks permission to quote from the following sources: *The Golden Road to Samarkand* by Wilfrid Blunt (published by Hamish Hamilton Ltd) by permission of the Rainbird Publishing Group Ltd; *Nanga Parbat Pilgrimage* by Hermann Buhl by permission of Hodder and Stoughton Ltd; *Alexander the Great* (published by Penguin Books Ltd) by permission of Curtis Brown Ltd; *Soviet Deserts and Mountains* by George St George by permission of Time-Life Books; *Annapurna* by Maurice Herzog (translated by Nea Morin and Janet Adam Smith) by permission of Jonathan Cape Ltd; *High Adventure* by Sir Edmund Hillary by permission of Hodder and Stoughton Ltd; *When Men and Mountains Meet* by John Keay, by permission of John Murray; *The Heartland* by Stuart Legg (published by Secker and Warburg Ltd) by permission of Laurence Pollinger Ltd; *Abode of Snow* by Kenneth Mason (published by Rupert Hart-Davis) by permission of Granada Publishing Ltd; *Continents in Collision* by Keith Miller by permission of George Philip and Son Ltd, *In and beyond the Himalaya* by S. J. Stone by permission of Edward Arnold (Publishers Ltd); *Early Jesuit Travellers in Central Asia* by C. Wessels by permission of Martinus Nijhoff Publishers BV; *Into Tibet* by George Woodcock (published by Faber and Faber Ltd) by permission of Anthony Sheil Associates Ltd; *The Call of the Snow Hispar* by H. W. and Fanny Workman by permission of Constable Publishers; and *Everest: the Challenge* by Sir Francis Younghusband by permission of Thomas Nelson and Sons Ltd; *Mountains of the Middle Kingdom* by Galen Rowell © 1985 Galen Rowell, by permission of Sierra Club Books.

The illustrations are mainly from the collections of the Royal Geographical Society, with the exception of the following. The cover photograph is by Roland and Sabrina Michaud from the John Hillelson Agency. *36* Robert Harding Picture Library; *38L* Aldus Archive/British Museum; *R* Aldus Archive/National Palace Museum, Taiwan; *41* Crown Copyright reproduced with the permission of the Controller of her Majesty's Stationery Office and the Royal Botanic Gardens, Kew; *42T* Aldus Archive/Bibliothèque Nationale, Paris; *B* Aldus Archive/British Museum; *43T* Aldus Archive/Topkapi Sorayi Museum, Istanbul; *B* Aldus Archive/Bibliothèque Nationale; *44* Neil Ray/Royal Geographical Society; *48* John Massey-Stewart; *52, 56* Fotomas Index; *67* India Office Library and Records; *77* Captain John Noel; *78* Susan Griggs Agency/Michael Wall; *79T* Daily Telegraph Colour Library/Chris Bonington; *B* Robert Harding Picture Library; *80TL* Jerry Young; *TR* Ardea/Mike Coleman; *B* Bruce Coleman Ltd/Chris Bonington; *83* National Portrait Gallery; *110L* India Office Library and Records; *113B* Royal College of Surgeons; *114T* Jerry Young; *B* Chris Bonington; *115* John Hillelson Agency/Roland Michaud; *134T* Chris Bonington; *134B, 135* Doug Scott; *136T* Chris Bonington; *136B* Doug Scott; *169* Susan Griggs Agency/David Beatty; *170* Crown Copyright/HMSO/Royal Botanic Gardens, Kew; *171* Crown Copyright/HMSO/Royal Botanical Gardens, Kew; *172* Jerry Young; *209* RGS/International Karakoram Project 1980/E. Smith; *210T* RGS/International Karakoram Project 1980; *210B* RGS/International Karakoram Project 1980/S. Wesley Smith; *206* RGS/International Karakoram Project 1980/Robert Holmes; *207T* John Hillelson Agency/Howard Sochurek; *B* John Hillelson Agency/Roland & Sabrina Michaud; *208* William Macquitty; *212* RGS/International Karakoram Project 1980/S. Wesley Smith; *213* RGS International Karakoram Project 1980/N. Winser; *214, 216* RGS/International Karakoram Project 1980.

INDEX